Institut für Volkswirtschafts-
theorie und -politik der
Wirtschaftsuniversität Wien
o. Prof. Dr. Leonhard Bauer
Augasse 2-6, 1090 Wien

Neo-Liberal Economic Policy

Neo-Liberal Economic Policy

Critical Essays

Edited by

Philip Arestis

University of Cambridge, UK and Levy Economics Institute, USA

Malcolm Sawyer

University of Leeds, UK

Edward Elgar
Cheltenham, UK • Northampton, MA, USA

© International Papers in Political Economy 2004

All rights reserved. No part of this publication may be reproduced, stored in a retrieval system or transmitted in any form or by any means, electronic, mechanical or photocopying, recording, or otherwise without the prior permission of the publisher.

Published by
Edward Elgar Publishing Limited
Glensanda House
Montpellier Parade
Cheltenham
Glos GL50 1UA
UK

Edward Elgar Publishing, Inc.
136 West Street
Suite 202
Northampton
Massachusetts 01060
USA

A catalogue record for this book
is available from the British Library

Library of Congress Cataloguing in Publication Data
Neo-liberal economic policy : critical essays / edited by Philip Arestis, Malcolm Sawyer.
    p. cm.
  Includes index.
  1. Liberalism. 2. Economic policy. I. Arestis, Philip, 1941– II. Sawyer, Malcolm C.

HB95.N426 2004
330—dc22

2004047146

ISBN 1 84376 794 5

Typeset by Manton Typesetters, Louth, Lincolnshire, UK.
Printed and bound in Great Britain by MPG Books Ltd, Bodmin, Cornwall.

Contents

List of figures	vi
List of tables	vii
List of contributors	viii
Preface	ix

1	Introduction *Philip Arestis and Malcolm Sawyer*	1
2	The theory of credibility: confusions, limitations and dangers *James Forder*	4
3	Financial fragility: is it rooted in the development process? An examination with special reference to the South Korean experience *Santonu Basu*	38
4	A 'third way' in economic policy: a reappraisal of the Rehn–Meidner model in the light of modern economics *Lennart Erixon*	71
5	The economic policy in Spain during the decades of the 1980s and the 1990s *Jesus Ferreiro and Felipe Serrano*	117
6	The costs of neomonetarism: the Brazilian economy in the 1990s *Alfredo Saad-Filho and Lecio Morais*	158
7	Macroeconomic policies of the Economic and Monetary Union: theoretical underpinnings and challenges *Philip Arestis and Malcolm Sawyer*	194

Index	233

Figures

2.1	The time-consistency problem	7
4.1	The R–M economic and wage policy model – means and objectives	75
4.2	Solidaristic wage policy, profit margins and number of firms	97
5.1	Unemployment and inflation rates	122
5.2	Wage growth approved in collective bargaining agreements and rate of inflation	124
5.3	Evolution of implicit deflators	127
5.4	Rates of growth of costs and prices in the manufacturing sector	128
5.5	Rates of growth of costs and prices in the services sector	129
5.6	Evolution of real GDP and wage earners' rates of growth	134
5.7	Employment rates of temporary workers	135
5.8	Inflation and real GDP rates of growth	141
5.9	Evolution of household consumption and saving	143
5.10	Evolution of public administration expenditure	146
5.11	Evolution of fiscal pressure	147
6.1	Brazil: monthly inflation rate, May 1990–December 1999	167
6.2	Brazil: real interest rate, 1990–1999	168
6.3	Brazil: domestic public debt, 1990–1999	174
6.4	Brazil: nominal exchange rate, June 1994–December 1999	184

Tables

2.1	Problems and effects of monetary policy	15
5.1	Real rate of growth of monthly average earnings	140
5.2	Distribution of salaried workers according to their labour revenues	150
6.1	Brazil: GDP, 1990–1999	163
6.2	External sector of the Brazilian economy, selected variables, 1990.I–1991.IV and 1992.I–1994.II	166
6.3	External sector of the Brazilian economy, selected variables, 1994.III–1995.I and 1995.II–1995.IV	170
6.4	Brazilian manufacturing industry, import coefficient, 1993 and 1996	171
6.5	Brazil: central government fiscal balance, 1991–1999	176
6.6	Brazil: central government financial expenditures, 1991–1998	177
6.7	Brazil: indexation and maturity of central government securities, 1991–1999	178
6.8	Brazil: foreign currency cover of the primary liabilities of the central government, 1991–1999	180
6.9	External sector of the Brazilian economy, selected variables, 1996.I–1998.II, 1998.III–1999.I and 1999.II–1999.III	182
6.10	Brazilian economy, selected variables, 1990.I–1994.II and 1994.III–1998.IV	186
7.1	Real GDP growth rates, inflation rates and unemployment rates	200

Contributors

Philip Arestis, Levy Economics Institute and University of Cambridge, UK.

Santonu Basu, South Bank University, London, UK.

Lennart Erixon, Department of Economics, Stockholm University, Sweden.

Jesus Ferreiro, Department of Applied Economics V, The University of the Basque Country, Bilbao, Spain.

James Forder, Balliol College, Oxford, UK.

Lecio Morais, economics adviser, Camara dos Deputados, Brasilia-DF, Brazil.

Alfredo Saad-Filho, School of Oriental and African Studies, University of London, UK.

Malcolm Sawyer, Leeds University Business School, University of Leeds, UK.

Felipe Serrano, Department of Applied Economics V, The University of the Basque Country, Bilbao, Spain.

Preface

This book, which contains revised and updated versions of contributions that have already appeared in the *International Papers in Political Economy*, seeks to contribute to a critical analysis and appraisal of neo-liberal economic policies. We wish to thank all the contributors to this volume and to the issues of *International Papers in Political Economy*. Without their support this and a companion volume, based on *International Papers in Political Economy*, would not have been possible. Edward Elgar and Dymphna Evans have been supportive publishers in this and other ventures, and we are grateful to them and their staff for their support.

1. Introduction

Philip Arestis and Malcolm Sawyer

The general shift in economic policy in many countries over the past two decades or more can at one level be put under the heading of the continuing rise of neo-liberalism – the doctrine that economic policy should take the form of 'leave it to the market' and for government to retreat from intervention in markets. In a more specific way, some of the notable shifts in economic policy have been:

1. the retreat from fiscal policy and the reliance on monetary policy, and the associated shift in the objectives of macroeconomic policy from concerns over employment and growth to the concentration on inflation and price stability;
2. the promotion of the notion that the causes of unemployment lie in the operation of the labour market, and that 'inflexibility' in the labour market is a major cause of unemployment. The shift in economic policy has taken the form that unemployment is to be tackled by labour market 'reforms', rather than through macroeconomic demand management policies and through regional and industrial policies designed to tackle structural unemployment. The perceived 'rigidities' in the labour market have been associated with trade union power, long-term employment contracts, minimum wages and so on, with the consequent 'flexible' labour market policies designed to remove the source of those 'rigidities;
3. a trend towards the liberalization and deregulation of markets and notably of financial markets (including the lifting of controls on the movement of capital between countries).

The chapters in this book present critical appraisals of these trends in economic policy. The rise in importance of monetary policy has been associated with a focus of monetary policy on the inflation objective, and with many central banks becoming 'independent' – that is, their operations are undertaken without direct reference to government though subject to the edict of using the instruments of monetary policy (notably interest rate) to achieve a pre-stated inflation target. The 'independence' of the central bank and the focus of monetary policy on inflation have been justified in the following way. An 'independent' central bank would be more 'conservative' than an elected government in that the bankers would be more averse to inflation and less inclined to promote lower unemployment (as compared with an elected government). This tendency can be reinforced by stating that the objective of the central bank should only be low inflation. Further, the 'independent' central bank was thought to be more 'credible' (especially in the eyes of the financial markets) in the pursuit of low inflation. A more 'credible' policy would then deliver lower expectations of inflation, and thereby enhance the achievement of low inflation.

In Chapter 2, James Forder provides a detailed critical examination of the theory of credibility, exposing confusions in the literature, limitations of the analysis, and dangers from accepting the 'credibility' of central bank argument. He concludes that excessively contractionary policies, the dismissal of distributive concerns and insinuation against democracy can arise from the applications of the conclusions of the literature on the credibility of central banks. There are also serious dangers for the conduct of monetary policy, specifically in a deflationary direction.

In Chapter 3, Santonu Basu considers the experience of South Korea with financial liberalization, and specifically the relationship between financial deregulation and financial fragility. He argues that, contrary to the claim made by the advocates of financial liberalization, there is a theoretical explanation as to why the interest rate alone cannot provide the link between savings, investment and growth. This chapter argues that financial liberalization, instead of delivering a higher growth rate, is more likely to affect the growth rate adversely through its effects on financial fragility and the likelihood of financial crisis. The author seeks to explain why intervention is necessary in the operation of the financial market, specially during the process of development.

The Swedish economy for many years represented a unique policy in combining full employment and equity with growth and price stability, and operated what has been termed the Swedish model, or the Rehn–Meidner (R–M) model. In Chapter 4, Lennart Erixon provides a reappraisal of this model in the light of modern economic analysis. The R–M model was based on a wage policy of solidarity and the use of selective instruments – primarily labour market policies and marginal employment subsidies – within the framework of a restrictive fiscal policy. Erixon notes that a main argument now against the R–M model is that the scope for an economic policy has narrowed by internationalization. However, he argues that while internationalization has served to limit the possibilities of any single country applying this model, there is still a role for modified versions of the model: 'International labour mobility is still limited in scope but certainly a real challenge of solidaristic wage policy. The road is long to coordinated wage policy actions on the European Union (EU) level. But the R–M model does not rule out wage differences between individuals based on differences in job content, competence and education'.

The Spanish governments of the past two decades, and notably the Socialist governments in power from 1982 to 1996, have pursued economic policies very much in line with the neo-liberal agenda. In Chapter 5, Jesus Ferreiro and Felipe Serrano examine the economic policies of those Socialist governments. They conclude that the general strategy of economic policy followed by the Socialist governments has been conditioned by a mistaken diagnosis of the core objective of the Spanish economic policy (inflation). It has also been conditioned by the implementation, first, of a tight monetary policy joined to a hard currency policy, and, second, of a set of institutional reforms focused on the labour market to solve a structural-nature problem.

Brazil provides a further example of a country which pursued what may be termed a neo-liberal or neomonetarist agenda during the 1990s. In Chapter 6, Alfredo Saad-Filho and Lecio Morais consider the costs of neomonetarism for the Brazilian economy in the 1990s. They conclude that the slow growth of the Brazilian economy during the 1990s (at 1.7 per cent per annum, the lowest of the century) arose from the costs of the neomonetarist economic strategy implemented in this period, especially through the Real Plan. Investment declined from 22.1 to 19.6 per cent of GDP, while domestic savings fell from 20.1 to 16.8 per cent of GDP. Manufacturing employment fell by one-third, and productive capacity declined in several important sectors, especially the capital goods industry. Industrial restructuring reduced the economy's employment generating capacity, and Brazil became more heavily dependent upon imports and foreign finance.

The economic policy regime surrounding the introduction of the European single currency fits with the characterization of neo-liberal policies given above. In Chapter 7, Philip Arestis and Malcolm Sawyer outline what they see as the theoretical foundations of the Economic and Monetary Union (EMU) model. They examine the policy implications of the EMU, along with its theoretical and institutional dimensions surrounding monetary and fiscal policies, and conclude that the present policy arrangements will not enable the EMU to achieve full employment and low inflation. Indeed the policy regime is overtly deflationary. The authors conclude with a range of policy measures designed to overcome the shortcomings of the present policies.

The contributions to this book serve to illustrate the ways in which neo-liberal policies have been applied (and how those policies fit in with the three shifts in economic policy identified at the beginning of the chapter). They also seek to show both the shortcomings of these neo-liberal policies and that there are alternative policies available.

2. The theory of credibility: confusions, limitations and dangers

James Forder*

INTRODUCTION

It has become a commonplace of discussion among academics, policymakers, and indeed in opinion-forming society at large, that because of political short-termism, monetary policy is affected by a time-consistency or credibility problem which leads to inflation. The solution to the problem is equally widely held to be the devising of some form of commitment to a policy leading to price stability. It is these doctrines which lie behind much of the conventional wisdom of current macroeconomic policy. They certainly sustain the case for central bank independence; they were clearly instrumental in advancing much of the Maastricht Treaty; and of course they go a long way to explaining the esteem in which central bankers are now frequently held, for in this vision, they are the guardians of our credibility.

Widespread as this general view now is, it owes a great deal more to confusion over time consistency and credibility than to the theory's actual characteristics. In particular, I wish to argue that, properly understood, the theory traces inflation neither to political opportunism nor to short-termism. Furthermore, the literature is far from conclusive in advocating solving the problem by firm commitment to price stability. The construction of the modern policy prescription, then, cannot truly be based on the theory of policy credibility at all. Rather, I shall argue, it is based on a pseudo-credibility theory which, taking common, although more or less unsubstantiated, intuitions and combining them with misstatements of the theory of credibility, arrives at its popular conclusions. The connection of pseudo-credibility theory with the real thing, and the connection of that real thing to short-termism and political advantage are almost completely illusory. There has been, in this area, a great intellectual débâcle, which should not be allowed to persist in a scientific community.

The process of exegesis has, then, the scholarly purpose of clarifying the claims made by credibility theory, and showing that they do not accord with what is commonly supposed. I hope thereby also to tackle what I believe is a widespread tendency to misuse the terminology of the theory of time consistency and credibility, often no doubt in error, but sometimes to give emotive support to some policy proposal, or occasionally policymaker.

But I have a further purpose because this tendency is far from being the benign shorthand as which it is sometimes defended. In fact it is a dangerous influence on policymaking and attitudes to it. In this connection, I hope to highlight the ways in which the pseudo-credibility theory has given support to the case for central bank independence and a firm policy of aiming for price stability in ways that the real thing does not. Furthermore, the theory of pseudo-credibility engenders a contempt for the democratic process which is in no way mandated by the true theory. Indeed, I believe the true theory argues far more powerfully for democratic control of policymaking than it does for central bank independence. But in the pseudo-theory, it is all too easy to present certain prior beliefs as the outcome of the rigorous analysis of the credibility theorists, thereby giving the impression of powerful support for independence. Central bank independence may or may not be a good idea, I shall conclude, but independence advocated, supported and believed in because of a perception of the importance of achieving credibility is simply dangerous on any reasonable, democratically-minded account.

The scholarly purpose, then, of clarifying in some detail the nature of the theory of credibility, and distinguishing it from its relations – although it occupies much space – is preliminary to the thoroughly utilitarian objective of influencing policy. It is because the intellectual débâcle so clearly threatens material and political well-being that the abandonment of what is called 'credibility' as a concern of policymakers is important and urgent. Whether this can be achieved while policymaking remains in the hands of independent central bankers remains to be seen.

THE TIME-CONSISTENCY PROBLEM

The problem of time consistency was identified by Kydland and Prescott (1977) who presented an argument that what they called a policy 'rule' would be better than 'discretion'. Their argument has certain clear resemblances to those of Friedman (1968 and 1977), and others to Lucas (1976). But there are also important differences between them and the other authors, both in their argument for a 'rule' and in what they understood following one to entail.

Friedman (1968) had argued that monetary policy could not achieve a target rate of unemployment in the long run because unemployment would always revert to its 'natural' rate. And further, he argued, continuing a major theme of Friedman (1948), that while there was no deep theoretical objection to the idea that policy could play a useful stabilization role, the attempt was as likely to do harm as good because the data and capabilities of the policymakers were so poor. Consequently, policy would be better off following a monetary rule, for example to achieve a steady rate of money growth. Discretion – that is setting policy without such a rule – is dangerous because it is difficult and therefore often does harm, and sometimes serious harm.[1]

Lucas argued for a similar conclusion, but by incorporating the idea that the private sector might understand the intentions of policymakers and therefore that changes of policy would lead to changes in private sector behaviour, he gave a firmer rationale for the difficulty of designing optimal policy – each design which appeared optimal on the basis of past experience would be likely to cease to be so when the private sector adjusted to its implementation. This argument is not in principle one against discretionary policy, but rather one that proposals to vary policy will be all but impossible to assess. That increases the practical importance of Friedman's argument that the automatic tendency of unemployment to revert to its natural rate, imperfect as it is, would be better than anything the policymakers were likely to devise.

Kydland and Prescott, however, suggested a particular way in which the private sector's understanding of policy might affect their behaviour and this led them to propose a policy rule not as a compromise with the unfathomable difficulty of ideal policy design, as it seems if one follows Friedman and Lucas, but rather as being the optimal policy bearing in mind the private sector's responses. They began by supposing the policymaker to have a loss function in which the marginal rate of substitution of unemployment for inflation rises with inflation. This means that as inflation rises by fixed amounts, it takes larger and larger falls in unemployment for the policymaker to remain on the same indifference curve. Subject to the requirements of differentiability of the indifference curve, this means that at a low enough level of inflation the policymaker will always favour an increase in inflation if that will bring any fall in unemployment.

Kydland and Prescott followed Friedman's argument in assuming a natural rate of unemployment, and an expectations-augmented Phillips curve so that there is a stable trade-off between unexpected inflation and employment. Unlike Friedman, however, they made the assumption that the policymaker has a perfect understanding of the structure of the economy, including all transmission lags. As to the private sector, Kydland and Prescott assumed that it forms its expectations of inflation on the basis not only of a correct understanding of the structure of the economy, but – as Lucas suggested – also of a correct perception of the way in which policy is set.

They characterized the different ways in which policy might be made as 'discretion' or a 'rule'. If operating by discretion, the policymaker sets policy at each point in time in order to maximize discounted social welfare. On the other hand, operating by the rule they proposed, again with a Friedmanite air,

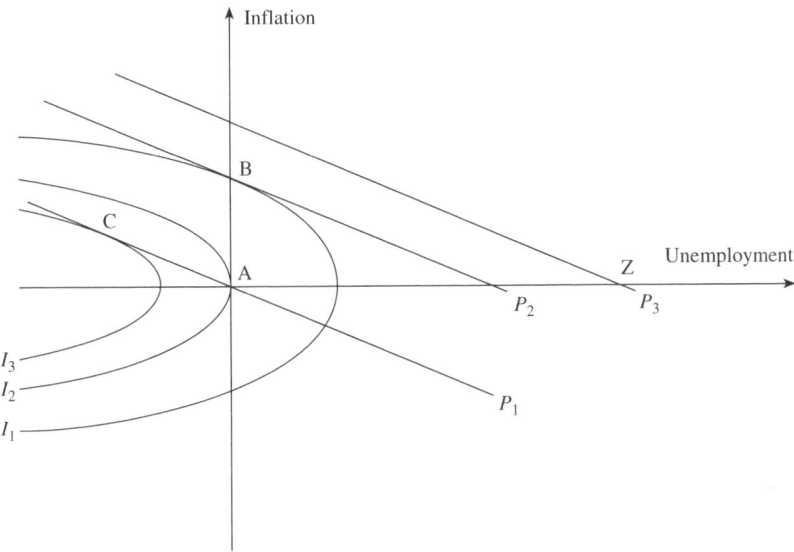

Figure 2.1   The time-consistency problem

the policymaker simply causes the money supply to expand at a predetermined rate. With the alternatives so characterized, it is fairly clear that a normal, commonsensical view would be that the discretionary policy can always mimic the rule, so the possibility of doing otherwise creates the possibility of improvement on the rule-based outcome, and therefore discretion is the better approach. But as so often with the best economic theory, its interest lies in the contradiction of common sense, and in this case Kydland and Prescott were able to argue that discretion might be inferior. Although this much is widely understood, their particular argument is frequently misstated. This argument can be analysed with a diagram like that of Figure 2.1. The indifference curves, I_i, and the Phillips curves, P_i, are drawn as assumed. The vertical axis shows the natural rate of unemployment which is defined as that rate which prevails when labour market expectations of inflation are satisfied, and the horizontal axis shows the optimal rate of inflation, for convenience often called 'zero'. On these assumptions and the private sector's understanding that policy is made by discretion, Kydland and Prescott argued that there is only one equilibrium, in the short or long run, which is at point B.

Their argument is best understood as a *reductio*. It works by making an assumption and seeking to deduce from it a contradiction. That being achieved, it follows that the assumption must be false. Here, for example, if it is assumed that the rational expectation of inflation is zero, the expectations-augmented Phillips curve would pass through the origin. In that case, the maximizing policymaker would set some positive rate of inflation to reduce unemployment, and the outcome is illustrated by point C. Inflation there is not zero, which means that, in this deterministic world, it is impossible for the rational expectation of inflation to be zero. Therefore the short-run Phillips curve does not pass through the origin. Therefore point C is never achieved. A similar argument can be made for any expectation of inflation other than that prevailing at point B. This point is unique in having the characteristic that on the assumptions made, if the private sector bargain on the basis that the policymaker will generate that rate of inflation, then the policymaker will do so. The Kydland and Prescott equilibrium, which is unique and stable, and prevails in all periods is therefore at point B, which is evidently socially suboptimal.

Kydland and Prescott's solution to this problem was to propose that the policymaker ceases the period-by-period optimization that leads the private sector to expect positive inflation, and instead follows the 'rule' of setting monetary growth to achieve price stability. The private sector, in understanding that the rule has been adopted, set wages appropriately to zero inflation, so that the natural rate of unemployment prevails and point A is reached.[2]

My own reaction to Kydland and Prescott's argument is that it offers a tremendous insight in social science. Of course one can doubt their market-clearing framework, but that is not essential to their underlying argument. There is a more general, and important, argument that in any framework, the private sector's understanding of how policy is made will affect its success, but this of course is attributable to Lucas. What Kydland and Prescott offered was an analysis of an important – and I believe, to date, the most important – special case of the Lucas critique. That is the case where the approach of doing what seems best at a point in time achieves society's objectives less well than the approach of giving up those opportunities in order to encourage desirable behaviour on the part of the private sector. Putting these cases, many of which are well known individually, into a general framework, is itself a valuable insight.[3]

Beyond this, however, I believe that one should be impressed by Kydland and Prescott's serious attention to what is, from the monetarist perspective, a genuine puzzle of their times. If it is the case that inflation is straightforwardly the result of excessive monetary growth, and monetary growth is readily controlled by the authorities, and inflation brings no benefits, what is one to say about its persistence in the post-war period? One possibility is to suppose that the policymaker is ill informed about the structure of the economy, in which case close attention to Friedman's argument for the natural rate would be the antidote. Another is that the policymaker is hamfisted and overambitious, in which case Friedman's argument on the difficulty of fine-tuning would be appropriate reading. Once these things have been clarified, however, it becomes a harder matter – from a monetarist perspective – to explain continuing policy failure. It could be that the policymaker is not trying to serve the public interest, which was indeed alleged by Friedman (1982), amongst others, and in which case, it would be appropriate to find a different policymaker. But Kydland and Prescott's argument should, I believe, be thought of as addressing this issue, in a striking and original way, and offering an explanation which seems to make clear why persistent inflation is a phenomenon of the age of macroeconomic management, but avoids attributing it to policymaker error or malice. Inflation is, surprising as it seems, the outcome of well-intentioned, well-informed policymakers setting policy in the public interest. It is, I suggest, in this diagnostic mode that Kydland and Prescott's serious attention to a scientific problem should be most highly regarded.

THE CREDIBILITY PROBLEM

The credibility problem was alleged to exist by Barro and Gordon (1983a). They pick up the argument where Kydland and Prescott left off, and simply raise the question of whether the private sector will believe that the policymaker is following the monetary rule. Their argument that they will not is again well conceived as a *reductio*. On the assumption that the private sector do believe the rule is being followed, they will set wages appropriate to price stability. If they do this, the actual Phillips curve will be P_1. In this case, the best option for the policymaker is to ignore the rule and set inflation so as to arrive at point C. The argument is, in all its essentials, the same as Kydland and Prescott's account of the result of discretionary policy. This similarity was no accident because Barro and Gordon's point was, in effect, that Kydland and Prescott's proposal that the policymaker simply adopt the 'rule' did not change any aspect of the underlying game, and therefore would not change the outcome. Nevertheless, the problems are distinct. Kydland and Prescott offered a diagnosis of persistent inflation based on the idea that the policymaker had not understood how the private sector form expectations. Barro and Gordon's point turns on the view that the private sector doubt either the consistency of purpose or the honesty of the policymaker.

Barro and Gordon (1983b) themselves offered one response to the problem of how to make the private sector believe that the rule would be followed. On certain heavy-handed assumptions about the response of the private sector to a broken commitment, they were able to argue for the existence of an equilibrium rate of inflation below that of Kydland and Prescott's discretionary equilibrium, but above the optimal rate. In other words, a certain degree of disinflation could be promised by the policymaker, and then anticipated by the private sector. The delivery of that rate would – as the private sector are assumed to understand – be optimal once it had been promised because of the response of the private sector if the promise were broken.

Some of the terminology adopted by Barro and Gordon may itself have been confusing. Even the use of the word 'credible' has been a mixed blessing. Intended to characterize whether the private sector believe a policy announcement, it has an inevitable flavour of describing the outward appearance of a certain kind of policymaker.[4] They were no doubt picking up the use of the same word by Fellner (1976) who had appreciated that convincing the private sector of the imminence of a decline in inflation would make it achievable at lower cost in lost output, but they added to that their very particular game-theoretic account of why the private sector would presume that the policymaker was acting under the permanent influence of an incentive to lie to them. The general idea that because of this incentive the achieving of credibility is the greatest of problems has become a central theme in the subsequent literature.

Second, in characterizing their equilibrium conditions, Barro and Gordon chose to label offsetting forces 'temptation' and 'reputation'. The former is simply the functional relationship between a promised rate of inflation and the benefit (on the detailed assumptions of the model) of breaking the commitment. The latter was similarly the relationship between the promised rate of inflation and the benefit of keeping to the commitment. Only when the benefit of keeping it is equal to or greater than that of breaking it, argued Barro and Gordon, would the promise be believed. The ideas of temptation and reputation have, however, been powerful in ways quite unrelated to this equilibrium. The reputation of certain central banks – the Bundesbank, for example – apparently goes without saying, but a host of assertions have been made about it and one has the impression that many of the authors feel that the word can be used in its ordinary English sense, with the full authority of economic theory also behind whatever claim is made.[5] Similarly, the 'temptation' in almost a biblical sense – not of central bankers so much as of politicians – has become a regular feature of cod theoretical discussion of the issues.

Standing beside their undeniably evocative language, however, there are aspects of the argument which, when clearly understood, seem to lack plausibility. The private sector was assumed to 'punish' broken commitments with a period of 'non-cooperation'. That is to say that if a commitment were broken, there would be exactly one period in which the private sector would not believe any other commitment. Although the assumption of such a strategy was shown to give rise to Barro and Gordon's equilibrium, the issues of why it would be adopted in the first place or how the private sector were supposed to coordinate themselves in applying it were left rather out of consideration.[6]

An alternative response to Kydland and Prescott, incorporating a different formalization of the idea of a reputation, was offered by Backus and Driffill (1985a). Not only is their model a more plausible representation of a popular way of thinking about monetary policymaking, but it is also, perhaps, a fair representation of what many people have in mind when they refer to 'Barro and Gordon'. Their idea was to suppose that there are two kinds of policymaker. One is identical in every way with Kydland and Prescott's policymaker who shares society's objectives; the other is more inflation averse. The inflation-averse policymaker can be represented diagrammatically as having more pointed indifference curves. It is then evident that the Kydland and Prescott equilibrium – that is, the point where the indifference curve is tangent to a Phillips curve at the natural rate of unemployment – for the more inflation-averse policymaker will be at a lower rate of inflation than for the other kind. Backus and Driffill suggested, however, that the public might be unable to distinguish the two types other than by their actions, in which case policymaking involves a signalling problem.[7]

If the private sector know the probability that the policymaker is of the inflation-averse kind, then one can think of the argument as beginning with the idea that some positive rate of inflation less than that prevailing at point B will initially be expected.[8] The private sector is presumed to update its estimate of the likelihood of the policymaker being of each type based on the behaviour they observe. Therefore, the policymaker has an incentive to set low inflation, in order to appear as the inflation-averse kind. To the extent that this is successful, the Phillips curve will move downwards, improving policy opportunities in the future. The policymaker who succeeds in causing the Phillips curve to move to a very low position is in an enviable position since it would then be feasible either to maintain low inflation together with low unemployment, or, if one were so minded, to create an inflation surprise moving to a point on the left-hand side of the diagram.

On an intuitive level, this account may have considerable appeal. All new policymakers assert their anti-inflationary intent; the public treats that assertion with some scepticism; those policymakers who deliver low inflation are gradually believed more and more. The argument also has the implication that one might see periods of persistently high unemployment and low inflation without treating that as a refutation of the natural rate model since expected inflation might be above actual inflation for a succession of periods.[9]

A characteristic of the model, which one does not tend to see noted, is that there must be some question as to whether building reputation is desirable. Certainly it is beneficial to have a good reputation. But if it is costly to acquire, it may not be worth the price. A crucial consideration would be how damaging it is to permit inflation at the level of the Kydland and Prescott equilibrium. It is not clear what that level is, but the experience of the 1970s suggests it is in single figures. At that time, when inflation rose into double figures it became clear that this was politically unacceptable.[10] If we suppose the Kydland and Prescott equilibrium is at 10 per cent, which would therefore seem to be the maximum reasonable estimate, the question that needs to be addressed is whether the benefit of establishing a reputation that would allow it to be kept lower is great enough to warrant the cost of doing so. If, as one seems forced by events to suppose, those costs are to be the levels of unemployment that have been experienced in the European disinflations, that would seem to be implausible. I suggest, then, that even in Backus and Driffill's world, the right response to the 'problem of credibility' could be to ignore it, and accept suboptimal equilibrium inflation.[11]

Actually to complete their argument, Backus and Driffill were forced to make certain simplifying assumptions. One of these, of course, was that there are only two kinds of policymaker. One would like the only distinction between them to be their degree of inflation-aversity, but Backus and Driffill also assumed another one. That is that the inflation-averse policymaker always sets the intended policy, but the less inflation-averse kind sets policy at random. Therefore, a policymaker who had always set low inflation could be either kind, but one that had ever set high inflation would be known with certainty to be of the less inflation-averse kind.[12] In the model, therefore, reputation is hard to establish, but can be lost in a moment, and this doctrine has certainly found its place in the conventional wisdom of today's policymaker. On an intuitive level one might have thought that a rise in inflation would merely cause an upward reassessment by the private sector of the probability that the policymaker was not powerfully inflation averse, but in the model, it destroys reputation altogether. It is worth noting, I think, that there is no sense in which this has been argued. It was simply an assumption of the model, designed to make the mathematics tractable. Like Barro and Gordon, Backus and Driffill described their model as an analysis of 'reputation', and this has no doubt contributed to the confusion that exists between the two. There are clearly different theoretical accounts of the nature, importance and acquisition of reputation between the two, and for accuracy, among other things, one should want to keep them separate.

Another response to Kydland and Prescott, and one that should be thought of as being of an entirely different character from either those of Barro and Gordon or Backus and Driffill was that of Rogoff (1985). His concern was not, as in the case of the others, that Kydland and Prescott's solution to their problem would not work, but rather that it would be dangerous. Kydland and Prescott's proposal was that price stability be the policymaker's target.

As Rogoff observed, in the presence of supply shocks, which, in diagrammatic terms can be thought of as exogenous shifts in the Phillips curve, such a policy would not be optimal. So, for example, if the policymaker is successfully following Kydland and Prescott's rule, and point A is normally reached, but on one occasion, the Phillips curve moves to P_3 then it is not optimal to maintain price stability at point Z since higher indifference curves are available.

If the alternative to following the rule were pure discretion in Kydland and Prescott's sense, one would have to choose between avoiding the inflation bias they diagnosed and the ability to stabilize employment to some degree when supply shocks occur. Rogoff, however, observed that there could be a middle course. He proposed operating a discretionary policy, but doing so while always leaning in a counterinflationary direction. The well-intentioned policymaker would, according to Rogoff, as it were, think of the policy of pure 'discretion' and then set something a little tighter.

Rogoff conceived of the decision as to how much tighter to make policy than it would be under pure discretion as a once-and-for-all choice, and presented his idea in terms of the notion of a 'conservative central banker'. He noted that being more inflation averse than society as a whole, such a central banker would behave in the way he was recommending: a tendency towards disinflation would partly compensate for Kydland and Prescott's inflation bias. But on the other hand, such a central banker would also give some weight to the stabilization of employment.

There are a number of issues relating to Rogoff's argument that are worth noting. First, and perhaps most obviously, Rogoff's idea is not an argument in support of 'rules' in either Friedman's or Kydland and Prescott's sense. It is precisely the opposite, a critique of Kydland and Prescott and an argument for discretion.[13] Second, the idea of a conservative central banker is certainly not presented as a solution to the time-consistency problem. It is at most an accommodation of it. The Rogoff-banker still generates an inflation bias, although a lesser one than Kydland and Prescott's discretionary policymaker. In fact the Rogoff-banker can be thought of as a policymaker who behaves like Backus and Driffill's inflation-averse policymaker, but without the necessity of demonstrating any inflation aversity.

A closely related point is that policymaking can be too inflation averse. Rogoff sought to calculate the optimal degree of inflation aversity, which depends on how much output stabilization is wanted and the distribution of shocks. Clearly this means that a more inflation-averse policymaker is not always to be preferred. On the other hand, some of the subsequent literature appears to suppose both that Rogoff made an argument for central bank independence and that – as might make sense in the model of Barro and Gordon or Backus and Driffill – there is some advantage in the policymaker exhibiting an extreme distaste for inflation. In fact Rogoff's point was the opposite one, that one does not want such a policymaker.

Indeed, another crucial distinction between Rogoff and Backus and Driffill is that the latter treat the central problem as being one of how to identify the policymaker's type. If Rogoff's proposal is taken literally as one to appoint a central banker of certain characteristics, then it would evidently be the case that he was assuming Backus and Driffill's problem does not exist. This is one of the considerations that led me to argue in Forder (1998) that it is a mistake to treat Rogoff as making a proposal as to who should be the central banker, but rather one should see him as offering a plan of action for a public-spirited person in that role. In any case, it must be recognized that there is a considerable tension between the argument of Backus and Driffill and that of Rogoff so that one can hardly imagine that it is desirable to appoint an independent central banker for the reason Rogoff gives, and believe that such a policymaker will nevertheless face a problem of reputation-building which should be thought about along the lines suggested by Backus and Driffill. The idea, for example, that the European Central Bank is desirable because it is known to be inflation averse, but must nevertheless always act pre-emptively to control inflation because of its need to build reputation is theoretically absurd.

These, then, I believe are the main lines of thinking of the credibility literature and some crucial characteristics of the models are summarized in Table 2.1. Kydland and Prescott discovered what they took to be a problem arising from the way policy is made, and an explanation of the continuous inflation of the post-war period. They also offered a solution, which involves making policy in a different way. Barro and Gordon chose to view the problem as one of game theory and alleged that the private sector could not be expected to believe that a policymaker had really adopted Kydland and Prescott's proposal, unless it was because of a reputational mechanism. The mechanism they suggested, however, seems poorly designed for the kind of problem in question, and so, at least in general outline, the reputational account given by Backus and Driffill seems to offer a closer correspondence with the intuitions that guide much thinking about monetary policymaking. Rogoff, on the other hand, was not seeking to solve the credibility problem at all,[14] but rather to refine Kydland and Prescott's solution to the time-consistency problem. Although any of the arguments can be taken considerably further, these, I believe, are the ones which, in one way or another, provide the theoretical ballast for almost all discussions of the design of monetary policy-making institutions and the 'credibility problem'.

Table 2.1 Problems and effects of monetary policy

Author[1]	Rational expectations?[2]	Policy ineffectiveness?[3]	Time-consistency problem?[4]	Credibility problem?[5]	Benefit of reputation?[6]	Electoral manipulation?[7]	Short-termism?[8]
Friedman	No	Yes	No	No	No	No	Perhaps
Nordhaus	No	No	No	No	No	Yes	Yes
Lucas	Yes	Yes	Yes	No	No	No	No
Kydland and Prescott	Yes	Yes	Yes	No	No	No	No
Barro and Gordon	Yes	Yes	Yes	Yes	Yes	No	No
Backus and Driffill	Yes	Yes	Yes	Yes	Yes	No	No
Rogoff	Yes	No	Yes	No	No	No	No

Notes:
1. The articles in question are those referred to in the text.
2. 'Rational expectations?' records whether the authors assume rational expectations.
3. 'Policy ineffectiveness?' records whether the authors either assume or argue for a role for policy in either determining long-run outcomes or in stabilization.
4. 'Time-consistency problem?' records whether there is a time-consistency problem in the model.
5. 'Credibility problem?' records whether the authors suggest that Kydland and Prescott's solution to the time-consistency problem will not work.
6. 'Benefit of reputation?' records whether the policymaker's record of policy is treated as a determinant of credibility.
7. 'Electoral manipulation?' records whether the model treats policymakers as having anti-social electoral objectives.
8. 'Short-termism?' records whether the model treats policymakers as excessively short-termist.

TWO KEY CONFUSIONS

There is no doubt that there are many criticisms of the theory of credibility. I have questioned the grounds for believing the problem is in any practical way important in Forder (2001) and whether it argues for central bank independence in Forder (1998). The present objective is, however, to identify ways in which relevance of the theory has been misunderstood, and there are two major areas in which this has occurred. One is that it seems to be widely believed that the credibility problem is caused by electoral objectives; the other that credibility problems are caused by short-termist policy. Both of these are mistaken, but in each case, some degree of confusion is understandable because there are a variety of forms of short-termism and electoral incentive, and some of these have certain resemblances to the credibility problem. Consequently, there is no escape from considering the issue in some detail.

Credibility and Elections

It is clear that if the policymaker places little weight on the achievement of price stability, then inflation is likely to be the outcome. There are a number of possible variations of this idea. The policymaker might like inflation. Or it may be that there is no unique 'social interest' to maximize, and inflation is the outcome of the policymaker's efforts to deal with social conflict. Kydland and Prescott, however, excluded both of these possibilities by specifically assuming that there is an agreed social welfare function relating inflation and unemployment, and that it is shared by the policymaker. The indifference curves of Figure 2.1 therefore are those of the policymaker, and they are also those of each member of society.

This is an important point in the development of the argument because it is persistently asserted – in some or other form of words – by the advocates of central bank independence that the time-consistency problem has something to do with the policymaker having electoral objectives. But electoral objectives are, evidently, sectional objectives, and consequently not shared by the private sector as a whole. Kydland and Prescott (1977 p. 475) say,

> 'An agreed upon social objective function ... is assumed to exist'

and

> 'it is assumed that there is some social objective function which rationalizes policy choice'.

These statements clearly leave no room for the view that it is the chasing after party advantage which lies at the root of the problem.[15] Consequently all statements to the effect that the quest for party advantage cause a time-consistency problem are false, and there is no room for further debate. Whatever the effects of that quest may be, they do not include generating that problem.

Even apart from this, it is difficult to see that a 'finding' that electoral objectives might distort policy would have attracted much attention. Is it really supposed that it took the economics profession until the 1970s to discover that if policy is set in the private, rather than the public, interest it might fail to maximize social welfare? Even the formalization of the point with respect to monetary policy pre-dates Kydland and Prescott, being attributable to Nordhaus (1975).[16] If voters can be fooled before an election into thinking that a fall in unemployment is attributable to good government, rather than a transitory monetary expansion, then governments seeking re-election have an incentive to pursue such policy. In this case, the problem can be attributed, according to taste, either to the politicians' unfortunate incentives, or to the voters' lack of acuity. But in Kydland and Prescott's argument, neither of these conditions pertains: they are both specifically assumed away. Furthermore, it is quite clear that Kydland and Prescott were thinking of 'the policymaker' as being the Federal Reserve, not an elected policymaker. The fact that they were diagnosing a failing of the policy of that institution is surely a knock-down of the view that the problem is traceable to electioneering and to regard them merely as restating Nordhaus is to trivialize their considerable insight.

If the time-consistency problem itself is not a consequence of electoral motivations, it might still be supposed that the credibility problem emerges because of elections. This too is a mistake, but the argument depends on which of the subsequent lines of thought one follows.

Barro and Gordon (1983a, p. 591) follow Kydland and Prescott precisely in saying: 'We view the policymaker as attempting to maximise an objective that reflects "society's" preferences on inflation and unemployment'. It should be noted that it is 'the policymaker' not 'the elected policymaker' whom they analyse and the problem that that person faces is therefore not dissolved by independence. Once again, to treat their problem as one of electoral motivation is to make a fundamental error and to misconstrue the essence of their argument.

Alternatively, in the case where policymaking is the kind of struggle to establish reputation that Backus and Driffill envisaged, a temporary, but renewable period of office would seem to be almost an ideal arrangement to provide appropriate incentives for the establishing and maintenance of reputation. If we think of the voter as caring only for the policy outcomes, then a policymaker who has a reputation for inflation aversity is desirable. Such a policymaker is precisely one who engenders the kind of expectation that leads to a low Phillips curve. And if the Phillips curve is lower, the menu of available combinations of inflation and output is preferable. Therefore the policy outcome will be better. This must mean that well-informed voters will tend to vote for a policymaker with such a reputation. Therefore – and this, of course, is the crucial point – all incumbent policymakers have every incentive to treasure a reputation for inflation aversity. It can only be an electoral asset. Indeed, this point, although it has been ignored by almost all of the advocates of central bank independence was perfectly clearly noted by Backus and Driffill (1985a, p. 536) themselves.[17] They said, 'If there were a chance of reelection, the incentive to preserve reputation may actually restrain the spending spree'.

Some authors nevertheless seem to be tempted to suppose that the policymaker might set about building a reputation during the early years in office in order to have a lower Phillips curve available towards the end so that a highly favourable position could then be created by surprise inflation. On this kind of reasoning it seems that there is room for both reputation building and electoral motivations, and one would expect to see a pattern of outcomes resembling that suggested by Nordhaus: contraction in the early years, and expansion in the later ones.

However, there are two fatal mistakes in this. First is that it does not take the idea of rational expectations seriously. The opportunity and incentive to build reputation – in the technical sense – only arise because of this assumption. But on that assumption, voters will not be impressed by the creation of a boom they know to be damaging. Quite the opposite. The idea that elections can be won by generating a high level of employment at the right time is an idea which, plausible as it may well be, depends on a lack of understanding among the electorate. It is no good, therefore, trying to reconstruct that argument in a model which has already assumed their full understanding of the structure of the economy. Therefore, if one is adopting the assumption of rational expectations one needs to carry that thought through to the analysis of electoral motivations.

Just as fatal to this view, although a more subtle argument, is the consequence of an understanding of how reputation is acquired. Backus and Driffill, following a long line of game-theoretic enquiry, supposed that if reputation is valuable, anyone will take any available costless actions that lead to its acquisition. But precisely for that reason, the private sector will take no notice of costless actions, and hence there will be none that has the desired effect. The private sector will uprate their estimate of a particular policymaker being of the inflation-averse kind only when they observe an action which it would be unlikely that another kind of policymaker would take.[18]

However, if it is postulated that policymakers care only for their re-election, and that reputation is therefore only valued because of the possibility of exploding it in a pre-election boom, the conventional ideas will not follow. On the assumption of such motivations, the consequence would be that – if it will be effective in building reputation – any policymaker will act in a counterinflationary way in the early period of government. But if that is true, then no such action will be effective in building reputation. Such action has become, on the electoral-motivation assumptions in play, the kind of thing that any policymaker would do. Therefore doing it does not convey information about what kind one is. Therefore, one cannot reconstruct an electoral cycle from Backus and Driffill's model.

If one prefers not to treat reputational considerations as the essential ones, there is a temptation to try to reconstruct an electoral cycle from the argument of Rogoff. In that case there is no issue of the policymaker's 'type' being unknown, but merely an issue as to how to select a candidate of the socially optimal degree of inflation aversity. Here, there is something of a temptation to suppose that individuals will vote for candidates who share their own preferences. Such an outcome is likely to be undesirable since Rogoff showed that optimally the policymaker will be more inflation averse than society as a whole. This may create the illusion of an argument for central bank independence. The reality – if one takes the model seriously – is that there is no compelling reason for people not to vote for a policymaker more inflation averse than they are themselves if that will improve policy outcomes. Since Rogoff's argument entails that it will, one must conclude that well-informed voters will elect a Rogoff-banker.[19]

While these results – the electoral advantages of preserving reputation and the electability of the Rogoff-banker – seem to indicate rather strongly that the theory of credibility argues against independence, this conclusion is not always accepted. Two attempts to escape the conclusion deserve attention.

One is to suppose that while economic agents have rational expectations, this assumption should not be extended to voters. In that case the conclusions of credibility theory might hold good, but there could still be an electoral benefit in mismanagement of the economy. The other is the idea that the policymaker might have an informational advantage over the private sector so that, in appropriate circumstances and with good timing, it would be possible to create the impression of successful economic outcomes at election times. The *ad hoc* nature of either of these moves will be evident. Why should it be that wage bargainers have this insight which is not available to voters?[20] Why should the government not be able to make available the information which, all the while it is private, curses them with the credibility problem? On the other hand, if there is some obstacle to creating the institutions to make this information public, then one would have thought that there might be an equivalent one to making the central bank independent.

In any case, the proponents of either view are alleging that there are two distinct sources of excess inflation: the time-consistency problem is one, and the electoral incentive to generate a Nordhaus boom, whether traceable to voter myopia or policymaker informational advantage, is the other. Then it is being claimed that central bank independence is the solution to both. Of course it is not. On the assumptions being made – that wage bargainers understand the credibility problem but voters are fooled by electorally motivated policy – there is a permanent (Kydland and Prescott) inflation bias and an electoral cycle. The independent central bank might eliminate the latter, but it does nothing for the former. It is therefore a pretence that the theory of credibility is adding anything to the case for independence.

It is, I think, clear that if one chooses to take the credibility models seriously, rather than adopting their assumptions long enough to generate an inflation bias and then jettisoning them in time to advocate central bank independence, and that if they are relevant to the issue at all, they make a case for democratic control of policymaking. Certainly, alluring as the terminology is, there is no particular 'temptation' on elected policymakers to pursue bad policy. That will only get, from the voters, what it deserves. Here at least, then, the case for independence rests on sophistry.

Short-termism

Another recurring mistake in the interpretation of both Kydland and Prescott and the later authors is the supposition that their results are the outcome of policymaker short-termism. This is a more difficult issue than that of electoral incentives because there are important terminological ambiguities, not least in the meaning of 'short-termist' itself, and there are problems related to that of time inconsistency which might loosely be described as the outcome of short-termism without thereby attracting opprobrium. But despite a great deal that has been written to the contrary no truly short-termist policy is involved in the time-consistency problem.

One source of confusion may simply be that the argument is made by reference to the 'short-run Phillips curve'. This, however, is merely a technical name for a particular theoretical construct. It does not justify the application of the powerfully normative description 'short-termist' to any policy that happens to come under consideration in such a model. It is true that the time-consistency problem arises because in certain circumstances, albeit only hypothetical ones, the policymaker (and society) would like to move up the Phillips curve, and it is also true that the policymaker would not then be acting under the impression that the beneficial effects of doing so would be permanent. But whether the effects of a policy are permanent does not determine whether the policy is 'short-termist'. Satisfying one's hunger, for example, is only temporarily effective. It is not therefore 'short-termist'.

Another possibility is that confusion arises from the temptation to think of Kydland and Prescott's argument as relating to a policymaker who ignores the future. It is not so. Kydland and Prescott explicitly note that if the policymaker is presuming that a policy of inflation raises the expected rate of inflation and thereby worsens the Phillips curve available in the future, that is a factor that will be taken into account by the policymaker. It does not, however, mean that the optimal rate of inflation will be zero.[21] They say (1977, p. 481): 'It is hard to fault a policymaker acting consistently [that is, with 'discretion']. The reason that such policies are suboptimal is not due to myopia. The effect of this decision upon the entire future is taken into consideration'. Unless the advocates of independence have an argument that Kydland and Prescott were mistaken in the interpretation of their own model, that would seem to resolve the issue.

Another possibility is that the label 'short-termist' is erroneously attached to Kydland and Prescott's problem because of certain similarities with other analyses. If we suppose the same structure of the economy as Kydland and Prescott did, but not that the private sector has rational expectations, then there are a range of possibilities. One is that we might imagine an economy which begins at the natural rate of unemployment, and zero inflation and expected inflation. This is a position that never arises for Kydland and Prescott so long as policy is set by discretion, because expected inflation cannot be zero. However, when expectations are adaptive, starting from that position, the policymaker does have the opportunity to raise inflation above the expected level and thereby reduce unemployment. It is routinely argued, following Friedman that such a policy would cause expectations of inflation to rise, thereby worsening the trade-off available in the immediate future. The policymaker might then, at some point in the future, choose to raise inflation further, again causing it to be above expectation, and achieving another temporary fall in unemployment. All benefits of such a policy cease when inflation and expected inflation reach such a level that a further increase in inflation is in itself so damaging to social welfare that the fall in unemployment is not worth the price that must be paid. There would therefore be an equilibrium rate of inflation where the marginal cost of surprise inflation is equal to the marginal benefit of the fall in unemployment that it would bring. The diagrammatic representation of this long-run equilibrium could well look like Figure 2.1, with the equilibrium at point B.

Some caution about whether to call such a policy 'short-termist' would still be in order. One possibility is that the policymaker has failed to recognize that current inflation worsens future opportunities. Friedman's arguments

(1968 and even more clearly 1977) can be understood to be precisely to this effect: policy was too inflationary because policymakers had not understood its intertemporal effects. If Friedman's understanding were thought to be correct, it would be natural, I suggest, to describe it as a case of policymaking which, because it was based on bad theory, is properly described as bad policy. On the other hand, I can see that the more tendentious label 'short-termist' might have rhetorical appeal to the policy's opponents. But to describe the resultant excess inflation as the result of 'time inconsistency' would be a clear mistake.

A second possibility is that policymakers do understand the structure of the economy, but accept the eventual equilibrium inflation because of the benefits in the form of increased output that it brings in the interim. It has frequently been assumed since Friedman (1968) that if it raises inflation, maintaining unemployment below the natural rate must be bad policy, and could then easily be regarded as short-termist. Indeed it is rather rare to see this view challenged.[22] But normal analysis would seek to estimate the costs and benefits before dismissing the policy. On Friedman's account the case for price stability would seem to be rather weak. He suggested that expected inflation might take decades to catch up with reality, and that in the interim, unemployment might be measurably below its natural rate. So if we say, on the basis of a policy of gradually raising inflation, that expected inflation might rise from zero to 10 per cent over 30 years, and that in the interim, unemployment might be kept 2 per cent below its natural rate, we can perform a thoroughly back-of-the-envelope cost–benefit calculation.[23] Over the 30-year period, the total of output in excess of the natural level will be about 60 per cent of one year's GDP.[24] At a rate of return of 5 per cent, that extra output, if invested, is worth 3 per cent of GDP per year in perpetuity.[25] On the cost side we have an equilibrium rate of inflation of 10 per cent. The question, therefore, is whether we would think such an increment in income is worth the price of the inflation. Obviously the decision depends, among other things, on how costly inflation is felt to be – a matter of some controversy. What is clear, however, is that it is a strikingly puritanical view to suppose that the eventual cost could not be a price worth paying for the temporary fall in unemployment.[26]

It might be argued that the 60 per cent increment in output is unlikely to be invested, more probably being consumed. This is not really relevant. From the perspective of those who find themselves in the high inflation equilibrium, it may then seem regrettable that a policy of allowing inflation gradually to rise was followed. But the fact that later generations suffer a cost of the policy is not in and of itself equivalent to its being a short-termist policy. It merely means that an intergenerational transfer has occurred – not something which is in general automatically condemned.

So, while it is not clear that such a policy is bad policy, or 'short-termist' at all, it should be perfectly evident that in any case it has nothing to do with Kydland and Prescott's problem. Their assumptions do not permit the temporary fall in unemployment in the first place. Second, Kydland and Prescott's policymaker is specifically assumed to share the private sector's preferences, including their discount rate. Therefore, whatever balance is being struck between immediate and future well-being is society's balance, not particularly the policymaker's. And third, even if the policymaker had some discount rate less than the private sector's, so that future generations were treated more favourably, Kydland and Prescott's *reductio* would still apply and therefore the time-consistency problem would, in some degree, still exist. This, I think, makes it clear that the issue of the policymaker's discount rate cannot be the source of the time-consistency problem.

One might, of course, still be inclined to argue that policymakers often have discount rates which are normatively too high. If this could be established, then it is clearly appropriate to call the resulting policy 'short-termist'. It would also be a case of bad policy, and perhaps of the wrong person setting the policy. Equally, it is clear that some argument for central bank independence might be crafted out of such an outcome, if one were inclined to make all the positive and normative arguments it would require. But even so, a case of bad policy due to the policymaker using the wrong discount rate is clearly not a case of a time-consistency problem. It is simply a case of bad policy.

Thinking of the problem of credibility, rather than that of time consistency, there is a possible role of the policymaker discount factor in determining the effectiveness of attempts to establish reputation. Since the benefits of reputation accrue in the future, its present value depends on the policymaker's discount rate. One with a lower rate will have a greater interest in building reputation. Therefore, the effectiveness of reputational solutions to the credibility problem depends on the policymaker's discount rate.[27] This may be a reason why the credibility problem is attributed to short-termism. But that is still an unwarranted move. It is true that credibility would be better established by a policymaker with a lower discount rate. That does not change the fact that the policymaker is presumed to have the same discount rate as society as a whole, and so the appellation 'short-termist' is churlish. There is a case for appointing an atypical policymaker, in a Rogoffesque manner – this time one with an unusually low discount rate. But, this leads nowhere in particular since again, if that is what is desirable, such a person can be elected. The temptation again exists to suppose that elected policymaker discount rates become very high when elections approach, but just as before, this creates no policy problem. It is the policymaker who adopts the policy favoured by the public who will achieve re-election. If the public have elected someone to behave as if they have a low discount rate, it is doing that which will win favour.

Another possible confusion arises from an entirely different kind of discounting issue. Discount functions are usually assumed to be exponential, and this leads to the characteristic that the marginal rate of substitutability between utility in any two periods will be the same however far in the future they lie. However, if a discount function is non-exponential, the result is that the rate of substitutability between two fixed times – 2051 and 2052, say – will depend on whether the issue is viewed from 2050 or from 2049. A consequence of this is that the situation can arise where a plan made at one point in time, and then partially executed, is no longer a maximizing plan at a future date. So, for example, if a fixed budget is to be consumed over three periods, the consumer will have different preferences between the second and third periods at the start of the second from those at the start of the first.[28]

This problem was systematically analysed by Strotz (1956) who observed that under certain conditions, it will generate behaviour of a familiar type that is sometimes regarded as irrational. For example, an individual might persistently feel that some point in the near, but not immediate, future will be the appropriate time to bear some cost. Whenever that near future arrives, however, the current consumption is valued more relative to the future than the consumption of that period was while it still lay in the future.[29] The bearing of the cost would then rationally be postponed. This behaviour pattern clearly resembles what might be called 'weakness of the will'.[30]

A further case, closely resembling the Strotz problem, and more distantly resembling the time-consistency case might also be distinguished. This occurs if there is an endogenous change of preferences, of which the most familiar case is perhaps the possibility of an acquired taste. This would not be attributable to any particular discount function, but rather to a change in the shape of the underlying utility function. This case is, I believe, the one that is correctly called 'the Odysseus problem'.[31]

The distinction between these three problems should be quite clear. Endogenous changes of preference lead to a new utility function; the Strotz problem leads to replanning of present and future activities as moments move from the distant future to the near future, not because of a change in the underlying utility function, but because of the peculiarities of the discount function. The time-inconsistency problem, however, has an entirely different source, being traceable to the reactions of other agents to the manner in which one agent chooses to make policy.

Confusion has set in, however, perhaps in part because of the terminology that has been adopted, and in part because of the similarity of treatments that have been prescribed for the different problems. As to the terminology, the Strotz problem was labelled by later authors, for example, Elster (1979 ch. II.5) as that of 'inconsistent time preferences'. The similarity to 'time-inconsistent policy' is not at all helpful, but it should still be clear that in one case it is preferences which are 'inconsistent', and the other label refers to a problem about policy. The two are quite distinct.

As to the solutions, Strotz proposed two for his problem. One – only a partial solution – he called the 'consistent plan', presaging, unfortunately, Kydland and Prescott's description of their discretionary policy in the same words. For Strotz, the plan was to act today to maximize the utility function embodying the current discount factors, accepting as a constraint the fact that future behaviour will be set to solve the future optimization problem. Kydland and Prescott's idea of 'consistency' was quite different, being merely that the same (discretionary) procedure be applied to determine policy in all periods.

It is perhaps also not too difficult to see a resemblance between Strotz's 'consistent plan' and Barro and Gordon's idea of a reputational equilibrium. In both cases, an accommodation is made with the impossibility of firmly binding future policy, and the agent plans on the basis of the future incentives to maximize current discounted welfare. Of course, the apparent similarity is here achieved by the vagueness of the description: the two things are again in reality quite different. In the Strotz case, the insight is to recognize the change in one's own time preferences as affecting future behaviour. The Barro and Gordon idea of reputation relates to what other people will believe.

All three problems might also be addressed by an initial commitment of future policy. Most famously, perhaps, this was Odysseus' method of finding his way past the Sirens. Strotz actually used the label 'precommitment' to describe this kind of solution to his problem. This same term is now commonly used in game-theoretic settings to describe a particular kind of strategy, of which creating a binding rule to guide monetary policy is a possible example. However, there is a clear distinction between 'precommitment' in a game-theoretic problem and in either of the other two. The paradigm in the game-theoretic case is the problem of entry deterrence. The assumed circumstances are that if a potential entrant to a market believes that their entry will be met by price cuts by the incumbent monopolist, they will not enter. However, the potential entrant generally speaking also knows that in the event of entry it will not be advantageous for the incumbent to cut prices.[32] If the incumbent can devise some mechanism whereby it evidently becomes either obliged or incentivized to cut prices in the event of entry, then entry will be deterred. That device is then called a precommitment, and its value and interest lies in the fact that in making the precommitment an agent's incentives are changed in a way that makes it rational for another agent to behave in a manner that suits the precommiting agent's purposes. The idea of precommitment in the Strotz and Odysseus problems is quite different. There is no issue of strategic interaction with another agent, and therefore no issue of influencing that other agent's decision. One merely binds oneself to carry out one's original plan.

Some may feel that monetary policymakers are susceptible to any of these problems. The Strotz case is perhaps the hardest to envisage, but in any case, one cannot deny the possibility of policymakers having such discount functions. The Odysseus case could be imagined as one of the public-spirited policymaker being elected, but recognizing in advance the danger of acquiring an excessive taste for power, and of subsequently seeking to pursue that rather than the public interest. It might then be rational to seek a binding arrangement that would make it impossible for that taste to lead to a distortion of policy.[33]

Whether it would be appropriate to call behaviour exhibiting either the Strotz or the Odysseus problem one of 'short-termism', I am not sure, but certainly this seems to be done fairly frequently. However, I hope it is clear that any tendency of monetary policymaking to be afflicted by either problem, even if that leads one to call it short-termist, is most certainly nothing to do with either the time-consistency or the credibility problem. Although one can understand where this confusion arises, then, it should not be allowed to persist.

THE DANGERS OF THE THEORY OF PSEUDO-CREDIBILITY

I can see that I might be thought pedantic to make too much of the misuse of words. It could be said, after all, that electoral motivations are widely felt to be important in explaining policy failure, and a perfectly clear, if debatable, case for central bank independence exists without reference to credibility theory. If the danger of the Nordhaus cycle is sometimes called 'time inconsistency' and the benefits of avoiding it 'credibility', it is not much to say that these words are inappropriate. After all, nearly all economists use theoretical terms in more or less metaphorical ways – think of 'moral hazard', 'second best' and 'liquidity trap'. If my complaint is only designed to appeal to the purist and the lexicographer, how long should it detain the practical economist? So 'credibility' has a classical sense and a demotic one, but so what? One response I should offer is that one can be too quick to disown pedantry. Presumably the value of the rigorous mathematical approaches to problems in economics is to be found in the accuracy of inference and precision of meaning that such techniques bring. If so, it is a pity to have those assets frittered away by casuistic or simply haphazard application of theory to problem. In that case, one lesson that might be drawn from the development of the theory of policy credibility and the case made for central bank independence is that, whatever the advantages of mathematical exactitude, economics would benefit, at the margin, from greater attention to the interpretation of theory.

But that is enough of economic scholarship, and I should move into utilitarian mode. If the theory of credibility were treated in either of the ways I believe it reasonably might be, I would have no concern. The theory might be dismissed out of hand for any of a number of reasons. One could deny its monetarist framework; rational expectations; or the tendency for it to be presumed that government commitments are not to be trusted. One might remain neutral on these theoretical issues, and be impressed by Posen's (1998) negative conclusions on the availability of evidence. Alternatively, the simple observation that monetary transmission lags are now thought to be 18 months or more, but most wage bargains are for a shorter period means that the move order supposed by Kydland and Prescott is incorrect. If policy is set, and then wages are set, there is clearly no problem. Although the idea of credibility has provoked much excitement and kept numerous mathematical researchers busy, that would only locate it somewhere in the no-man's land between academic curiosity and job creation scheme. It would not make it a matter of concern.

On the other hand, one might prefer to take the theory seriously, as I have tried to take it in this chapter. But then it would be readily appreciated that it has little if anything to do with short-termism, electoral politics, or central bank independence. These things might also need to be taken seriously, but whatever argument were made could not invoke credibility theory in its support.

In fact, however, I believe that the theory is widely treated in a third way, which makes it worthy of study by Bricmont and Sokal (1998). In this theory of pseudo-credibility, lessons are only selectively drawn, and the result is an amalgam of ideas which appears scientific, but in fact is not. Borrowing an intuition of Nordhaus, it is said that booms at election time lead to success for the government; borrowing one from Barro and Gordon, it is said that the private sector will anticipate this behaviour to the extent that the policymaker is ineffective in building credibility. The establishment of this credibility is presumed to be a proper policy priority irrespective of the cost–benefit analysis. But, it is felt – perhaps on the basis of a misunderstanding of Rogoff – that it is hard, if not impossible for elected governments to have credibility. The case for independence having thus presented itself, some ideas from Backus and Driffill might still, in this hallucination, seem relevant to the issue of how that independent central banker goes about building reputation. In particular this conception seems to emphasize that it is a long struggle, requiring determination at all points, and one in which all reputation can be lost in a moment of weakness, or perhaps, returning to the origins of the myth, in a moment where the impression is created that there has been political influence on policy.

The first danger that arises from this is that opportunities for increases in output might be lost because of the fear of increasing inflation and thereby losing credibility. As Stiglitz (1998) among others has suggested, a policy of 'cautious expansionism' might reveal that a lower level of unemployment than currently believed is sustainable. If it did, the benefits would be great. But his proposal stands in stark contrast to the prevalent attitudes that 'prudence' – meaning pre-emptive counterinflationary action – is important, and that policymakers should 'err on the side of caution' – meaning caution about inflation, not about lost output. This excessive caution and the consensus which appears to surround it are hard to explain on the basis of proper economic analysis. As Stiglitz says, the worst that could happen if his policy were followed is that inflation might rise, and he implies that his policy is not followed because of one of three fears about this outcome. These are that a low rate of inflation will itself be very damaging, which is not the case. Alternatively it might be felt difficult to reverse. Again, he says, as far as one can tell, the Phillips curve is linear so that the costs of reducing inflation are no greater than the benefits of having allowed it to rise. Third, it might be feared that inflation has some more or less automatic tendency to acceleration – but where is the evidence for that?

But I fear that however successful Stiglitz may be in correcting these three mistakes, his argument will not lead to the adoption of his policy while the theory of pseudo-credibility holds sway. That theory paralyses policy with the fear that a small rise in inflation will destroy reputation. It is a curiosity, evidently, but no less dangerous for that, that so many of those who assert that their monetary policy is based on the view that it can have no long-run effects except on the price level, should be so enthralled by the idea of reputation. The danger is not that inflation will rise, but that credibility will be lost. And this we 'know', as a pseudo-scientific fact, because it is assumed by the models, will result in a great and lasting deterioration of opportunities.

A second danger can be identified by reflection on Kydland and Prescott's true insight at this point. Supposing that the private sector understands, as they certainly seem to be invited to at present, that policy will take whatever steps are necessary to stabilize the price level. And suppose, furthermore, that they understand – correctly, as I have suggested – that the modish 'prudence' will be exercised, so that when the outlook is uncertain, it will tend to be presumed that the main danger is a rise in inflation. This, I believe, can only be detrimental to private investment, and perhaps consumption as well. The potential investor is warned, in effect, that policy will be on average excessively contractionary. Investment must be planned, therefore, in the expectation of low levels of domestic demand, and so long as the control of inflation is implemented by monetary policy, an unfavourable exchange rate, and it must be understood that signs of booms, not just the reality, will result in policy aimed at appreciation. From this line of thinking, we might infer that rather than the inflation bias of policy analysed by Kydland and Prescott, we should be concerned at the danger of a credibility bias arising from a misinterpretation of the literature which they initiated.

A third danger is of a slightly different character. It arises from the attitude that the theory of credibility invites one to take towards distributive concerns. Kydland and Prescott assumed an agreed social welfare function. Their motive in this, I have suggested, was merely to lead to the demonstration that they could explain equilibrium inflation without reference to sectional interests. There was no argument that it was a good representation of reality. Nevertheless, on the basis of this assumption, adopted by later authors, it follows that all members of the private sector benefit equally from the establishment of credibility. This gives the policymaker's credibility the character of a public good. If a more favourable Phillips curve becomes available, and the natural rate of unemployment is then achieved at a lower rate of inflation, this benefits all equally. Although this is an assumption, not a finding, as regards the benefits of low inflation, it might be argued that it is not too far from being accurate.[34] On the other hand, a point which is rather easily overlooked is that the costs of establishing credibility can hardly, in reality, be supposed to be borne equally by all. Reputation, at least in the more plausible Backus and Driffill framework, is established only by accepting unemployment. The costs of establishing credibility therefore fall on those who are in insecure employment, have few savings and live in depressed regions.[35] It is no consolation to those who bear these costs that the benefits they earn are shared with others. So here, the pseudo-theory invites the dismissal of an important concern, but offers only an assumption, no argument, that it should be dismissed.

A further consequence arises from a further development of the idea of pseudo-credibility. This suggests that credibility is assessed – or one might say, conferred – by the financial markets. This has no warrant in the actual models usually under consideration, since it is the expectations of the labour market which are important.[36] Nevertheless, many versions of pseudo-credibility theory seem to suggest that credibility can only be achieved by satisfying whatever happen to be the current demands of spokespeople of the financial sector. So it is never too much of a surprise to find that, for example, the view is gaining ground that labour market deregulation, a certain arrangement of tax policy, or even the trade arrangements desired by financial markets are essential to the maintenance of credibility.[37]

But the fifth, and perhaps the greatest danger arises from the attitude one is invited to take towards the value of democracy. It is hard to see where the point has been argued, but the idea that democracy damages the people's welfare is enthymematic in almost all discussion of central bank independence. Indeed, while Rogoff joked that the noun 'central banker' seems to demand the adjective 'conservative', it now seems at least as common to presume that 'short term' is an inevitable description of 'political objective', and with it comes contempt.[38]

There are, of course, many arguments that democracy is an undesirable system of government, and there is a certain fashionable disdain for it. It is not to be wondered at, then, if the constant repetition of the undesirability of 'political objectives' influencing monetary policy gradually contaminates the discussion of politics more generally. This is not the place to advocate democracy, but it should be noted that there are also many arguments in its favour and certainly that more attention should be given to its value before it is given up, even in limited areas.

It is in the area of the deprecation of democracy, I think, that the pseudo-credibility theory serves the purposes of the advocates of central bank independence particularly powerfully. If one were forced to argue the general undesirability of policy being formed on the basis of 'political objectives', it would evidently be necessary to accept that the case for democracy was being doubted. Instead of being required to accept this challenge, the advocates of central bank independence have been favoured with the support of theoretical illusions which suggest a special and distinct failing of democracy in the area of monetary control. By pretending that it is monetary policy alone that requires insulation from democracy, the theory of pseudo-credibility allows the advocates of independence to avoid a crucial challenge to their case.[39]

The striking significance of this possibility is particularly apparent when one considers the affinity between some popular arguments for democracy and some key presumptions of neo-classical economics, with the general sense that people know their own interest being central to both. This view would have to be abandoned in a strictly selective way if the case for central bank independence were to be made without either the support of the theory of pseudo-credibility, or alternatively inviting a wider reconsideration of economic policy. When the illusions of pseudo-credibility are stripped away, and replaced by the real thing, it becomes clear that the case for central bank independence rests only on the failure of individuals to secure their own interest. If we are assuming rational expectations, and we believe that policy is short-termist, it is because voters are short-termist. Alternatively, if a boom before an election does favour the incumbent, that must be due, if not to an extreme short-termism, and a willingness to reward such policy on the part of the private sector, then to a failure of their understanding as to what occurs.

To this, one might respond, by all means, assume that voters are myopic. Let the thought not just be entertained, but believed, acted upon, that the American voter is myopic and will reward the creators of unsustainable booms with re-election. Let a case for central bank independence or other devices to restrict democracy be argued clearly on these grounds. But how is it then to be argued that there can be no question of seeking to counteract those same households' tendency to a high level of consumption and an accumulation of international debt? Let us also, in this spirit throw away the ideas of policy invariance: neither Ricardian equivalence, nor the Permanent Income Hypothesis nor even the neutrality of money are defended on such assumptions as we would then be making. Let it be said, similarly that the market is not all-knowing. The voters may be fooled by the electorally-motivated window-dressing of the national economy. But then why should the markets not be equally fooled by transient or cosmetic characteristics of corporate performance? And what is then the case for the efficiency of capital markets?

Clearly, once one adopts the view that the biological creature caricatured as *homo economicus* is quite so blinkered, or quite so prey to the whims and pleasures of the moment, it may well be easy to make a case for central bank independence. But there will be no hope for the broader framework of the adoration of the market which so dominates the discussion of economic policy. A whole range of interventions might become desirable to assist the now benighted private sector in fulfilling their own objectives. The restraint of consumption; the direction of investment; restriction of financial markets; regulation of the labour market; even the command of key industries are all easy to advocate if one is permitted the assumption that the private sector cannot tell benefit from harm.

The pseudo-credibility theory, however, seeks to have it both ways. There is a pretence that there exists a mystical 'time-consistency problem' which is 'understood' by the invocation of its mysterious and confusing terminology, by the malice of politicians, by their alleged professional incentive to disregard the public interest, and by their short-termism. This problem, of course, does not arise from any failing of the private sector, but rather from the metaphysics of the model. Therefore, no more general conclusion is to be drawn than that in this one, convenient, policy area, control of policy should be removed from democracy. 'Credibility', similarly, in the great jumble of assumption, deduction and prejudice which characterizes the use of the term is easily supposed to be something uniquely associated with central bankers, and uniquely necessary in the conduct of monetary policy.

Without the ideas that credibility is important, achieved only by unbreakable commitment, and that those whom we elect can certainly not be trusted with our interests, it is impossible, I think, to explain, let alone justify Article 107 of the Maastricht Treaty,[40] which says,

> Neither the European Central Bank nor a national central bank, nor any member of their decision-making bodies shall seek or take instructions from Community institutions or bodies, from any government of a Member State or from any other body. The Community institutions and bodies and the governments of the Member States undertake to respect this principle and not to seek to influence the members

of the decision-making bodies of the European Central Bank or of the national central banks.

And the prohibition of seeking to influence, if it is not a drafting error, is surely a testimony to pseudo-credibility's power in undermining democracy. How else could it be thought reprehensible for the elected representatives of the people to seek to influence – by persuasive argument perhaps – the central aspects of policy?

And in Europe there is a further fear. Should it come about that price stability in some countries and pseudo-credibility for the European Central Bank is paid for by recession in other countries, it can hardly be expected that harmonious relations will be preserved and it is a pity that the European project might be endangered by what is so often regarded as its greatest achievement. In the normal course of events, one might expect a political reaction to prevent an undue burden being borne by some. But in the case in question, an extravagant conflict might then seem to threaten since the theory of pseudo-credibility can hardly escape the conclusion that an 'attempt to influence' the central bank is itself something that damages credibility, since it is, by that theory, in the nature of political objectives that they are contrary to the public interest. For that reason, one supposes, any such attempt should lead to firmer policy, required by the dictates of pseudo-credibility. In such an environment, the 'independence' of the central bank, and its own interest in displaying it, can therefore become a great curse.

CONCLUSION

Excessively contractionary policies; the dismissal of distributive concerns; and insinuation against democracy are always likely to arise from prejudice and interest. But the intellectual imposture which is the theory of pseudo-credibility creates the impression of a source of scientific support for these things which it does not have. It is a separate danger, then, that bad policy might be followed because of theoretical confusion. Far from being mere matters of theory, therefore, the concerns I have raised point to serious dangers for policy.

And so doubts about central bank independence, at least in one aspect, easily arise from the thought that central bankers of our time are the least well placed to dismiss concerns of pseudo-credibility from their thinking. Indeed, it could be said that they have an interest in maintaining it, since it, in turn, maintains their status. One can hope that wisdom and insight will prevail, as in the long run perhaps they do. But the status of central banks – the esteem in which they are held – now depends so much on the idea that they supply 'credibility' that one might well fear that it is asking too much for their policy to ignore it. If this is so, then the achievement of policy which is not dominated by the fantastic versions of this theory may in itself call for a reconsideration of the institutions of monetary control.

NOTES

* I am grateful for the comments of Philip Arestis and Malcolm Sawyer on an earlier draft.
1. Which is not to say that Friedman had no other objection to discretionary policy. He clearly did, believing it to raise issues of political acceptability which are hinted at in Friedman (1948), but made much clearer in Friedman (1962 and 1967).
2. In Forder (1998, p. 310) I was either confused or confusing when I wrote that in the Kydland and Prescott world, the time-inconsistency problem 'can be solved by making explicit a rule which guides private sector expectations in a helpful direction or by keeping it implicit and following it for long enough'. As Jörg Bibow has pointed out to me, on the view I had adopted that the policy process is transparent so that the private sector just know whether policy is set by a 'rule' or 'discretion', all that is required is that the policymaker adopt the rule. The private sector can be relied on to see and understand what has happened. If such transparency is not assumed, they need to be told, obviously.
3. As they noted, the patents problem is similar. It would clearly enhance economic performance today if patents were abolished. Equally, the approach of allowing patents (presumably) affects the rate of innovation so that it is easy to suppose that the 'rule' of allowing them serves us better than the 'discretionary' policy of deciding at each point in time whether existing patents are serving the public interest.
4. And unfortunately, the researches of Blinder (2000) seemed designed to perpetuate muddle. Although he is on record as finding little practical value in the Barro–Gordon theory (see, for example, Blinder 1997), by conducting a survey of attitudes of academics and central bankers to 'credibility' without further specifying what he meant, he left himself no way of telling whether the responses related to 'credibility' in the Barro–Gordon sense; in the ordinary English sense; in some muddled combination of the two; or something else entirely. A reasonable guess may be that central bankers tended to answer about ordinary English 'credibility' and academics about the Barro–Gordon kind, and this would indeed go some way to explaining aspects of the results that puzzled Blinder, but who knows?
5. There no doubt are important issues of 'credibility' in the ordinary English sense that arise in monetary policymaking. But 'credibility' in that sense is not to be acquired or maintained in the ways suggested in the models under discussion.
6. The adopting of this punishment strategy lacks rationality in the clear sense that once the offence has been committed, the punishment can do no good. The threat to continue with such a punishment strategy is therefore something that should itself lack credibility in the technical sense. The idea that the whole of the private sector can nevertheless be costlessly assumed to embark on the strategy, when from the point of view of each one, there is every incentive to free ride on the punishment delivered by the rest, clearly lacks credibility in the ordinary English sense.
7. Again, it could be said that Fellner (1979) made an earlier argument with some similarities and captured much of the point without formalization.
8. This discussion cuts some theoretical corners in order to highlight the aspects of the Backus and Driffill argument which I believe are both intuitive and have been influential. The mathematical chapter and verse is of course readily available for those who want it in Backus and Driffill (1985b).
9. A characteristic which leads to a useful excuse for failed monetarist stabilizations, since when inflation falls but unemployment remains, this can be blamed on the supposedly

10. poor, but unobservable, reputation of the policymaker. There is of course nothing to be done but stick it out until the reputation improves.
10. Whether it was unacceptable because it was genuinely damaging or for some other reason is immaterial. Permitting inflation at that level was clearly not maximizing the private sector's utility.
11. It should be noted that this argument is not vulnerable to a critique based on the presumption of a natural rate of unemployment. Throughout the period of reputation building the inflation outcome is lower than the private sector (probabilistically) expected, and therefore unemployment is, by that theory, above the natural rate.
12. A certain degree of intuitive justification of this assumption is available along these lines: all policymakers 'try' to set the low inflation policy (either because they prefer it, or to build reputation), but the will of the, presumptively soft-hearted, less inflation-averse one might crack at an unexpected moment.
13. And it may of course be vulnerable to a Friedmanesque critique of discretion.
14. To recall: the 'credibility problem' is the one that arises from the private sector's behaviour being presumed to be dominated by their perception of the policymaker's incentive to lie.
15. Nothing is fundamentally different in Backus and Driffill or Rogoff. Although the possible existence of policymakers of different 'types' is introduced, there is still presumed to be an underlying agreement on social objectives. Elections feature in none of these accounts as explanations of policy failure.
16. Which is the latest possible dating of this 'insight'. The basic idea is evident in Plato's *Republic*.
17. They also, it must be admitted, said that a response might be to appoint central bankers with a reputation for controlling inflation. But this seems to be a much weaker piece of analysis, since they gave no hint of how the central banker might have acquired that reputation prior to being appointed.
18. This is only the application of Bayes' rule.
19. The distinction between having a certain objective function and achieving a certain objective is well known in the principal–agent literature. If it is thought reasonable for shareholders to appoint a manager who is not a profit maximizer in order to increase profits by deterring entry, why should voters not elect a policymaker more inflation averse than they? This result has, in effect, been noted first by Alesina and Grilli (1992) and then by Lippi and Swank (1999), without either seeming to think it brought the idea of central bank independence into much question.
20. Some are tempted to suppose that unionization makes the difference, but they fail to reflect on how much unionization has declined; how hard it is to find cases of reference being made to credibility issues in wage disputes; or why in such a case we would not all look to unions for guidance on how to vote.
21. Sargent (1999) is confusing without quite being wrong. In Chapter 3 he presents what he calls the time-consistency problem for the case where there is only one period, saying that the policymaker 'forgets' there is a future. In Chapter 4, he then reconstructs the problem for the case of infinite time, just as Kydland and Prescott first stated it. His motive appears to be to introduce some terminology he is going to use later in the book, but it is very much to be hoped that the impression is not given that Chapter 3 alone offers some kind of simplified, but serviceable, statement of Kydland and Prescott's problem. It does not.
22. Galbraith (1997) therefore being unusual.
23. These numbers are, I think, somewhat more generous to the anti-inflation case than a reading of Friedman would suggest. He wrote that it might take 'decades' for expected inflation to catch up with actual inflation, but in 1968 that referred to rates of inflation well below 10 per cent. One would expect, therefore, to be able to set inflation at, say, 3 per cent before having to raise it to 6 per cent and later to higher levels while spending 'decades' at each level, benefiting from low unemployment all the while. A total transition period of 30 years to reach expected inflation of 10 per cent can therefore hardly be too optimistic.
24. Again, an unfavourable assumption from my point of view. I have assumed that 2 per cent

25. extra employment in each of these years leads to 2 per cent extra output. An application of Okun's law would entitle me to double that amount.
26. And it is worth noting that if one thinks of the extra output associated with inflation being invested, then (depending on the growth theory one adopts) it may not even be the case that the benefit of the policy is only temporary, making its rapid dismissal from consideration even harder to understand.
27. If I may be permitted a small jibe at one of my elders and betters, I note that Friedman (1948, p. 245) disparages the tendency of economists 'to act and talk as if any improvement, however slight, in control of the cycle justified any sacrifice, however large, in the long-run efficiency, or prospects for growth of the economic system'. Twenty years later he had apparently moved over to the view that any increase in inflation, however small was too high a price to pay for other benefits, however large.
28. This is true in one way or another in the Barro and Gordon and the Backus and Driffill models.
29. A consumer has the utility function $U = C_t^{1/2} + \frac{1}{3}C_{t+1}^{1/2} + +\frac{1}{6}C_{t+2}^{1/2}$ and the budget constraint $C_1 + C_2 + C_3 = 82$, where C_i is consumption in period i. At $t = 1$, maximization of the utility function leads to $C_1 = 72$, $C_2 = 8$ and $C_3 = 2$. Supposing the consumer acts on this plan, then at $t = 2$, the remaining budget is 10, and re-optimizing, with the utility function now in effect simply $U = C_t^{1/2} + \frac{1}{3}C_{t+1}^{1/2}$ leads to $C_2 = 9$ and $C_1 = 1$.
30. Strotz was writing before the invention of the snooze button, but he would surely have thought it emblematic of his idea.
31. A discount function that prioritizes the present, but treats all the future periods in the normal exponential way will lead to behaviour which persistently exhibits 'weakness of the will' in this sense. It should be noted that it is far from clear that this characterization properly captures the notion of weakness of the will. Akrasia – Aristotle's idea, considered principally in *Nicomachean Ethics* VII, of acting against one's own better judgement – is clearly a candidate for that term.
32. The 'Ulysses problem', as our Latinist teachers are apt to say. Unaccountably, Strotz himself notes the Odysseus story as if it is thought to be relevant to his problem. But I think a reading of the *Odyssey*, book XII will reveal that what Odysseus feared was a change of his utility function, not his own propensity to non-exponential discounting.
33. I am enjoying again the cutting of corners. The object is merely to contrast the game-theoretic problem with the Strotz problem, not to give a precise account of the theory of entry.
34. Disinclined as I am to make the case on behalf of its advocates, central bank independence would clearly be one response to this problem. Whether there is persuasive evidence of policymaker preferences changing in this kind of way; if so, whether there is a particular effect in the area of monetary policy; if so whether the effect is strong enough to overcome the electoral incentives to good policy; if so, whether the issue is of great enough significance to warrant attention in institutional design; if so, whether independence rather than, say, term limits, are the best response; and if so, whether the compromise with democratic values that would be entailed is a price worth paying are all further questions.
35. The point could be argued. In practical politics, we may be inclined to think of the control of inflation being a preoccupation of the right, but Galbraith (1960) for example, identified it specifically as a goal of the liberal.
36. And once again, one might say that if disinflation is achieved by overvaluation, those who have the misfortune to be in the tradables sector bear the cost for the benefit of those elsewhere.
37. Nor is it easy to see how an interesting financial market (true-) credibility model could be constructed. If policymakers fear that financial markets expect high inflation, and therefore will only lend at high rates of interest, a simple solution is to issue index-linked debt. The idea that institutional changes like the creation of monetary unions are necessary to solve this problem is ridiculous.

37. This version of the pseudo-credibility theory almost seems to recall Crompton's (1925) creation of Violet Elizabeth Bott whose threats to scream until she was sick induced numerous policy changes.
38. One of the distressing aspects of the central bank independence literature is the way that authors persistently equate 'short-term objective' with 'political objective' and clearly regard both as reprehensible. Apart from their failure to acquaint themselves with the theory they routinely invoke, these authors appear not to have comprehended that a 'political motive' can be a paradigm of legitimate motivation of democratic governments.
39. In Forder (2003) I try to show how various conceptions of the benefits of democracy are relevant to the issue of central bank independence, and to draw attention to the failure of the advocates of independence to address the issues.
40. Renumbered, but retained, in the Treaty of Amsterdam, as Article 108.

REFERENCES

Alesina, A. and V. Grilli (1992), 'The European Central Bank: reshaping monetary politics in Europe', in V. Canzoneri, V. Grilli and P. Masson (eds), *Establishing a Central Bank: Issues in Europe and Lessons from the United States*, Cambridge: Cambridge University Press, 49–77.

Backus, D. and J. Driffill (1985a), 'Rational expectations and policy credibility following a change in regime', *American Economic Review*, **75**, 530–38.

Backus, D. and J. Driffill (1985b), 'Rational expectations and policy credibility following a change in regime', *Review of Economic Studies*, **52**, 211–21.

Barro, R. and D. Gordon (1983a), 'A positive theory of monetary policy in a natural rate model', *Journal of Political Economy*, **91**, 589–610.

Barro, R. and D. Gordon (1983b), 'Rules, discretion and reputation in a model of monetary policy', *Journal of Monetary Economics*, **12**, 101–21.

Blinder, A. (1997), 'What central bankers can learn from academics – and vice versa', *Journal of Economic Perspectives*, **11** (2), 3–19.

Blinder, A. (2000), 'Central-bank credibility: why do we care? How do we build it?', *American Economic Review*, **90** (5), 1421–31.

Bricmont, J. and A. Sokal (1998), *Intellectual Impostures*, London: Profile Books.

Crompton, R. (1925), *Still William*, London: Newnes.

Elster, J. (1979), *Ulysses and the Sirens*, Cambridge: Cambridge University Press.

Fellner, W. (1976), *Towards a Reconstruction of Macroeconomics: Problems of Theory and Policy*, Washington, DC: American Enterprise Institute.

Fellner, W. (1979), 'The credibility effect and rational expectations', *Brookings Papers on Economic Activity*, **1**, 167–90.

Forder, J. (1998), 'Central bank independence – conceptual clarifications and interim assessment', *Oxford Economic Papers*, **51**, 307–34.

Forder, J. (2001), 'The theory of credibility and the reputation bias of policy', *Review of Political Economy*, **13** (1), 5–25.

Forder, J. (2003), 'Central bank independence: economic theory, evidence, and political legitimacy', *International Papers in Political Economy*, forthcoming, reprinted in P. Arestis and M. Sawyer (eds), *Recent Developments in Political Economy*, Cheltenham, UK and Northampton, MA, USA: Edward Elgar, 2004.

Friedman, M. (1948), 'A monetary and fiscal framework for economic stability', *American Economic Review*, **38**, 245–64.

Friedman, M. (1962), 'Should there be an independent monetary authority?', in

L. Yeager (ed.), *In Search of a Monetary Constitution*, Cambridge, MA: Harvard University Press, 219–43.
Friedman, M. (1967), 'The monetary theory and policy of Henry Simons', *Journal of Law and Economics*, **10**, 1–13.
Friedman, M. (1968), 'The role of monetary policy', *American Economic Review*, **58**, 1–17.
Friedman, M. (1977), 'Nobel lecture: inflation and unemployment', *Journal of Political Economy*, **85**, 451–72.
Friedman, M. (1982), 'Monetary policy', *Journal of Money, Credit and Banking*, **14** (1), 98–117.
Galbraith, J.K. (1960), *The Liberal Hour*, New York: Houghton Mifflin.
Galbraith, J. (1997), 'Time to ditch the NAIRU', *Journal of Economic Perspectives*, **11**, 93–108.
Kydland, F. and E. Prescott (1977), 'Rules rather than discretion: the inconsistency of optimal plans', *Journal of Political Economy*, **85**, 473–91.
Lippi, F. and O. Swank (1999), 'Policy delegation and elections', in Lippi, *Central Bank Independence, Targets and Credibility*, Cheltenham, UK and Northampton, MA, USA: Edward Elgar, 73–86.
Lucas, R. (1976), 'Econometric policy evaluation: a critique', in K. Brunner and A. Meltzer (eds), Carnegie-Rochester Series on Public Policy, Amsterdam: North-Holland.
Nordhaus, W. (1975), 'The political business cycle', *Review of Economic Studies*, **42**, 169–90.
Posen, A. (1998), 'Central bank independence and disinflationary credibility: a missing link?', *Oxford Economic Papers*, **51**, 335–59.
Rogoff, K. (1985), 'The optimal degree of commitment to an intermediate monetary target', *Quarterly Journal of Economics*, **100**, 1169–90.
Sargent, T. (1999), *The Conquest of American Inflation*, Princeton, NJ: Princeton University Press.
Stiglitz, J. (1998), 'Central banking in a democratic society', *De Economist*, **146**, 199–226.
Strotz, R.H. (1956), 'Myopia and inconsistency in dynamic utility maximization', *Review of Economic Studies*, **23**, 165–80.

3. Financial fragility: is it rooted in the development process? An examination with special reference to the South Korean experience

Santonu Basu*

INTRODUCTION

The purpose of this chapter is twofold. First, it is to examine why financial liberalization, despite its claims,[1] is unable to deliver a higher growth rate or efficiency in the financial sector. This means that some form of intervention will be required in the operation of the financial sector, specially in developing countries, in order to promote growth. In recent years, there has been a growing body of literature which rightly points out the reasons for intervention and its beneficial effect in promoting growth.[2] However, experience suggests that in the past, intervention has adversely affected the performance of the financial sector. This means that there is a problem, especially in the form of the intervention that has taken place, but the existing literature may be somewhat limited in its ability to assist in the investigation of the negative aspects of intervention. Thus the second purpose is to investigate what went wrong with the intervention and why. This will be investigated with reference to South Korea. We chose the South Korean economy, as opposed to any other developing nation, for obvious reasons.

South Korea is one of the most successful nations in terms of its economic performance, and is where government intervention played a positive role in the process of development. Yet it also followed the path of liberalization. In fact, financial liberalization followed by financial crisis can be traced back to weaknesses that seemed to have crept in during the period of intervention, which will enable us to understand why liberalization simply made the country more vulnerable, leading to the crisis. This in turn could alert policy makers to the need to take some precautionary measures when intervening in the functioning of the financial market and perhaps may enable them to strike a balance between intervention and the free market.

Accordingly, this chapter has been divided as follows. First, we shall critically investigate why liberalization cannot bring efficiency to investment, and therefore cannot improve the nation's growth rate. Second, we shall investigate why it is necessary to intervene and the nature of the intervention adopted by the South Korean government. Third, we shall investigate what went wrong with the intervention and why. This is followed by the conclusion and policy prescriptions.

LIMITATIONS TO THE SUCCESS OF LIBERALIZATION

The basic tenet of liberalization is centred on the postulation that there is an explicit link between financial development and growth rate. Goldsmith (1969) observes that there was an upward drift in the ratio of financial institutions' assets to gross national product (GNP) for 35 countries, which includes both developed and less-developed countries, between 1860 and 1963. Interestingly, he also observes that in the early stage of development, bank finance plays a crucial role, however in the later stage of development, the importance of the banks to some extent declines as a result of the growth of either the Non-Banking Financial Intermediaries (NBFI) or the stock market. However, Goldsmith is very cautious in deriving any particular conclusion from this observation as to whether financial factors were primarily responsible for the acceleration of economic development or whether the financial development reflected economic growth. In Goldsmith, the process of growth has a feedback impact upon the financial sector as he observes that the process of growth itself creates incentives for further financial development and this gives the impression that the financial intermediation may be an endogenous process. McKinnon's (1973) and Shaw's (1973) main thesis is centred on the postulation that government intervention can have an adverse impact upon this process. They mainly focus on exogenous factors such as the impact of government policy regarding financial markets on savings and investment, and argue that financial repression reduces the incentive for savings, resulting in lower investment and growth. However, despite their strong theoretical claim, there was no endogenous model to support it, that is, in the absence of any intervention, the endogenous process will produce a higher growth rate.

Following the development of the endogenous growth model (Romer 1986 and 1990),[3] recent literature on finance and development has incorporated the role of financial factors within the framework of this model, where financial intermediation is also considered as an endogenous process. The proponents of models that take financial intermediation and growth as endogenous argue that there exists a positive two-way causal relationship between economic growth and financial development. The essential argument in this literature is that the process of growth encourages higher participation in the financial markets, which in turn facilitates the creation and the expansion of financial institutions. It is also argued that financial institutions, by collecting and analysing information from potential borrowers, enable the allocation of funds for investment projects to be more efficient and thus promote investment and growth (Greenwood and Jovanovic 1990).

Banks and other NBFIs play a crucial role in the process of development. These financial intermediaries open up the opportunity for individuals to hold their savings in the form of deposits, thereby reducing the need to hold savings in the form of non-liquid unproductive tangible assets, thus increasing liquidity in the economy. Banks then can use these deposits to invest in currency and capital. While an individual's need for liquidity remains unpredictable, banks, by the law of large numbers, face a predictable demand for deposit withdrawals, and this in turn allows banks to invest funds more efficiently. In other words, by applying the law of large numbers, banks can avoid the unnecessary premature liquidation of capital that otherwise would have emerged in the absence of banks, where individual investors may have been forced to liquidate their non-liquid assets prematurely when liquidity needs arise. Thus banks avoid resource misallocation, provide liquidity to savers and at the same time offer long-term funds to investors. Thus the essence of the argument is that inducing savers to switch from unproductive assets to productive assets must stimulate productive investment.[4] Accordingly King and Levine (1993b, p. 517) argue that, 'Financial repression ... reduces the services provided by the financial system to savers, entrepreneurs, and producers; it thereby impedes innovative activity and slows economic growth'.[5]

The most important contribution of this literature is that it points out the active and positive role that financial factors play in the process of economic development.[6] In order to highlight this aspect of finance, the focus is on the interest rate as a primary channel for the intermediation between savings, investment and growth. But the authors of this literature overlook the crucial role that the credit standard and credit risk play in the process of intermediation between savings and investment,[7] a consideration of which may suggest that the result that they derived may not be achieved via liberalization.

It is argued that under the liberalized system, competition between lending institutions for depositors will cause a rise in the interest rate on deposits, which in turn will raise the deposits. In other words, higher interest rates will induce households to increase their level of savings. This in turn will increase the availability of credit and thereby will cause a rise in investment growth. Furthermore, it is argued that although investment responds to the interest rate negatively, the growth rate responds to the interest rate positively. It is argued that as the higher interest rate discourages low-return investments, investors will be induced to undertake high-return investments, thereby bringing efficiency to investment, which in turn will improve the growth rate to a greater extent than that which is possible under financial repression. Thus the key link here is the interest rate. Now let us briefly examine whether the interest rate alone can play such a crucial link between savings, investment and the growth rate.

To begin with, it is assumed that savings are a function of the interest rate. Extensive empirical investigation of this relationship so far remains inconclusive. For example, Fry (1978 and 1980) in a sample of 14 Asian developing countries and Turkey, found the existence of a positive relationship between the interest rate and savings ratios. Giovannini (1983) reproduced Fry's equation using the same set of seven Asian countries that was used by Fry and applied it to a different sample period and found that the result that was obtained by Fry cannot be found in a different sample period. This raises some serious doubts about the evidence that was produced by Fry. Gupta (1987) further tested the above hypothesis using 22 Asian and Latin American countries, and while he found support for income growth as a determinant of savings, he could not find much support for the above hypothesis.

Interestingly, Gupta observed that the results reveal a significant regional variation. There could be two possible explanations for this variation between regions: the first is that if two regions have a different growth in income then it is reasonable to assume that they should produce a different savings rate, other things being equal; the second is that this variation may have emerged due to the fact that, as Khatkhate (1988) and Cho (1989) observed, a higher interest rate mainly helps in the mobilization of savings. In other words, a higher interest rate changes the composition of savings portfolios, that is, the savings that were previously held in the form of inventory are now transformed into financial assets. In this situation, the impact of the interest rate on the mobilization of savings will largely be determined by the value of the savings that were held in the form of inventory.

Thus if two nations have two different levels of inventories, changes in the interest rate are likely to reveal different levels of savings. It is the second possible explanation which may also provide a clue as to why Giovannini's different sample period produced a result which is in sharp contrast to the result obtained by Fry. Interestingly, Demetriades and Luintel (1996) found that the extension of branch facilities played a positive role in the mobilization of savings in the case of India.[8] This inconclusive nature of the findings may have led Modigliani (1986, p. 304) to conclude: 'despite a hot debate, no convincing general evidence either way has been produced, which leads me to the provisional view that s [the saving ratio] is largely independent of the interest rate'. Common sense suggests that a person who has an insufficient income and struggles to survive on a basic diet will never be able to save, irrespective of the level of interest rate. On the other hand, if we assume that we save for our future consumption, then a higher interest rate instead of inducing higher levels of savings should in fact reduce our urge for higher levels of savings (see Marshall 1920 and Keynes 1936 on this issue). The above argument simply suggests that savings are residual and arise from the difference between income and consumption. Allocation of savings is largely governed by the level of interest rate, liquidity preference and our taste and preference for risk and uncertainty. The above argument therefore may explain why all empirical investigations are unable to establish a direct link between interest rate and savings. If interest rate plays any role in inducing higher levels of savings, its role is a minor one.

Regarding the relationship between the availability of credit and investment growth, it is also assumed that the interest rate will play a key linking role. In other words, interest rate will intermediate between savers and investors, or more precisely lenders and borrowers will intermediate via the interest rate. The crucial assumption behind this argument is that there is certainty about the loan repayment. Given this assumption, we do not need to make a distinction between the availability of credit and access to credit, as a rise in the former will automatically improve the latter.

But the problem here is a critical one, as the loan market operates in the presence of uncertainty. This uncertainty principally arises from the fact that there remains a time gap between the advancement of loans and the repayment of loans. Assume that the borrower is an investor who borrows with a specific purpose to invest such funds in a project, and promises to repay the principal plus interest rate from the expected proceeds from the project. The issue of expectation mainly enters into such an equation, due to the fact that the investor's decision to invest in a project has more than one probable outcome, neither of which is known to the investor with absolute accuracy. As a result, the investor tries to form an expectation in relation to his/her project's return. In the absence of future information in relation to the factors that are likely to influence the outcome of the project, in most cases the investor relies on his/her past experience or current information in relation to the project's outcome. But the problem is, the past experience may not repeat itself, or the probability value of the factors that influence the outcome of the project may change. This means that we cannot calculate the expected value of a project's outcome with absolute accuracy. In other words, there remains a possibility that the expected value may deviate from its actual value.[9] This in turn introduces the possibility that the borrower may not be able to honour his/her promises.

This possibility therefore introduces the need for the separation of the concepts of availability of credit from access to credit. In other words, as uncertainty enters into the equation in relation to the loan repayment, it is implied that promises to pay the interest rate alone cannot clear the loan market. Lenders have to take measures to ensure that should the borrowers' projects fail, lenders do not lose their loan capital. Therefore, lenders will investigate whether the borrower has an alternative means of income or asset, to honour the debt obligation. In this situation, loan approval to any borrower will depend upon whether the borrower can offer an alternative means of payment should the borrower's project fail. In other words, banks will ask for collateral whose value should be equivalent to the value of the principal, as an alternative means of payment, should the return from the borrower's project fail to maintain the repayment rate. The measure introduced by banks in order to protect their loan capital should the borrower's project fail is referred to as the credit standard.

This therefore suggests that the borrower's access to the loan market depends upon whether the borrower can meet the bank's credit standard, and this is independent of the merits of the project.

Now given this analysis, let us assume that the interest rate increases as a result of liberalization. This will increase the deposits, either as a result of a change in the composition of savings portfolios where savers prefer to hold financial as opposed to unproductive assets, or as a result of a rise in access to the foreign savings market, resulting in a rise in the availability of credit. But the rise in the deposit rate will also cause a rise in the loan rate, and with a given size of loan, this in turn will also increase the contractual repayment rate. This means that the credit standard that has been set in accordance with the size of the loan and the previous interest rate, is no longer capable of protecting the bank's entire loan capital when the interest rate increases. In this situation, the portion of the loan which is not secured by the credit standard is that portion of the contractual repayment rate which has increased as a result of a rise in the loan rate. The portion which is not secured by the credit standard will not be recouped from the proceeds of the collateral, and this is referred to as credit risk. We are assuming banks' main aim is to protect the entire loan capital by the credit standard, so that no shortfall will arise in meeting the depositors' demand should there be a failure in borrowers' projects. In other words banks would like to take zero credit risk. Thus banks will raise the credit standard to the level where the credit risk becomes zero.[10] If some borrowers cannot meet this higher credit standard, then they will receive loans of a lesser size than demanded or will be denied loans altogether. This means that a rise in the availability of credit does not necessarily imply a rise in the borrowers' access to the loan market. In fact as just shown above, a rise in the availability of credit can be accompanied by a reduction in the access to the loan market for some borrowers who may have qualified for the loan previously.[11]

This problem is further complicated by the fact that the level of credit risk that banks wish to take is not entirely determined by their taste and preference for risk and uncertainty, but rather is determined by the competitive atmosphere under which they operate. By competitive atmosphere we mean the level of competition that a bank faces when competing with other lending institutions for borrowers as clients. This level of competition that banks face varies from one borrowing group to another. The borrowing groups that have larger firms with assets of a larger value demand bigger loans as opposed to those that have smaller firms with assets of a lesser value. As the administrative or transaction costs of large loans falls well below the administrative cost of small loans, this suggests that with a given interest rate, large loans will offer a higher expected rate of return compared to any small loans.

Furthermore, owing to the economies of scale of operation, large firms are more likely to enjoy a lower cost per unit of production compared to their smaller counterparts, given the market price of the product. Furthermore, due to their larger size of operation they do have some control over the price of their product as opposed to their smaller counterparts. This suggests that firms with a bigger scale of operation will be in a better position to absorb any adverse shock that may follow from fluctuations in the aggregate demand compared to their smaller counterparts. In addition to this, as they have assets of a larger value, this suggests that even if the project's (for which they seek loans) return falls below the expected return, they have more than sufficient alternative means to maintain their contractual payment. The combined impact of the lower administrative costs with a lower possibility of default, offers a much higher level of expected rate of return on larger loans compared to any smaller loans.

The demand for borrowers who offer a higher expected rate of return, given the level of interest rate, will be high in the lenders' market compared to those who offer a lower expected rate of return on loans. This higher demand in turn provides a choice to those borrowers who offer a higher expected rate of return on loans. That is, they can either borrow from banks or else they can borrow from other lending institutions, and they can also raise funds directly from the stock market. Thus when banks compete for these borrowers in the lenders' market, then banks have little option other than to make concessions in order to attract these clients as borrowers. These concessions include relaxation of the credit standard requirements, interest rate concessions and better terms and conditions for the loan repayment. However, as the borrowers' ability to offer higher expected rates of return falls, given the level of interest rate, with a decreasing size of operation and with lower asset backing, so the demand for such borrowers falls in the lenders' market. This means that these borrowers will have less choice in raising external funds from alternative sources. In a majority of cases, most borrowers have the option either to raise external capital by borrowing from banks or by borrowing from private money lenders or from friends and relatives. Thus as the borrowers' choice of alternative means to raise external funds shrinks, it increases banks' monopoly power over such borrowers and this power shrinks as borrowers' ability to offer higher expected rates of return increases. Accordingly banks set their credit standards, that is, where they have a monopoly power they will set the credit standard at a level where the credit risk will be zero, and as the monopoly power erodes so too does their ability to insist upon credit standards that can fully secure their loan capital. This therefore suggests that not all borrowers will have equal access to the loan market.

Assume again that the interest rate increases as a result of liberalization. Banks then will raise their credit standard where they have, or are able to maintain, a monopoly or near monopoly power, in order to ensure that the credit risk remains either zero or close to zero. Their ability to raise the credit standard is more likely to remain the same for borrowers (comprising mainly smaller and medium-sized borrowers) who demand smaller loans. If these borrowers fail to meet the banks' new credit standards, then either their access will be denied or they will receive less than that demanded. But banks' ability to raise the credit standard for those who seek large loans will be further restricted by the higher level of competition that follows from liberalization of the lenders' market. This therefore suggests that if liberalization increases the interest rate then it is more likely that the smaller and medium-sized borrowers' access to the banks' loan market will be reduced. For example, Jaramillo et al. (1996) investigated whether there was any improvement in the small firms' access to loan market during the post-liberalization period as opposed to the pre-liberalized period, for Ecuadorian firms. Their investigation was based on a rich panel data set containing balance sheets and profit and loss statements for 420 manufacturing companies during the 1983–88 period. Of these firms, 22 per cent were considered to be large firms with assets over US$600 000 (at 1975 prices), 47 per cent of the sample was represented by young firms, that is, those who were established after 1970. The year 1986 was taken as the dividing line between the pre- and post-liberalization period on the basis of the fact that the interest rate was fully deregulated in 1986 and the real rate reached positive levels. Jaramillo et al. found that while there was no change in access to the loan market either in the pre- or post-liberalization periods for the large firms, the small and young firms had difficulty in gaining access to it in both periods and this further increased during the post-liberalization period.[12] This is mainly because these borrowers are often unable to meet banks' higher credit standards. On the other hand, as liberalization in the short term will increase the intensity of competition among the lending institutions for large borrowers as clients, banks will have to relax their credit standard requirements even further than they would have done in the absence of liberalization. This therefore suggests that liberalization will not only further aggravate the unequal access to the loan market beyond that which already exists,[13] but will also make the banking system fragile as their loan portfolios will carry a higher level of credit risk than they would have carried in the absence of liberalization.

Now let us examine their third link, which is that higher interest rates will discourage low-return investment while it will encourage higher-return investment, which in turn will bring efficiency in the growth rate. This proposition is based on simple logic, that is, as the higher interest rate reduces the net return for the project that succeeds, it therefore will induce investors to switch from low- to high-return projects. Let us assume that there is no problem with the first two links constructed by the school of liberalization. Thus the proposition here is whether the higher interest rate will induce investors to undertake high-return investments, since low-return ones reduce the net return in the presence of higher interest rates. The crucial assumption therefore is that the selection of a project may vary with the level of interest rate. Central to this assumption is the claim that a higher interest rate will improve the growth rate. But two important factors that must be considered by an investor when making the decision to switch between projects, following changes in the interest rate, are overlooked: (a) there is a cost associated with selection and switching between projects, and (b) the possibility of an adverse impact from the 'crowding-out' effect.

The issue of the switching cost arises due to the fact that investment expenditure is largely irreversible. That is, these are mostly sunk costs and therefore cannot be recovered. Thus, if an investor (or a firm) wishes to switch from a low- to a high-return project, which often involves switching from one industry to another, or may involve switching from a cheaper product to an expensive one, he/she must consider the net loss that would accrue as a result of the sunk costs from the old project. This is because a firm's capital (that is, plant and equipment), marketing techniques and advertising techniques are all to some extent specific to that project. These, therefore, in their present form, will have little or no use for other projects or for other industries, and so are sunk costs. In principle, a firm should be able to sell its plant and equipment to any other firm which is involved in that specific project within that industry. However, as the value of plant and equipment will be about the same for all firms within that industry, it is unlikely that one firm will gain much, if anything at all, from selling it.

Furthermore, in the event of changes in the interest rate, if a firm considers that its current project's net return is not sufficient in comparison with the high interest rates, then this view is likely to be shared by other firms operating in that industry. Therefore, all firms in that industry would have the same inducement effect. In these circumstances, firms either will have no buyers for their plant and equipment, or will be forced to sell well below the current market value in order to induce other firms to buy it. In either case, this suggests that a switch between projects involves a substantial loss to a firm, due to the irreversible costs. It follows that once we consider the incorporation of the switching cost as well as the selection cost, the firm's net expected rate of return may not rise sufficiently to induce it to switch from low- to high-return projects, even when the new project offers a higher expected rate of return. If we assume that switching between projects does not necessarily imply switching from one industry to another, the sunk costs may be small but we cannot ignore the adverse impact of the crowding-out effect. That is, if all firms within the industry decide to switch from low- to high-return projects (that is, from low- to high-return products), then this movement will in turn not only reduce the return of the so-called high-return projects, but will also increase the risk of the projects, because of the greater competition that is brought in as a result of the greater supply of firms. This is equally applicable to the case of switching between industries.

The above argument suggests that switching between projects in the event of changes in the interest rate is possible, provided we assume that capital is malleable (since malleable capital has properties that eliminate the additional costs involved in switching) and there exists an unlimited demand in the market to absorb all additional firms without adversely affecting the price of the products. From the above it follows that if the switching between projects involves satisfying the above two conditions, then it is unlikely that existing firms that are already committed to projects will be in a position to make any possible additional gain by switching. Thus the possibility of receiving a lower expected net return remains high in the event of high interest rates, irrespective of the choice of projects, that is, whether they choose to remain with the old project or switch to a new one. This therefore suggests that the higher interest rate or liberalization for that matter, is unlikely to deliver a higher growth rate.

In fact, in the case of Latin America, De Gregorio and Guidotti (1995) found the existence of a very strong negative correlation between financial intermediation and growth during the 1970s and 1980s, a period when their financial market was liberalized. Real GDP in Argentina declined by 11 per cent between 1980 and 1982, in Chile by 15 per cent between 1981 and 1983 and in Uruguay by 14 per cent between 1980 and 1983 (Diaz-Alejandro 1985). Similarly, in Mexico, the GDP growth rate declined by 20 per cent between 1994 and 1995. In Thailand, Malaysia, South Korea and Indonesia, the GDP growth rate declined by 10 per cent between 1996 and 1998 (Mishkin 1999). A study by Arestis and Glickman (2002) also found that in Thailand, South Korea, Indonesia, Malaysia and the Philippines, the GDP growth rate declined by almost 11 per cent between 1995 and 1998.

The problem with financial liberalization is that it opens up the opportunity for investors who carry substantial financial assets in their portfolios to take advantage of the higher interest rate and greater flow of credit.[14] The financial assets do not have a direct link, as their link with physical capital is an indirect one via the purchase of shares, and therefore the sale of these will not incur sunk costs. But it may often involve a capital loss if investors wish to switch from a low- to a high-yield investment, when the interest rate increases (for reasons already explained above). In other words, in the absence of sunk costs the total capital loss that will be incurred is much lower compared to the loss that will be incurred by an investor who is involved in a productive activity and who wishes to sell his/her investment in order to switch to a new venture. This therefore suggests that investors who carry financial assets will have the opportunity to switch from low- to high-yield securities when the interest rate increases.

As large investors in general carry substantial financial assets in their portfolios, with a greater access to credit they will be in a position to take advantage of this high interest rate. These are the investors who are also likely to carry high levels of credit risk. The issue here is not whether these investors will switch from low- to high-yield securities, but whether this greater flow of credit to the stock market will be accompanied by an equivalent rise in the supply of new shares. As the latter does not depend upon the former, but upon the growth of the corporate sectors, which in general depends upon overall economic growth, it is unlikely that this greater flow of credit will be accompanied by a rise in the supply of new shares. In this situation it is more likely that the greater flow of credit will cause a rise in the price of shares. This in turn introduces the possibility of making a profit from the expected change in their price. As the profit from the purchase, and subsequent sale, of shares will rise, loan capital will be further attracted to the stock market, thereby increasing stock market activity. This introduces the possibility of attracting a substantial portion of the banks' loan capital to move away from the productive areas of the economy in favour of financial assets.[15] This obviously raises a concern about the efficiency gain via liberalization.[16] Furthermore, in the process, as the link between the share market and the real sector gets weaker, share prices will tend to deviate substantially from the fundamentals upon which the initial share price was set. In other words, the yield on shares will not be able to justify the rise in the price of shares. More importantly, in this process the return on loans will no longer be linked with the yield on shares; rather it will be interlocked with the return from the expected change in the price of shares.

This is where a serious problem arises, that is, if the actual price falls short of the expected price, then these borrowers may have difficulty in meeting their commitment to banks. In this situation, banks will not be able to recoup the entire portion of the loan capital from the proceeds of the collateral. This problem arises because the banks could not maintain the credit standard requirements for these borrowers. In other words, banks advanced loans which exceeded the aggregate value of the borrowers' assets. Thus the centre of the problem lies with the fact that banks have had to take a higher level of credit risk on large loans as a result of liberalization. This may have caused the banking crisis to emerge following liberalization of the financial market. Between 1976 and 1996 there were 59 banking crashes in developing countries and the total cost of these crashes was $250 billion which is over 9 per cent of the GDP (Caprio and Honohan 1999). This is without taking account of the Asian crisis. In the case of Asia we are yet to determine the cost of bank failures, but we know that the total equity losses were over $700 billion between June 1997 and January 1998 (Arestis and Glickman 2002). The banking crisis was not confined to developing countries, but has also been observed in developed nations. For example, between 1976 and 1993, there were 104 incidences of large bank failures, in 24 developed nations (Goodhart 1995). In the United States, altogether 1150 commercial and savings banks failed between 1983 and 1990 (Benston and Kaufman 1997).[17] It is the possibility of bank failures which introduces the seeds of financial crisis.

AN ANALYSIS OF WHY INTERVENTION MAY BE NECESSARY

Given the analysis presented in the last section, it should be clear that in the functioning of the financial market, government intervention will be required whether the country is categorized as a developed, or as a third world, country. Intervention will take the form of some regulations in order to protect depositors' funds, and also some other forms of intervention often will be required for the allocation of funds to ensure that certain sections of the community are not being deprived of access to the loan market. However, the level and the nature of intervention that will be required for developing countries will differ considerably from the type of intervention that is normally required for developed nations.

In order to understand why this is so, we shall now examine the problems being faced by developing countries when they achieved independence. Their economies then were described as being in a backward state, with high poverty, low education, high mortality rates and so forth and so on. It was recognized that in their current state they could not escape from these problems, nor did there exist any internal mechanism which indicated that this state was likely to change by itself in the near future. Yet in order to address these problems, it was essential to transform these economies from their backward, to an advanced industrial, state without necessarily following the evolutionary stages that already-developed nations underwent. But this involved changing the structure of the economy from one state to another, where the principal aim was to improve the economic well-being of every member of the society. The ultimate objective of development is therefore to expand the existing entitlement set, specially for those who otherwise would remain in a deprived state.[18] It is this situation that will allow us to understand why the nature, and the levels, of intervention differ considerably in developing countries from those which we experience in the context of developed countries.

The problems of developing countries, specially in transferring the economy from one state to another, is most succinctly described by Rosenstein-Rodan (1943), Nurkse (1953) and Scitovsky (1954). It was recognized from Kuznets's (1955) work that the process of development requires a higher accumulation of capital. But there was a problem in the process of capital accumulation, arising from both the supply side as well as the demand side. The supply problem principally arose from the low per capita income, which itself prevented the generation of sufficient savings that are required to increase the stocks of reproducible capital (Nurkse 1953). The demand problem in the capital formation also arose from the low per capita income, where the greater proportion of income went on necessities, leaving little to spend on industrial products. Consequently, the demand for industrial products remained low, causing a lack of incentive for private investors to invest in such industries. This problem is further exacerbated by the fact that the production process in modern industries represents complex sets of interdependent relationships among firms. In this situation, if the coordination among firms is to be propelled by the price-guided system, then investment in a firm may give rise to pecuniary external economies, and consequently its private profitability will understate its social desirability (Rosenstein-Rodan 1943 and Scitovsky 1954). This possibility of externalities arising from the intertemporal dependence among firms presented a serious impediment to the growth of developing countries. These problems particularly arise in multi-linkage industries, where, in the absence of simultaneous growth in the interdependent industry, one industry may not adjust to the growth in the other industry due to difficulties in achieving economies of scale. The fact that these problems are particularly acute for developing countries, principally arises not only from the deficiency in overall demand, but also from the further complication of the unequal distribution of income and wealth causing difficulty in capturing the right pattern of demand. The central problem in multi-linkage industries is whether a complementary decision will be made or not, which has a direct bearing upon the future market, and whether the product will be sold.

In other words, it was recognized that the investment decision involves undertaking some risk and uncertainty, where uncertainty principally arises from the fact that under these conditions investors are unable to approximate the future demand.[19] Furthermore, Scitovsky argues that private return is an imperfect indicator of social return.[20] Thus while Rosenstein-Rodan's and Scitovsky's work pointed out the important impediments to development by identifying some of the exogenous factors, from Solow's (1957) work, it was recognized that the process of development is a much more complex issue than that which can be fully comprehended from the previous authors' writings. The latter concentrated only on the exogenous factors that presented an impediment to growth, but overlooked the importance of endogenous factors that also stood as a barrier to development.

Solow's (1957) work suggests that technical progress plays a much greater role in the context of growth than savings. This therefore suggests that in the process of growth, one needs to address not only the exogenous, but also the endogenous factors, for which one needs to develop economic organizations whose principal task will be to address micro-level issues. These organizations will play the role of information gathering and dissemination of information, and assist firms and industries in the more efficient utilization of productive resources over time.

It was recognized that the process of development does not just involve how to mobilize savings and how to eradicate deficiency in demand, but there is also the necessity to address a complex set of processes of learning how to operate newly created production facilities to cope with a changing structure of production.[21] These all involve development of a new set of institutions, whose principal task is to provide support to firms in exchange related activities, such as marketing, communications, transport, the transfer of technology, credit and insurance. Thus the principal aim of these institutions would be to remove the externalities that exist in the information-processing and other exchange-related activities, and also to provide economies of scale and scope in these activities.[22]

Thus the process of development involves the mobilization of savings, channelling these savings into the most productive sectors of the economy, and in the presence of deficient demand, inducing firms to undertake projects which not only provide private returns but are also accompanied by a social return. In addition, development also involves the dissemination of information about the new opportunities, technology availability and how to use them. While various informational and learning problems can be overcome by establishing specific types of institutions,[23] the mobilization of savings and the allocation of credit has to be carried out by banks. This means that intervention will not only be required to develop the real sector, but will also be required in the financial sector to assist the development of the real sector. Here banks have a very important role to play.

Banks are profit-seeking organizations just like any other business organization. Their principal task is to raise the deposit by offering the interest rate, to relend these deposits to borrowers in the form of credit at a higher interest rate, and make a profit from the difference between the loan rate and the deposit rate. Accordingly, any borrower who can meet a bank's credit standard requirements and who promises to pay the interest rate with a project which expects to be profitable, will obtain a loan. Should the borrower fail to meet his/her obligations, banks will resort to the credit standard. Banks as profit-seeking organizations would not be concerned with whether these borrowers are using their loanable funds for productive or unproductive purposes; nor would they be concerned whether the project for which the borrower seeks a loan, produces any social return or not.

The above argument therefore suggests that the development process will require a change in the bankers' culture, that is, not only are they required to investigate borrowers' creditworthiness, but also they have to assess the merits of borrowers' projects, in terms of both their expected private rates of return and also their social rates of return.

Banks, in the early stages of the independence of developing countries, were engaged in advancing loans for trade-orientated activities and meeting working capital requirements. They were advancing loans for short-term purposes. But the process of development requires long-term and large loans. The size of operation of most of these banks was small and most of their dealings with short-term loans comprised smaller-sized loans, and their survival depended upon short-term returns. Thus they developed neither the capital nor the necessary skill that is required to assess the merits of projects which involve large long-term loans. In addition to this, the greater proportion of the money market was controlled by the informal credit market.

The first problem that any government from developing countries faces, is how to bring the informal credit market under the umbrella of the formal credit market, so that a greater proportion of savings can be brought under the orbit of the formal market. One option is to open a number of branch facilities not only in the metropolitan area but also outside it. But the problem is that opening branch facilities, specially outside the metropolitan area, is costly, and a private bank whose principal motivation is to make profit is unlikely to participate in such a venture. In addition to this, banks may not have sufficient capital that is required to open additional branch facilities. But in the absence of higher levels of savings, a country cannot finance its development programme.

Given the complex issues involved in the development process, the South Korean government after a brief experiment with import substitution, adopted the path of export-led growth policy. The adoption of this policy has allowed South Korea to avoid the problem that arises from internal demand deficiency. In fact, criticisms were often made against the Nurkse–Rosenstein-Rodan–Scitovsky model (Datta-Chaudhuri 1990), because their model essentially concentrated on the internal demand condition when examining the problem of capital formation. This may be largely because of their experience with stagnating trade in the first half of the twentieth century. However, this changed dramatically in the 1950s. High growth rates in the Organisation for Economic Co-operation and Development (OECD) countries during the two decades following the Korean War led to a massive expansion in world trade. Rising wage rates in the developed countries also changed the pattern of the international division of labour, implying that poorer countries do not have to rely upon the internal market to generate demand for capital formation.

Furthermore, cold war tensions between the Western nations and Eastern European countries put South Korea in a very favourable position to take advantage of the export opportunities. But the problem was that while government had to provide information about these opportunities to firms and to induce them to participate in such ventures, it also had to induce banks to participate in such ventures. The government recognized that private banks are unlikely to participate in the promotion of export ventures and industry development programmes in their infancy. This is because their markets are not established. In other words, whatever potential profit opportunities these markets may offer, the future viability of these industries is not known to banks. Furthermore, would-be participating firms in these markets often have neither an established track record as a successful operator in these industries nor sufficient assets to offer as collateral to banks in order to obtain loans. As the government was the principal initiator of these programmes, it could not ask the participating privately owned firms to comply with the banks' credit standard requirements, specially when the firms themselves did not have sufficient information about these markets, a reason for which the government established the trading companies. Thus the South Korean government's second problem was how to induce private banks to participate in the development process.

The above argument suggests that successful implementation of the development strategy will require not only that banks increase their efforts to mobilize greater amounts of savings by offering a higher rate on deposits and by opening a larger number of branch facilities, but also that banks relax their credit standard requirements and offer cheaper credit facilities. Neither of these can be expected from private banks, since both of these strategies will result in a reduction in the banks' profit margin. At the same time, banks will become more vulnerable in the event of borrowers' default, arising directly as a result of the reduction in the credit standard requirements and the reduction in the difference between loan and deposit rates. While the former implies that the banks will be carrying a higher credit risk, the latter implies that very few, if any, banks will be able to make provision for non-performing loans. The government recognized that, while the establishment of trading companies may provide support to producers in exchange-related activities, producers cannot take advantage of the support that will be offered by these trading companies unless cheaper credit facilities can be provided.

WHERE INTERVENTION WENT WRONG

The complexities described above suggest that the implementation of such a policy would make the banks extremely fragile, and that this is similar to the situation that we observe when the financial system is liberalized. Therefore there is a need to undertake additional measures not only to ensure that the firms' reduction in revenue does not have a direct adverse impact upon the banks' loan performance, but also to ensure a minimization of the banks' credit risk in the near future. Experience suggests that most governments have not recognized the fundamental weakness that emerges from this form of intervention. The South Korean government is no exception to this and therefore it also made no attempt to reduce the fragility of its banks. In order to highlight this issue, we shall draw attention to three incidences, one of which is associated with the 1965 financial reform, the second with bailing out its troubled indebted firms in 1972 and the third with its restructuring of these indebted firms in 1982.

In 1961 the South Korean government nationalized its major banks with the aim of establishing firm control over the financial system in order to execute its task of the more effective mobilization of savings and to channel savings in order to finance its five-year development plan. But neither the government nor its economic advisers recognized that having control over savings and allocation of credit does not give any control over the return on these financial assets. Therefore, undertaking a development programme, whose financing requires a reduction in the banks' credit standard, means that much of the banks' own performance will be largely interlocked with the performance of the projects for which the banks have advanced loans. In this situation, it is essential to ensure that the debt/equity ratio does not rise to a level where it will be difficult to make up any shortfall in the loan repayment that may arise as a result of the firm's loss of revenue due to demand deficiency, from the return on equity.

Furthermore, the government needed to adopt two subsequent policies, one of which was to encourage these firms to develop an alternative pool of assets from the retention of their profits. This in turn would allow banks to take these alternative assets as collateral in the future, thereby unlocking the fate of the bank's loan capital from the performance of the indebted firms. The first policy, to be fully effective, would take a considerable number of years, and therefore the government needed to develop a second one, which we refer to as an intertemporal policy, which was to allow banks to monitor whether firms' production targets were in line with the demand for their output. At any point in time, if the supply of output exceeds its demand, then an unsold product will cause a reduction in the banks' earnings, and therefore it is often necessary to revise the production targets. It will be argued below that of the three incidences mentioned above, two are largely the result of not undertaking these precautionary measures. In other words, neither the South Korean government nor its advisers recognized that the relaxation in the credit standard is strictly a provisional measure. In fact, unprecedented growth in the loan capital is largely the result of not maintaining the credit standard, although it resulted in a high growth rate of GDP, but in the process the banks' loan capital was exposed to high credit risk. In other words, in the event of borrowers' default, a large portion of the banks' loan capital will not be recouped from the sale of collateral, and therefore bank failures would be inevitable.

The government brought the Bank of Korea (the central bank) under the control of the Ministry of Finance and established several specialized banks. In order to raise the capital that was required to finance its development programme, the government actively sought foreign capital and, following the advice of the US aid mission team (Gurley et al. 1965), raised the interest rate on time deposits, which is often referred to as financial reform, and established new banks. The interest rate on time deposits was raised from 15 to 30 per cent in 1965, and although this rate gradually declined, it remained above 20 per cent up to 1971 (see Amsden 1989 and Cho 1989). As a result of this high rate on deposits, the M2/GNP ratio rose from a little less than 9 per cent to a little over 33 per cent between 1964 and 1971 (see Cole and Park 1983).[24] This rapid growth of the formal financial sector was largely the result of high deposit rates, which induced asset holders to shift a portion of their funds from the informal credit market to banks. In other words, higher rates allowed the government to bring in part of the savings that were kept in alternative forms, under the umbrella of nationalized banks. This higher rate also helped to increase the capital inflow, specially from Japan.

In order to provide cheaper credit facilities to its development programme, the government divided the loan portfolio into two groups. Export and infant industries formed one group and received a preferential loan rate of 6 per cent, which remained below 10 per cent up to 1980. The rest of the economy formed another group and received loans at a non-preferential rate. This rate rose from 16.9 to 26 per cent between 1964 and 1965 and remained roughly around 24.4 per cent between 1966 and 1970. By 1971 the rate had come down to 17 per cent, and remained on average between 17 to 18 per cent up to 1980 (see Cho 1989 and Amsden 1989, 1994). In the absence of any other information, it appears that the preferential loans were subsidized by charging a very high rate on non-preferential loans. In this situation, a significant margin of difference should appear between the non-preferential loan rate and the rates on time deposits. But this was not the case. To begin with, between 1965 and 1968, rates on time deposits remained higher than those on non-preferential loans, implying that banks were running at a loss, independent of the projects' performance for which the banks advanced loans.[25] From 1969 the interest rate on non-preferential loans exceeded the interest rate on time deposits. But this was marginal, that is, the interest rate on time deposits was 24 per cent while the interest rate on non-preferential loans was 24.5 per cent. This margin of 0.5 per cent was so small that perhaps it was only able to cover the administrative cost, and this margin hovered around 0.4 to 1 per cent (see Cho 1989), implying that no provisions were made for non-performing loans. The above fact suggests that the interest rate subsidization on preferential loans did not come from non-preferential loan rates. It must, then, have come directly from the government or from cheaper foreign capital. This suggests that the success of the 1965 financial reform was made at the cost of banks.[26]

Despite this higher interest rate on time deposits, domestic mobilization of savings was not sufficient to finance its investment expenditure, and as a result South Korea had to rely on foreign capital. However, this higher rate made the foreign loan much cheaper compared to domestic loans, which in turn encouraged Korean borrowers to seek overseas loans.[27] Korea borrowed mainly to finance its balance of payments deficits and its long-term investment programme. Korea's foreign debt rose from US$206 million to US$2.922 billion and the ratio of foreign debt/GNP rose from 7 to 30 per cent between 1965 and 1971 (Amsden 1989). With the government providing guarantees on foreign loan repayments, firms resorted to foreign loans in order to finance imports of capital goods that are required for the production of export items and used the domestic loans in order to finance other exporting activities. As the economy grew, large firms in order to maintain a high rate of investment, not only relied on foreign and domestic bank loans but often resorted to the informal credit market for short-term loans when the need arose. Initially this was not a problem when exports used to constitute only a small fraction (5–7 per cent) of the GNP, but when the share of exports exceeded 20 per cent of the GNP, the importance of the outflow of credit in the context of its inflationary impact was recognized (see Cole and Park 1983). But what was not recognized was that the magnitude of the problem is not confined only to the issue of inflation but it has much wider ramifications for the financial system in the long run.

The fundamental problem with the Korean economy is that it is a debt-financing investment growth economy. That is, as the economy grew, firms instead of gradually remitting past debts and placing a greater emphasis on internal funds to grow, placed a greater emphasis on external capital for their growth rate. Initially, the problem with this form of financing growth was not recognized, mainly because as the economy grows, so does its ability to service the contractual debt commitment also grow, other things being equal. This steady flow of return on loans in turn increases firms' credit rating. Consequently, lenders' willingness to offer larger loans to these firms also increases.[28] With the increasing access to credit, investors (that is, borrowers) also do not feel the necessity to rely upon internal funds to any great extent for growth, and as a result their share of internal funds in relation to total funds shrinks. This in turn causes the debt/equity ratio to rise with the growth of the firm, thereby causing the debt service ratio to rise, which in turn, in the absence of an appropriate credit standard, exposes banks' capital to very high levels of credit risk. For example, as the share of exports rose from 5–7 per cent in the mid-1960s to over 20 per cent of GNP by the 1970s (Cole and Park 1983), the firms' share of internal funds in relation to total funds shrank from 47.7 per cent during 1963–65 to 25.4 per cent during 1966–71, while the share of external funds rose from 52.3 to 74.6 per cent during the same period (Amsden and Euh 1993).

During the same period, that is, between 1963 and 1971, the debt/equity ratio rose from 92 to 328 per cent and the debt service ratio as a percentage of merchandise exports rose from 5.20 to 28.34 per cent (Amsden 1989). The problem is that if the export earnings fall and as a result if the return from the total investment then falls below the repayment rate on the debt commitment, then the return from the internal funds may not be sufficient to meet the shortfall on the debt commitment. Firms have to borrow in order to meet their debt commitments. South Korea faced this problem in 1972.

As the economy grew, the cost of production increased, exporting firms started to face increasing difficulty in meeting the ever-rising export target. This problem was further magnified by the fact that there was a growing resistance from two of its main importers, namely Japan and the United States, to importing certain products, such as textiles, which in turn further added to the cause of slowing down the growth in export earnings. In order to rectify this problem the government devalued the currency with the hope that this in turn would pick up the demand for the export industry. But the devaluation instead caused a corresponding rise in the cost of servicing the foreign loans, which further added to the total cost of servicing loans. The return from the equity (that is, internal fund) which constituted only 25 per cent of the total investment, was not sufficient to meet the shortfall in the cost of servicing the loans. Firms have no option other than to borrow in order to meet their debt obligations.[29]

Many large firms turn to the informal credit market in order to meet short-term cash shortages. An increasing number of firms found that they were unable to meet the principal and interest rate payments to their foreign creditors. By 1971, the number of bankrupt firms receiving foreign loans rose to 200 (Cho 1989). As the banks neither imposed a credit standard when advancing loans to firms nor made any provision for non-performing loans, this suggests that the bankruptcy costs had to be borne by the banks. This means that the depositors also had to incur a loss. On the other hand, as the government provided guarantees on every single foreign loan in order to keep firm control over the foreign capital inflow, now it had an obligation to honour these overseas debts. Furthermore, as South Korea never had sufficient domestic savings that are required to achieve a high growth rate, it had to rely on overseas loans, and the government could not afford to default on foreign loans.

Following the advice of the indebted firms, in August 1972 the government issued the Presidential Emergency Decree, which gave it the power to invalidate all the loan agreements between firms and informal credit lenders, and institute a new agreement, that is, lenders had the option to transfer the loan into shares in the borrowing firms.[30] Thus the 1972 emergency decree, which bailed out troubled firms, did so mainly at the cost of depositors with both the informal credit market and the banks. This desperate act by the government might have allowed these firms to meet their overseas debt obligations, but for the fact that the government did not recognize that the problem might have emerged from overinvestment.

The possibility of overinvestment particularly arose for the two following reasons: (a) a reduction in the credit standard allowed borrowers to borrow more than they would have been able to borrow if the normal credit standard requirements were implemented; (b) a reduction in the credit standard requirements may encourage firms to borrow more, since the borrowers know that the higher the credit risk, the greater the likelihood that lenders would organize a rescue package in the event of an adverse performance of the project. This possibility of organizing a rescue package may make the borrower indifferent to risk or what is popularly referred to as the possible source of moral hazard.[31] In fact, the limit on a bank loan that a given firm can obtain, when determined by the credit standard requirements, itself prevents firms from undertaking overinvestment. This is because the firm knows that in the event of an unsuccessful venture it is the firm which has much to lose, since its income from other assets will be used to repay the loans.

However, it was recognized that in the early stages of development often it is not possible to maintain credit standard requirements, and in this situation it was essential to ensure that entrepreneurial capital constituted a larger share in the investment projects. This in turn would have ensured that in the event of an unsuccessful venture a reduction in the entrepreneurs' income may not have prevented them from maintaining their loan repayment. Nevertheless, one would imagine that one learns from one's own mistakes, but experience suggests that this did not make the government more prudent in its lending policy. The government neither encouraged firms to rely more upon internal funds as opposed to external funds for their growth, nor allowed banks to make provisions for non-performing loans, and to introduce credit standard requirements. Instead, the government embarked upon its next expensive project.

In the 1970s, the government decided to develop heavy and chemical industries. It appears that this decision was principally undertaken due to the fact that despite its high growth performance in the export-orientated sector, South Korea's reliance on imported inputs for the production of export items remained high. As a result, from every dollar it earned from the sale of its export items, 67 cents went to pay Japanese import bills (Chakravarty 1987). The combined impact of this import bill in addition to its reliance on overseas capital did not ease South Korea's foreign debt problem, despite its high performance in the export sector. Consequently, it was necessary for South Korea to attempt to reduce its reliance on imported inputs. But this venture was so risky that even many large firms were reluctant to embark on such a project. This is largely because of the fact that the development of these new industries required a very large investment in fixed capital and technology, with a long lag and an uncertain return. Furthermore, it was not clear whether the export industry was sufficiently large to allow these industries to achieve economies of scale, which meant that this industry too had to capture new markets. Given the difficulties, the government used a similar method that it had used in the past to encourage firms to enter into priority industries, which was to offer a strong package of tax and financial incentives to encourage some of the largest firms with minimum equity to enter into them. In addition to these incentives, the government introduced local content regulations and these also applied to the export sector.[32]

Throughout the 1970s the output of heavy and chemical industries increased considerably. Their share of the export market grew rapidly, but it was not sufficient to achieve economies of scale. By the late 1970s these industries were carrying a substantial amount of excess capacity, and coupled with the collapse of foreign markets in construction, shipping and shipbuilding in the early 1980s, the GNP turned negative for the first time in Korean history since the Korean War. As the share of internal funds in relation to the total investment was not sufficient to meet the shortfall that arose in their debt commitment, firms started to borrow again in order to meet this shortfall. As a result, firms' share of internal funds shrank from an average of 21.1 during 1975–79 to 16.4 per cent by 1980, while their share of external funds rose from 78.9 to 83.6 per cent (Choong-Hwan 1990). The debt/equity ratio rose from around 370 per cent during the late 1970s to 488 per cent by 1980 and as a result of this heavy borrowing Korea's external debt as a percentage of GNP rose from 32 to 48 per cent between 1979 and 1981 (Amsden 1989). By 1982, a growing number of highly indebted firms found it difficult to service their debt. The South Korean government once again was forced to assist in restructuring industrial firms that faced financial difficulties. Thus the problem of 1971 repeated itself, that is, the problem of overinvestment.

It appears that the South Korean government failed to recognize that this likelihood of overinvestment periodically will emerge in the absence of credit standard requirements, specially when firms' own share of capital, in relation to the size of the investment, is small. Thus it was essential for the government to introduce credit standard requirements. But the government neither addressed the issue of the credit standard, nor attempted to increase firms' share of internal capital as opposed to external capital. Instead, preferential lending rates were eliminated in 1982, and the government decided to abstain from further directed credit programmes. Furthermore, NBFIs were further deregulated and corporations were allowed to issue bonds with a guarantee by commercial banks. The government privatized the commercial banks, but in the presence of large non-performing loans, the government could not abstain from maintaining its control over the banking sector, as the restructuring of the industrial sector required government supervision of credit allocation. The government maintained its control over the interest rate and the credit allocation of the banking sector, which was fully lifted in 1991, along with its control over the foreign capital inflow. But the external as opposed to internal share of the total investment remained very high. In fact during 1987–91, the share of external funds constituted 73.6 per cent while the internal share constituted merely 26.4 per cent of the total investment (Amsden and Euh 1993). Thus the banking sector remained overexposed. By 1994, banks had to increase their allocated funds in order to make provisions for bad loans (see Bank of Korea 1994), but there is no evidence to suggest that the government made any systematic attempt to reduce the debt/equity ratio. For example, even in 1996 the average debt/equity ratio for the top 30 *Chaebol* was 898.49 per cent. This means that these firms borrowed on average 8.98 dollars against each dollar they owned, and the greater proportion of the loans either came directly from the banks, or else was raised via issuing corporate bonds, which were also guaranteed by the banks. Fourteen of these 30 *Chaebol* were making a negative profit in 1996, while for those who were making a positive profit, their profit remained marginal, compared to their total invested assets, including loans (Lee 1997). Thus it was only a matter of time before these firms' aggressive unsuccessful ventures would lead to massive bank failures.

CONCLUSION

The analysis that has been presented in this chapter suggests that the link that the school of liberalization has claimed to have established via the interest rate under the free market mechanism, cannot be established via the interest rate alone. This therefore may suggest that the policy of financial liberalization is unlikely to produce a higher growth rate. Instead, as the process of liberalization raises the interest rate, this will cause a rise in the banks' credit standard requirements for smaller and medium-sized firms. This in turn will aggravate unequal access to the loan market even further. In addition, the overall credit standard requirements will fall largely as a result of a relaxation in the credit standard requirements for large borrowers. Thus if these borrowers default on loans then a substantial portion of the principal would not be recouped from the sale of collateral. It is this possibility which introduces the seeds of financial crisis.

This means that intervention will be required, not only to maintain the stability in the financial system, but in the case of developing countries, intervention will be required in order to transfer the economy from a backward to an advanced industrial state. But this process often requires a relaxation of the banks' credit standard requirements. This means that there will also be an increase in the fragility of the banking system. Thus the process also requires adequate measures to be taken to reduce this fragility over time. Unfortunately it is the latter issue that has been overlooked by almost every developing country, and South Korea is no exception to this.

NOTES

* I would like to thank P. Arestis, S. Dasgupta, M. Hughes, J. Pullen and M. Sawyer for their comments on the draft of this chapter. Needless to say I alone am responsible for the errors that may remain.
1. McKinnon (1973), Shaw (1973) and Fry (1997) argue that interest rate controls and government-directed credit programmes cause a distortion with which savings are intermediated. Thus they argue that financial liberalization is the pre-condition for a higher growth rate. See also Roubini and Sala-i-Martin (1992) and King and Levine (1993a and 1993b).
2. This literature follows from the asymmetric information constraint which may cause market failure and as a result it is argued that intervention will be necessary. See Stiglitz (1993) and Gertler and Rose (1994) for further details.
3. The main feature of the endogenous growth model is that technological change is assumed to be an endogenous process; as a result capital stock does not necessarily suffer from a diminishing return, and consequently growth becomes a positive function of investment (Fry 1997).
4. See also Bencivenga and Smith (1991), Levine (1992), Roubini and Sala-i-Martin (1992), Saint-Paul (1992) and King and Levine (1993a and 1993b). A number of authors (Roubini and Sala-i-Martin 1992; King and Levine 1993a and 1993b; Fry 1997) including the

World Bank (1989) have empirically investigated the above relationships and found a positive result. King and Levine's work is probably the best known, however their method of using cross-section data in relation to causality effect was questioned by Arestis and Demetriades (1996). They use the time-series analysis for 12 countries (France, Germany, the UK, Japan, the USA, Korea, India, Greece, Spain, Turkey, Mexico and Chile) and found that the causal link between finance and growth depends upon the nature and operation of the financial institutions and policies pursued by each country (Arestis and Demetriades 1997).

5. Similarly, Fry (1997, p. 758), wrote: 'discriminatory taxation of commercial banks, investment banks, mutual funds, and stock markets through high reserve requirements, interest and credit ceilings, directed credit programmes ... reduces the growth rate by impeding financial development'. See also Roubini and Sala-i-Martin (1992) who argue that financial distortion has a negative effect. Contrary to this claim, Arestis and Demetriades (1997) found that financial repression has a positive impact upon the growth rate in the case of South Korea. Even the World Bank's (1993) report concedes that 'mild' repression may have a positive impact on the high-performing Asian economies. One cannot draw the same conclusion from the Indian experience (Demetriades and Luintel 1996). Rajan and Zingales (1998), on the other hand argue that whether the development of the financial market is determined by historical accident or as a result of government regulation does not really matter, since in either case a well-developed financial market will have a beneficial impact on the industries that are dependent on external capital.

6. In economics the role of finance in general is a passive one, the state of the art of the literature was that, 'By and large, it seems to be the case that where enterprise leads finance follows' (Robinson 1979, p. 20). The role of finance in the context of economic development is also a much neglected area in the literature on economic development. Chandavarkar (1992) provides an impressive list of authors who are pioneers of economic development, including three Nobel Laureates (for example, Peter Bauer, Colin Clark, Albert Hirschman, William Arthur Lewis, Gunnar Myrdal, Raul Prebisch, Paul Rosenstein-Rodan, Walt Rostow, Hans Singer and Jan Tinbergen) who also did not even mention finance as a factor in economic development. Furthermore, Chandavarkar points out that the recent surveys of economic development by Stern (1989) also ignore the role of the financial sector in the context of development.

7. Similarly, there are some authors (for example, Bencivenga et al. 1996; Levine and Zervos 1996) who argue that there is an explicit link between the development of stock markets and long-run growth. Their argument is centred on the notion that many high-return projects require long-term capital. However, investors are often reluctant to commit their savings to long-term projects. Stock markets provide the opportunity for firms to undertake long-term projects by offering liquidity to savers. That is, they issue equities to raise funds for long-term high-return projects, and these equities are held by savers, who then can offload them cheaply when a liquidity need arises. Hence in the process it should promote growth. Apart from the fact that new equity issues account for a very small fraction of corporate investment (Mayer 1988), they overlook an important issue, that is, only firms with a well-established reputation and with a large asset backing are able to raise funds via issuing shares. This means that only large corporations, big banks and other large NBFIs will be able to raise funds from the stock market. An important point to note here is that offering a return or a yield on shares is not a sufficient criterion to raise funds; issuing firms must have a large asset backing. This is independent of whether the firm is an innovative one or offering a high or low return on shares. In other words, the majority of the businesses comprising small and medium-sized firms, including farmers, will be excluded from this market. Therefore development of the stock market would not contribute to the growth of these sectors, and thus would not improve economic welfare. Furthermore, as a sizeable part of the economy would be excluded from the stock market, it remains a difficult proposition to prove whether or not development of the stock market would promote growth. And this is irrespective of whether or not one finds a correlation between the stock market and long-run growth, since a correlation does not tell us anything about the causality of such a link; it could be the growth which promotes the

stock market. In either case, the benefit from the growth of the stock market is a highly controversial issue, as other authors (for example, Devereux and Smith 1994; Obstfeld 1994) found that the internationally integrated stock market can depress savings rates, slow down the growth rate and reduce economic welfare. See also Singh (1997) for more on this issue; he suggests that on efficiency grounds evolution of the stock market should be curbed.

8. See also Dornbusch and Reynoso (1989), who find that financial savings are not related to a positive interest rate. See Arestis and Demetriades (1997) for more on this issue. For earlier work on this issue, see Chandavarkar (1971), Mikesell and Zinser (1972), and for an earlier survey on this issue, see Dougherty (1980). As far as financial liberalization is concerned, Diaz-Alejandro (1985) noted that domestic savings in South America did not increase as a result of liberalization. In fact, the Chilean gross national savings fell from 16.3 per cent of GDP during the 1960s to 12.4 per cent during 1975–81. Even Fry (1995, p. 158) who in his earlier works finds a positive effect of interest rates in Asia, following liberalization, finds that this effect disappears, as he wrote: 'even in Asia the effects appear to have diminished over the past two decades, possibly because of financial liberalisation'. This might have led him to concede that the impact of interest rates on the savings ratio may not be significant.

9. It is important to note that while Greenwood and Jovanovic (1990), King and Levine (1993b) and Fry (1997) argue that financial intermediaries play a key role in evaluating prospective entrepreneurs and finance the most promising one, however in their model these institutions' investment strategies are determined by the knowledge they have in relation to the 'current-period aggregate shock' (Fry 1997, p. 757). But they do not recognize that there remains a possibility that the future-period shock may deviate from the current-period one. This possibility can only be eliminated provided we assume that time is reversible. But time only moves forward; furthermore, the law of entropy suggests that it may not be sufficient for the assumption of reversible time to rely on current-period aggregate shock. See Georgescu-Roegen (1971) on this issue. However, as they overlook this issue the form of the contract that institutions devised became unimportant. King and Levine (1993b, p. 516) explicitly point out that their 'model does not focus on the precise forms of contracts and institutions that provide these services'.

10. For existing loans, banks instead of increasing the contractual repayment rate, may increase the repayment period, as they often do when recognizing that borrowers may have difficulty in meeting the rising repayment rate.

11. The above argument therefore may suggest why a high interest rate may have a negative supply-side effect on working capital (Taylor 1983; van Wijnbergen 1983). For example, Diaz-Alejandro (1985, p. 15) pointed out that, 'In Chile gross fixed investment during the 1960s averaged 20.2 percent of GDP; during 1974–82 it reached only 15.5 percent of GDP', and this is not because of a contraction in the growth of credit. In fact, liberalization is always accompanied by a surge in the expansion of credit, for example, the domestic credit in Chile expanded by 41 per cent between December 1981 and June 1982 (Diaz-Alejandro 1985). Similarly Arestis and Glickman (2002) observe that the financial liberalization in Asia (that is, Indonesia, Malaysia, South Korea, Thailand and the Philippines) was followed by a surge in the expansion of credit between 1995 and 1996, but the growth in the real GDP in fact fell from 8.3 to 7 per cent during the same period and it was only 4.4 per cent in 1997. A study by Greene and Villanueva (1991), whose samples cover 23 developing nations from 1975–87, also found that a high interest rate has a significant negative effect on private investment.

12. One of the key elements of the policy of financial liberalization is that under the free market mechanism all borrowers' access to the loan market will be improved irrespective of their age and size of operation. Thus government assistance would not be required. Contrary to this claim, throughout the 1980s in the United States, about 25 per cent of all loans were either originated by government agencies or carried government guarantees. The government organized these loans in order to assist students, small business, housing, exports and for a host of other worthy causes (Stiglitz 1993). See also Jappeli (1990) in the context of the United States, who also found that the smaller and marginal borrowers'

access to the loan market has not improved. Similarly, Basu (1989) observes that in Australia, despite deregulation, a variety of government programmes continued in order to ensure that smaller borrowers' access to the loan market was not adversely affected as a result of deregulation. In India, which also embraced the policy of financial liberalization from 1991, there was a growing concern not to abolish government-assisted loan programmes for small businesses, because of the fear that liberalization would reduce these borrowers' access to the loan market (Sen and Vaidya 1997). The above evidence therefore suggests that governments had to intervene in the loan market in order to ensure that the small businesses were not disadvantaged as a result of liberalization, as occurred in the United States, and when these assistance schemes were removed we observe that the smaller firms' access to the loan market was further reduced, as in the case of Ecuador.

13. For example, Diaz-Alejandro (1985, p. 9) notes that in Chile, 'The process of financial liberalisation had also led to a widely noted ... concentration of potential economic power in the hands of a few conglomerates or economic groups, which combined financial and non-financial corporations'. Similarly, Basu (1994, p. 282) in the case of Australia also noted that, 'the distribution of loans in general favoured the large borrowers rather than the smaller and medium sized borrowers'.

14. As Singh (1993 and 1995) observed, the 1980s financial liberalization simply led to portfolio substitution of bank deposits by tradable securities.

15. See also Morisset (1993) who suggests that the positive effect of a rise in domestic credit as suggested by McKinnon and Shaw could equally be offset by a portfolio shift from capital goods in favour of monetary assets. This possibility principally arises from the fact that banks have an incentive to offer loans for the acquisition of financial assets as opposed to fixed investments since the former increases liquidity as opposed to the latter.

16. The issue of efficiency gain via growth in the stock market is principally based on the postulation of the switching possibility from low- to high-yield securities. That is, a higher interest rate may encourage investors to abandon their low-yield securities in favour of high-yield securities. It is this possibility which brings discipline to firms who offer a lower yield on their securities, and thereby may bring a higher form of efficiency to these firms. See King and Levine (1993a and 1993b) and Levine and Zervos (1996 and 1998) on this argument. But in reality this involves investors switching from low-yield productive investment facilities to high-yield productive facilities. However, due to the irreversibility of investment expenditure, a considerable amount of doubt remains as to whether investors will be able to make the adjustment, to the satisfaction of shareholders, quickly enough. This limits the efficiency gain through stock market activity; perhaps we are asking too much from the stock market. Conveniently, we often ignore the other observed fact, which is that much of the stock market activity is not particularly followed by the fundamentals of securities but rather by expected changes in the price of the stocks. This caused concern to Singh (1997), following Nagaraj (1996) in the case of India, who notes that despite the stock market boom in the 1980s, and substantial resources raised by Indian corporations, their investment in fixed assets actually declined.

17. For a further analysis of bank failures, see Calomiris and Mason (1997) and Kaminsky and Reinhart (1999).

18. It is important to recognize that development and growth are not the same thing, as the latter is a prerequisite for the former, where the former involves improving the economic well-being of every member of society. See Streeten (1981) and Sen (1983) on this issue. Unfortunately, the school of liberalization does not recognize the importance of this distinction, and this may be largely because the model they use to promote their view is based on the assumption that everyone starts with equal endowments. Observation reveals that such an assumption is simply not a reflection of reality.

19. See Chakravarty (1993) for further details.

20. See Sen ([1982] 1984) on this issue although it is discussed in a different context.

21. See Arrow (1962), where he explains how worker productivity increases over time during the production process as they acquire skills. See also Haavelmo (1954) where he emphasizes the role of education, Kaldor (1961) on the technical progress function and Romer (1986 and 1990) who introduces learning and technical change.

22. For further details, see Datta-Chaudhuri (1990) and Lall (1994).
23. South Korea was particularly successful in developing various trading companies, which provided many exchange-related facilities. These institutions are largely responsible for the high-growth performance. See Jones and Sakong (1980), Amsden (1989), Westphal (1990), Datta-Chaudhuri (1990), Lall (1994) and Singh (1994) for further details.
24. See also Cho (1989) and Kim (1991) on the above issue. However Amsden (1989) pointed out that although household savings as a percentage of GNP increased from 0.18 per cent in 1965 to 4.15 per cent in 1966, it declined in the following year. Thereafter no systematic relationship can be observed between interest rate and saving behaviour.
25. For example, the tables that we have consulted from the authors (Cho 1989 and Amsden 1989 and 1994) indeed suggest that the interest rate on time deposits remained higher than the rate on non-preferential loans between 1965 and 1968. In the absence of any other information this suggests that banks were running at a loss during these 4 years. However, neither author makes any comment on this disparity between the rates on non-preferential loans and deposit rates. On the other hand, Cole and Park (1983) point out that this higher rate of between 24 to 28 per cent per annum on regular commercial loans, which remained below the rate paid on the time deposits of more than one year of maturity, or in other words, this reverse margin, attracted criticism from the banking community.
26. That is unless we would like to assume that the banks invested part of the deposits in the unregulated financial market, since the interest rate on loans in this sector was higher than the rate on time deposits.
27. On average there was 12.9 per cent difference between Korean loans and foreign loans (that is, the USA and Japan) during the period from 1966–70 (Amsden 1989). See also Park (1985) who pointed out that between 1965 and 1970, the divergence between domestic and foreign borrowing rates ranged from 4.4 to 18 per cent.
28. The last 20 years of experience of greater banking crises in developing countries than in developed countries indicates that this willingness is perhaps greater in the case of the former than of the latter. This difference in willingness between the two categories of nations may have emerged due to the gap in experience in that one achieved through an evolutionary process while the other was too young as yet to go through the necessary preliminaries that are involved in the process of development.
29. This problem can be more clearly observed from Choong-Hwan (1990), who presents figures for the internal and external share of funds for the 1963–69 and 1970–74 periods, which show that while in the former this on average was 33.3 and 66.7 per cent, respectively, for the latter this share changed to 25.7 and 74.3 per cent, respectively. This shows that as the economy slowed down, firms started to have difficulty in meeting their debt commitment, and in order to meet this commitment they resorted to borrowing and as a result this further reduced their share of internal funds.
30. For further details, see Bank of Korea (1973), Cole and Park (1983), Amsden (1989) and Cho (1989).
31. An issue which has been exhaustively discussed within the game theory framework in various contexts. See Jensen and Meckling (1976), Stiglitz and Weiss (1981), De Mezza and Webb (1987) and Gertler (1992).
32. For further details, see Cole and Park (1983) and Westphal (1990).

REFERENCES

Amsden, A.H. (1989), *Asia's Next Giant: South Korea and Late Industrialisation*, New York: Oxford University Press.

Amsden, A.H. (1994), 'Why isn't the whole world experimenting with the East Asian model to develop?: Review of the East Asian Miracle', *World Development*, **22**, 627–33.

Amsden, A.H. and Yoon-Dae Euh (1993), 'South Korea's 1980s financial reforms:

good-bye financial repression (maybe), hello new institutional restraints', *World Development*, **21**, 379–90.

Arestis, P. and P. Demetriades (1996), 'Finance and growth: institutional considerations and causality', Paper presented at the Royal Economic Society Annual Conference, Swansea University, April.

Arestis, P. and P. Demetriades (1997), 'Financial development and economic growth: assessing the evidence', *Economic Journal*, **107**, 783–99.

Arestis, P. and M. Glickman (2002), 'Financial crisis in South East Asia: dispelling illusion the Minsky way', *Cambridge Journal of Economics*, **26**, 237–60.

Arrow, K. (1962), 'The economic implications of learning by doing', *Review of Economic Studies*, **29**, 155–73.

Bank of Korea (1973), *Report on the Results of the August 3, 1972 Presidential Emergency Decree*, Seoul.

Bank of Korea (1994), *Annual Report*, Seoul.

Basu, S. (1989), 'Deregulation: small business access to the capital market, some theoretical issues with special reference to the Australian banking sector', *Australian Economic Papers*, **28**, 141–59.

Basu, S. (1994), 'Deregulation of the Australian banking sector: a theoretical perspective', *Australian Economic Papers*, **33**, 272–85.

Bencivenga, V.R. and B.D. Smith (1991), 'Financial intermediation and endogenous growth', *Review of Economic Studies*, **58**, 195–209.

Bencivenga, V.R., B.D. Smith and R.M. Starr (1996), 'Equity markets, transactions costs, and capital accumulation: an illustration', *World Bank Economic Review*, **10**, 241–65.

Benston, G.J. and G.G. Kaufman (1997), 'FDICIA after five years', *Journal of Economic Perspectives*, **11**, 139–58.

Calomiris, C.W. and J.R. Mason (1997), 'Contagion and bank failures during the Great Depression: the June 1932 Chicago banking panic', *American Economic Review*, **87**, 863–83.

Caprio, G. and P. Honohan (1999), 'Restoring banking stability: beyond supervised capital requirements', *Journal of Economic Perspectives*, **13**, 43–64.

Chakravarty, S. (1987), 'Marxist economics and contemporary developing economies', *Cambridge Journal of Economics*, **11**, 3–22.

Chakravarty, S. (1993), 'Theory of development planning: an appraisal', in Chakravarty, *Selected Economic Writings*, Delhi: Oxford University Press, pp. 270–88.

Chandavarkar, A.G. (1971), 'Some aspects of interest rate policies in less developed economies: the experience of selected Asian economies', *IMF Staff Papers*, March, International Monetary Fund, Washington, DC.

Chandavarkar, A. (1992), 'Of finance and development: neglected and unsettled questions', *World Development*, **20**, 133–42.

Cho, Y. Je (1989), 'Finance and development: the Korean approach', *Oxford Review of Economic Policy*, **5**, 88–102.

Choong-Hwan, R. (1990), 'Korean corporate financing', *Monthly Review*, Korean Exchange Bank, **24**, April, 3–13.

Cole, D. and Y.C. Park (1983), *Financial Development in Korea, 1945–1978*, Cambridge, MA: Harvard University Press.

Datta-Chaudhuri, M. (1990), 'Market failure and government failure', *Journal of Economic Perspectives*, **4**, 25–39.

De Gregorio, J. and P.E. Guidotti (1995), 'Financial development and economic growth', *World Development*, **23**, 433–48.

De Mezza, D. and D.C. Webb (1987), 'Too much investment: a problem of asymmetric information', *Quarterly Journal of Economics*, **102**, 281–92.
Demetriades, P.O. and K.B. Luintel (1996), 'Financial development, economic growth and banking sector controls: evidence from India', *Economic Journal*, **106**, 359–74.
Devereux, M.B. and G.W. Smith (1994), 'International risk sharing and economic growth', *International Economic Review*, **35**, 535–50.
Diaz-Alejandro, C.F. (1985), 'Good-bye financial repression, hello financial crash', *Journal of Development Economics*, **19**, 1–24.
Dornbusch, R. and A. Reynoso (1989), 'Financial factors in economic development', *American Economic Review*, **79**, 204–9.
Dougherty, C. (1980), *Interest and Profit*, London: Methuen.
Fry, M.J. (1978), 'Money and capital or financial deepening in economic development?', *Journal of Money Credit and Banking*, **10**, 464–75.
Fry, M.J. (1980), 'Saving, investment, growth and the cost of financial repression', *World Development*, **8**, 317–27.
Fry, M.J. (1995), *Money, Interest and Banking in Economic Development*, 2nd edn, Baltimore, MD: Johns Hopkins University Press.
Fry, M.J. (1997), 'In favour of financial liberalisation', *Economic Journal*, **107**, 754–70.
Georgescu-Roegen, N. (1971), *The Entropy Law and the Economic Process*, Cambridge, MA: Harvard University Press.
Gertler, M.L. (1992), 'Financial capacity and output fluctuations in an economy with multi-period financial relationships', *Review of Economic Studies*, **59**, 455–72.
Gertler, M. and A. Rose (1994), 'Finance, public policy and growth', in G. Caprio, I. Atiyas and J. Hanson (eds), *Financial Reform: Theory and Experience*, New York: Cambridge University Press.
Giovannini, A. (1983), 'The interest elasticity of savings in developing countries: the existing evidence', *World Development*, **11**, 601–7.
Goldsmith, R.W. (1969), *Financial Structure and Development*, New Haven, CT: Yale University Press.
Goodhart, C.A.E. (1995), *The Central Bank and the Financial System*, London: Macmillan.
Greene, J. and D. Villanueva (1991), 'Private investment in developing countries', *IMF Staff Papers*, **38**, 33–58.
Greenwood, J. and B. Jovanovic (1990), 'Financial development, growth, and the distribution of income', *Journal of Political Economy*, **98**, 1076–108.
Gupta, K.L. (1987), 'Aggregate savings, financial intermediation and interest rates', *Review of Economics and Statistics*, **69**, 303–11.
Gurley, J.G., H.T. Patrick and E.S. Shaw (1965), 'The financial structure of Korea', draft, United States Operations Mission to Korea.
Haavelmo, T. (1954), *A Study in the Theory of Economic Evolution*, Amsterdam: North-Holland.
Jappeli, T. (1990), 'Who is credit constrained in the U.S. economy?', *Quarterly Journal of Economics*, **105**, 219–34.
Jaramillo, F., F. Schiantarelli and A. Weiss (1996), 'Capital market imperfection before and after financial liberalization: an Euler equation approach to panel data for Ecuadorian firms', *Journal of Development Economics*, **51**, 367–86.
Jensen, M. and W. Meckling (1976), 'Theory of the firm: managerial behaviour, agency costs, and ownership structure', *Journal of Financial Economics*, **3**, October, 305–60.

Jones, L.P. and I.I. Sakong (1980), *Government, Business, and Entrepreneurship in Economic Development: The Korean Case*, Cambridge, MA: Harvard University Press.
Kaldor, N. (1961), 'Capital accumulation and economic growth', in F.A Lutz and D.C. Hague (eds), *The Theory of Capital*, London: Macmillan, pp. 177–222.
Kaminsky, G.L. and C.M. Reinhart (1999), 'The twin crises: the causes of banking and balance-of-payments problems', *American Economic Review*, **89**, 473–500.
Keynes, J.M. (1936), *The General Theory of Employment, Interest and Money*, London: Macmillan.
Khatkhate, D. (1988), 'Assessing the impact of interest rates in less developed countries', *World Development*, **16**, 577–88.
Kim, K.S. (1991), 'The interest-rate reform of 1965 and domestic saving', in Lee-Jay Cho and Kim Yoon Hyung (eds), *Economic Development in the Republic of Korea: A Policy Perspective*, An East–West Centre Book, Honolulu: University of Hawaii Press.
King, R.G. and R. Levine (1993a), 'Finance and growth: Schumpeter might be right', *Quarterly Journal of Economics*, **108**, 717–37.
King, R.G. and R. Levine (1993b), 'Finance, entrepreneurship, and growth: theory and evidence', *Journal of Monetary Economics*, **32**, 513–42.
Kuznets, S. (1955), 'Towards a theory of economic growth', in R. Levachman (ed.), *National Policy for Economic Welfare at Home and Abroad,* New York: Doubleday, pp. 12–85.
Lall, S. (1994), 'The East Asian Miracle: does the bell toll for industrial strategy?', *World Development*, **22**, 645–54.
Lee, S.J. (1997), 'Financial crisis in Korea', mimeo, Yale University.
Levine, R. (1992), 'Financial structure and economic development', Working Paper WPS 849, Washington, DC: World Bank.
Levine, R. and S. Zervos (1996), 'Stock market development and long-run growth', *World Bank Economic Review*, **10**, 323–39.
Levine, R. and S. Zervos (1998), 'Stock markets, banks, and economic growth', *American Economic Review*, **88**, 537–58.
Marshall, A. (1920), *Principles of Economics*, London: Macmillan, 8th edn, reprinted in 1982.
Mayer, C. (1988), 'New issues in corporate finance', *European Economic Review*, **32**, 1167–88.
McKinnon, R.I. (1973), *Money and Capital in Economic Development*, Washington, DC: Brookings Institutions.
Mikesell, R.F and J.E. Zinser (1972), 'The nature of the savings function in developing countries: a survey of the theoretical and empirical literature', *Journal of Economic Literature*, **11**, 1–26.
Mishkin, F.S. (1999), 'Global financial instability: framework, events, issues', *Journal of Economic Perspectives*, **13**, 3–20.
Modigliani, F. (1986), 'Life cycle, individual thrift, and the wealth of nations', *American Economic Review*, **76**, 297–313.
Morisset, J. (1993), 'Does financial liberalization really improve private investment in developing countries?', *Journal of Development Economics*, **40**, 133–50.
Nagaraj, R. (1996), *India's Capital Market Growth: Trends, Explanations and Evidence*, New Delhi: Indira Gandhi Institute of Development Research.
Nurkse, R. (1953), *Problems of Capital Formation in Under-Developed Countries*, Oxford: Oxford University Press.

Obstfeld, M. (1994), 'Risk-taking, global diversification and growth', *American Economic Review*, **84**, 1310–29.
Park, Y.C. (1985), 'Korea's experience with external debt management', in G. Smith and J. Cuddington (eds), *International Debt and the Developing Countries*, Baltimore, MD: Johns Hopkins University Press.
Rajan, R.G. and L. Zingales (1998), 'Financial dependence and growth', *American Economic Review*, **88**, 559–86.
Robinson, J. (1979), 'The generalisation of the general theory', in *The Generalisation of the General Theory and Other Essays*, 2nd edition, London: Macmillan, pp. 1–73.
Romer, P. (1986), 'Increasing returns to scale and long-run growth', *Journal of Political Economy*, **94**, 1002–37.
Romer, P. (1990), 'Endogenous technical change', *Journal of Political Economy*, **98**, S71–S102.
Rosenstein-Rodan, P.N. (1943), 'Problems of industrialisation in Eastern and South-Eastern Europe', *Economic Journal*, **53**, 202–11.
Roubini, N. and X. Sala-i-Martin (1992), 'Financial repression and economic growth', *Journal of Development Economics*, **39**, 5–30.
Saint-Paul, G. (1992), 'Technological choice, financial markets and economic development', *European Economic Review*, **36**, 763–81.
Scitovsky, T. (1954), 'Two concepts of external economics', *Journal of Political Economy*, **62**, 143–51.
Sen, A.K. (1982), 'Approaches to the choice of discount rates for social benefit–cost analysis', in R. Lind (ed.), *Discounting for Time and Risk in Energy Policy*, Baltimore, MD: Johns Hopkins University Press, reprinted in A.K. Sen (ed.), *Resources, Values and Development*, Oxford: Basil Blackwell, 1984.
Sen, A.K. (1983), 'Development: which way now?', *Economic Journal*, **93**, 745–62.
Sen, K. and R.R. Vaidya (1997), *The Process of Financial Liberalisation in India*, Delhi: Oxford University Press.
Shaw, E. (1973), *Financing Deepening in Economic Development*, New York: Oxford University Press.
Singh, A. (1993), 'The stock market and economic development: should developing countries encourage stock markets?', *UNCTAD Review*, No. 4, 1–28.
Singh, A. (1994), 'Openness and the market friendly approach to development: learning the right lessons from development experience', *World Development*, **22**, 1811–23.
Singh, A. (1995), *Corporate Financial Patterns in Industrialising Economies: A Comparative International Study*, IFC Technical Paper No. 2, Washington, DC: World Bank.
Singh, A (1997), 'Financial liberalisation, stock markets and economic development', *Economic Journal*, **107**, 771–82.
Solow, R.M. (1957), 'Technical change and the aggregate production function', *Review of Economics and Statistics*, **39**, 312–20.
Stern, N. (1989), 'The economics of development: a survey', *Economic Journal*, **99**, 597–685.
Stiglitz, J.E. (1993), 'The role of the state in financial markets', *World Bank Economic Review*, Proceedings of the Annual Conference on Development Economics, pp. 19–52.
Stiglitz, J.E. and A. Weiss (1981), 'Credit rationing in markets with imperfect information', *American Economic Review*, **71**, 393–410.

Streeten, P. (1981), *Development Perspective*, London: Macmillan.
Taylor, L. (1983), *Structuralist Macroeconomics*, New York: Basic Books.
van Wijnbergen, S. (1983), 'Credit policy, inflation and growth in a financially repressed economy', *Journal of Development Economics*, **13**, 45–65.
Westphal, L. (1990), 'Industrial policy in an export-propelled economy: lessons from South Korea's experience', *Journal of Economic Perspectives*, **4**, 41–59.
World Bank (1989), *World Development Report 1989*, New York: Oxford University Press.
World Bank (1993), *The East Asian Miracle*, New York: Oxford University Press.

4. A 'third way' in economic policy: a reappraisal of the Rehn–Meidner model in the light of modern economics

Lennart Erixon

INTRODUCTION

Since the emergence of Sweden in the mid-1930s as 'the middle way', the Swedish model has interested both social scientists and politicians. A strong welfare state, a powerful trade union movement, extensive equalization of pay and incomes, and priority of full employment was seen as either an example to follow or an extreme expression of European sclerosis. But adherents and critics of the model alike have shared one thing in common – an overriding interest in its practical aspects. Less attention has been paid, especially outside Sweden, to the theories behind or motivations for Swedish economic policies. In fact, it is easier to distinguish a Swedish model in theory than in practice. At the beginning of the 1950s, two economists at the LO (the Swedish Trade Union Confederation), Gösta Rehn and Rudolf Meidner,[1] devised a unique model for economic policy. Their exposition questioned the Keynesian policy of full employment while rejecting the non-interventionism and one-sided emphasis on price stability of the monetarists. What came to be known as the Rehn–Meidner model (henceforth R–M model) thus represented a 'third way' in economic policy. A major objective of the R–M model is to obtain full employment without inflation but also to combine economic growth with equity. Rehn and Meidner recommended labour market policy measures, solidaristic wage policy and deflationary fiscal policies to simultaneously achieve full employment, low rates of inflation, equity and growth.

It is still possible to consider the R–M model as a 'third way' in macroeconomics. Its scepticism to fine-tuning in economic policy and reliance on supply-side and market-adjustment measures to combine high employment levels with price stability are shared by critics of Keynesian economics. This consensus may seem paradoxical to people who, correctly, have noticed the importance of the art of social engineering and the strategic role of trade unions in the R–M model. But at the same time, the designers of the R–M model were post-Keynesians (or US 'orthodox' Keynesians) rather than neo-Keynesians (or (neo-) classicals), since they had doubts about the possibilities of avoiding macroeconomic imbalances by greater real wage flexibility. They also emphasized the negative effects of real wage flexibility on inflation, income distribution and growth. Rehn and Meidner reduced the possibility of underbidding in labour markets by their recommendation of a selective policy for full employment.

The R–M model is one of the few innovations in Swedish economics in the post-war period. I would even claim that it is one of the few coherent visions of economic policy beyond Keynesianism. Even friendly observers of Swedish labour market policies have failed to appreciate the scope of the R–M model where instruments and priorities of economic policy are concerned. Among other things, the model is a remarkable mix between a market-conforming policy to satisfy national goals on the one hand and measures to mobilize and strengthen the position of labour on the other.

The R–M model was not consciously applied in Sweden in all respects, even in its 'golden age' from the late 1950s to the mid-1970s. Not only foreign but also Swedish scholars (see Lindbeck 1997, pp. 1291–2) have sometimes exaggerated its importance as the rudder of Sweden's economic policy. But labour market and solidaristic wage policy would hardly have expanded to their current scope if Rehn and Meidner had not placed them in a larger economic and political context. The applications of the model in Sweden are analysed in (Erixon 1997a and 2001b). In this chapter I shall focus on the theory, not the practice, of the R–M model.

The R–M model gives two valuable contributions to positive economics; the first one concerns the analysis of wage formation in a country like Sweden. Rehn and Meidner laid strong emphasis on relative-wage preferences long before the birth of the modern theory of fair wages. But more important, their description of the (Swedish) wage process is more dynamic and comprehensive than that found in most wage models today. In the R–M model, wages are determined by competitive forces, X-inefficient firms, and by 'wage-setting' phenomena such as labour market policy, solidaristic wage policy and relative wage preferences. Bargaining and trade union theorists in particular tend to underestimate the role of competitive market labour markets both *per se* and as guidelines for collective wage negotiations. Friendly observers have often placed the R–M model in a trade union or bargaining theoretical context that conceals much of its underlying view of wage formation, inflation and growth. The second contribution of the R–M model to positive economics is in the field of growth economics. The model was not only a forerunner of X-inefficiency and vintage theories by assuming that productivity is stimulated by profit-margin squeezes. It has also paved the way for a general theory of transformation pressure by defining the pressure in terms of wage and stabilization policy.

The R–M model is both an economic (and wage) policy programme and a theory of wages, inflation, profits, employment and growth. Which of these two aspects of the model I am discussing at any given point will be obvious from the context. I shall begin by describing the content of the Rehn–Meidner economic policy programme. Then in the next two sections, I outline the positive theory behind the R–M model, with particular emphasis on inflation and growth, and survey the findings of some studies that have put hypotheses in the model to test. In the final section, some reflections will be made on the relevancy of the R–M model with a particular eye on the effects of globalization and European integration.

THE CONTENT OF THE R–M MODEL

The Shortcomings of Keynesianism

I shall define a Keynesian policy as a countercyclical fiscal and monetary policy (possibly including exchange-rate policies) with a bias towards expansionism to guarantee full employment and *ad hoc* measures to fight inflation. A more narrow definition of Keynesian policy will be avoided, for example one that emphasizes the use of fiscal rather than monetary instruments to stabilize the economy in line with Keynes's recommendations in the *General Theory* (Keynes 1936, p. 375). A similar priority of fiscal rather than monetary measures for stabilization purposes is also found in the R–M model.

Rehn and Meidner published their criticisms of Keynesianism at the end of the 1940s when expansionary fiscal and monetary policies to achieve low rates of unemployment had led to high inflation in Sweden (Rehn 1952a [1948]). They warned of the high costs even to the trade union movement of inflation and 'overemployment', pointing out that high aggregate-demand levels have negative effects on resource allocation and growth, and that full employment achieved through excess demand would lead to high absenteeism, excess labour turnover and a greater risk of accidents at work. Keynesianism is inflationary in its effects not only on aggregate demand but also its unpredictable and unintentional effects on income distribution. A high demand for, and limited availability of, skilled labour in particular is a cause for wage drift, that is, pay in excess of what has been negotiated in central agreements.[2] Wage drift leads to compensation demands from other groups of employees anxious to maintain their relative wage positions. A Keynesian policy of full employment therefore aggravates the conflict between those wage earners who benefit from market forces and those who do not. The conflict results in inflationary wage–wage spirals where, for example, 'wage drifters' try to preserve their initial wage advantage. Too expansive a general economic policy thus generates tensions between different wage-earner groups that not only lead to inflation but also threaten cohesion within the labour movement.

Rehn and Meidner also thought that any measures other than a restrictive general economic policy to fight inflation (and improve the balance of payments) were ineffective or arbitrary. Inflation, they said, cannot be curbed by means of controls on prices and investments as in a Keynesian policy of full employment. Regulations can hardly be comprehensive and from a growth viewpoint it is often the 'wrong' companies and sectors that suffer their effects. Nor did Rehn and Meidner hold any great hope that inflation in an overheated economy could be prevented by incomes policy, even one covering all the employee organizations, since central agreements will be obstructed by local trade union and individual wage drift. They came to the conclusion that incomes policy is ineffective in a boom and unnecessary in a recession. Further, if statutory, incomes policy threatens the autonomy of labour market organizations,[3] while the combination of high wage drift and 'voluntary' incomes policy undermines the redistribution policy of and solidarity between trade unions and weakens their legitimacy in the eyes of their members. Clearly, declarations of 'wage restraint' are incompatible with the main task of a trade union, which is to achieve the highest possible pay rises for their members.

The two economists presented their alternative to Keynesianism in a report to the 1951 LO Congress entitled *Trade Unions and Full Employment* (Meidner and Rehn et al., 1953 [1951]). Hereafter I equate the R–M model with this LO report. The report was primarily concerned with the inflation–unemployment dilemma; Rehn and Meidner did not pronounce the growth aspects of their model until the 1960s. However their subsequent work did not actually add anything to their original policy model apart from Rehn's proposals of marginal employment subsidies and Meidner's proposal of wage-earner funds. The marginal employment subsidies, enthusiastically advocated by Rehn in the 1970s and later, are considered as a component of the R–M model while wage-earner funds are not treated as parts of the model. The exclusion is primarily for the sake of convenience. (There was also some disagreement between Rehn and Meidner over wage-earner funds, which is another reason why I do not deal with them as parts of the model.) Basic arguments behind wage-earner funds were to appropriate 'excess profits' from solidaristic wage policy and increase labour's share of national income and wealth, fundamental parts of the R–M model. Revaluations of the currency, seen by Rehn in the 1960s and the 1970s as appropriate general tools to achieve price stability in an open economy, are also excluded from the R–M benchmark model. Means and objectives of the model are shown in Figure 4.1.

A reappraisal of the Rehn–Meidner model 75

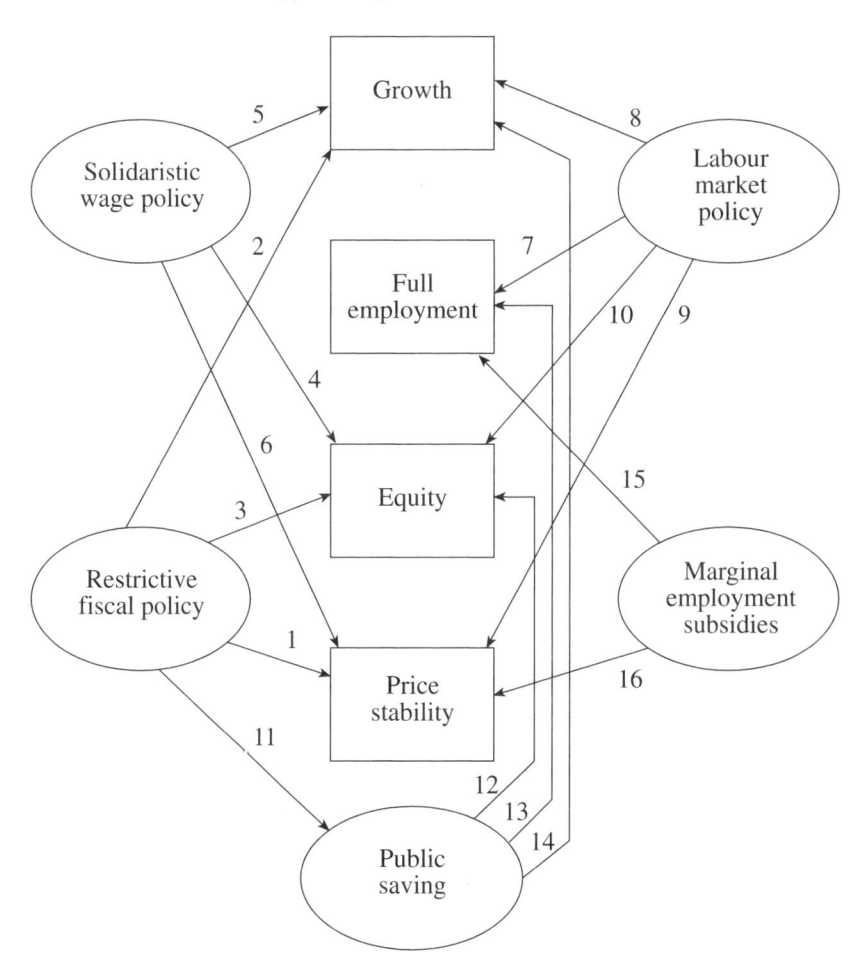

Figure 4.1 The R–M economic and wage policy model – means and objectives

A Restrictive Fiscal Policy

The R–M model recommends a restrictive general economic policy, especially fiscal restraints, to curb the rate of inflation (arrow 1 in Figure 4.1). Fiscal restraints will, *ceteris paribus*, depress flexible prices in the model (as in the *General Theory*) but more important, it is one component in a strategy to control inflation by keeping down profit margins in the medium and long terms (Meidner and Rehn et al 1953, pp. 92–4 and 99 [1951]; Rehn 1977, p. 212). Rehn even recommended in other publications than the LO report that fiscal policy should be predominantly tight over the business cycle, thus in the medium term (Rehn 1952a, pp. 36 and 51 [1948]). One purpose of fiscal restraint over the business cycle is to create a public saving surplus (arrow 11).

In the R–M model, a restrictive general economic policy is also expected to encourage rationalizations and structural change (arrow 2 in Figure 4.1); the positive effects of a tight general economic policy on productivity and growth were explored by Rehn in the 1960s (Rehn 1969, p. 151). Furthermore, the tight economic policy is to support the equity principles of the trade union movement by leading to smaller wage gaps between 'wage drifters' and other employees (arrow 3). More precisely, the policy reduces the risk of wages reflecting differences in profitability between firms rather than the content of work. Further, the advocacy of a permanently tight general economic policy is part of a strategy to change functional income distribution in favour of labour, thus to increase labour's share of value added.

Solidaristic Wage Policy

The main task of a coordinating trade union organization in the R–M model is to pursue a solidaristic wage policy, the common denominator being that wages should not be determined by company profitability. Identical work must be remunerated with the same rates of pay and wage differentials should reflect real differences in working environment, difficulty, responsibility, experience and education required. Solidaristic wage policy presupposes a systematic comparison of jobs by central trade unions, possibly in collaboration with central employer organizations, where the job evaluation has two components, the definition of identical jobs and the decision on a fair wage structure. Thus, the wage policy of solidarity is both a policy of identical rates of pay for the same work and a policy of fair wage differentials. Foreign economists often disregard this latter aspect of solidaristic wage policy (see Blanchflower et al. 1995, pp. 88–9). The R–M model is not a recommendation of wage equalization in general. A clear distinction must be made between the theory and practice of solidaristic wage policy.[4] Nor should the solidaristic wage policy of the model be confused with trade unions' strivings for compensation for wage drift because of relative wage preferences. The wage norm of solidarity is set after a comparison of jobs by central bodies in the labour market, not by wage earners in the leading sector. Solidaristic wage policy can be seen as a crude instrument of planning, typical of the early post-war period. It is nevertheless a policy aimed at simulating a long-run equilibrium in competitive labour markets. Here, the same wages are paid to homogeneous labour and wage differentials are explained by differences in worker qualifications and work content, *inter alia*, its degree of (un)pleasantness.

The wage principle of solidarity, already adopted by the LO in the 1930s, is governed by a concern for equity (arrow 4). Rehn and Meidner's contribution was to show that the principle also has implications for growth and price stability. They considered solidaristic wage policy as a means of achieving economic growth, primarily through structural change (arrow 5). Coupled to a restrictive general economic policy, this wage policy threatens to obliterate the least-profitable firms and sectors. The pressure on profit margins will create the incentives and release the resources for structural change. At the same time, solidaristic wage policy leads to 'excess profits' in firms and sectors which could have paid more than the wages of solidarity. These profits will increase the self-financing capabilities of established profitable firms and strengthen the motivation to set up new firms and transfer resources to dynamic sectors. Hence, solidaristic wage policy is compatible with economic growth since the expansion of fast-growing sectors is speeded up by larger profit differences and more closures. Firms that exhibit low productivity must engage in rationalizations in order to survive.

The R–M model freed the trade union movement from the straitjacket of incomes policy, particularly in an overheated economy. Government carries the main responsibility for the general level of wages, while the trade union movement is responsible for pay structure. Yet, as indicated above, it would be a simplification to say that the R–M model ignores the effects of stabilization policy on wage and industrial structure. Rehn and Meidner also expected that the wage structure may influence the rate of inflation. One aim of solidaristic wage policy is to bring down inflation by, first, weakening the direct influence of free market forces on wage formation and, second, countering the demands for compensatory wage increases that have no rational foundation (arrow 6). As already noted, the object of solidaristic wage policy is not to increase the intensity and scope of collective pay increases to preserve or improve a relative wage position. Rather, the aim is to prevent the inception of wage compensation spirals. Rehn and Meidner thought that compensation demands for other groups' pay rises or higher wage levels is less intense in the absence of challenging wage differences. Thus, a determination of fair wages would prevent inflationary wage drift and compensatory leapfrogging (Meidner and Rehn et al. 1953, p. 96 [1951]; Meidner 1974, p. 15; Rehn 1980, pp. 36 and 39–40). Central wage bargaining can provide wage moderation in the R–M model, but only indirectly by being conditional for solidaristic wage policy.

Solidaristic wage policy by itself is a poor instrument in the fight for equity and price stability, according to Rehn and Meidner. The incentives for dynamic firms to offer higher wages are not really affected by solidaristic wage policy. In fact, this policy will even increase the room for wage drift, *ceteris paribus*, since it leads to 'excess profits' in the most profitable firms. A solidaristic wage policy can therefore only contribute to lower wage drift if combined with a restrictive general economic policy and a mobility-enhancing labour market policy.

Labour Market Policy

A restrictive general economic policy will, *ceteris paribus*, cause unemployment, especially in some sectors of the economy if profit conditions vary. Further, 'structural unemployment' is bound to appear in the wake of a solidaristic wage policy. Rehn and Meidner's main recommendation to obtain full employment is labour market policy measures (arrow 7).

Labour market policy can be divided into three parts, selective demand policy, supply-orientated measures and actions to improve the matching process on the labour market. Demand-orientated measures should have the smallest possible effects on aggregate product demand and therefore be directed towards specific employee groups, companies and regions (particularly specific relief work and regional policy). The supply side of the labour market was to be affected by the introduction of relocation and retraining grants and occupational training programmes. The matching of job applicants to vacancies would be achieved through employment services by public agencies.

One objective of the supply-side and matching measures is to increase or reallocate the availability of labour and to improve the labour market's ability to make adjustments. Thus, labour market policy could stimulate economic growth by facilitating dynamic sectors' recruitment of labour (arrow 8). In addition, labour market policy is an important weapon in the struggle against inflation. Here, Rehn and Meidner emphasized not only that the alternative employment policy, that is an expansionary general economic policy, is inflationary, but also that some labour market policy has an inflation-dampening effect (arrow 9). Stimulation of labour mobility would moderate the rate of pay increases in sectors with high demand and labour market bottlenecks.

It is wrong to conclude, however, that labour market policy will moderate the pace of wage increases in the R–M model. The policy prevents open unemployment, and therefore a tendency to wage reductions in a recession.[5] Rehn and Meidner assume that these wage-increasing effects of labour market policy are decisive over the business cycle. A restrictive general economic policy is *inter alia* meant to counter the inflationary effects of labour market policy. In fact, Rehn and Meidner did not deny that labour market policy could be at least as inflationary as an expansive general economic policy to obtain full employment; their model is thus not hurt by some evidence that Swedish labour market policy has been inflationary or even more inflationary than an expansive general economic policy (see the survey of the empirical literature in Erixon 2000, pp. 66–9).

The prime object of labour market policy in the Rehn–Meidner programme for price stability is to assist fiscal policy in the strategy to lower inflation by holding down profit margins in the medium and long terms. Rehn and Meidner's main idea was that the combination of labour market policy and a restrictive general economic policy would result in a better trade-off between employment and inflation than the combination of an expansive general economic policy and incomes policy. Even Swedish economists have failed to uncover the essential idea of the Rehn–Meidner stabilization programme – labour market policy should lead to a 'downward shift in the Phillips curve' (using a later terminology) through the policy's contribution to a profit-margin squeeze, not through its stimulation of labour mobility (see Rehn 1969, p. 170). In the R–M model, the tendency to lower inflation by improvements in the functioning of the labour market is efficiently offset (during recessions and over the business cycle) by the wage-rigidity effects of selective policy measures aimed at avoiding open unemployment.

Labour market policy is also a vehicle in the endeavour for greater equity in the R–M model. The significant wage differentials between sectors that emerge when dynamic firms try to attract labour by higher wages are offset by measures to improve the mobility of labour from stagnating to expanding sectors (arrow 10). In particular, solidaristic wage policy is facilitated by government measures to speed up labour mobility (Meidner and Rehn et al. 1953, p. 97 [1951]; Meidner 1969, p. 190). Further, by guaranteeing full employment, labour market policy is one of the scissor blades, fiscal policy is the other, to squeeze profit margins and therefore change functional income distribution in favour of labour.

Public Saving

Rehn and Meidner argue for public saving in the medium and long terms. In particular, fiscal policies should increase the public share of total saving at the expense of company saving by reducing profit margins (Rehn 1952a, pp. 52–4 [1948]). Public saving is an intermediate goal in the R–M model. Rehn and Meidner prefer public saving in terms of income and wealth distribution (see arrow 12). They also consider it preferable from the viewpoint of achieving certain employment and growth ambitions in the field of industrial policy (arrows 13 and 14, respectively). These ambitions make public saving the least market-conforming component of the R–M model.

Further, according to Rehn and Meidner, large public budget surpluses during a boom will increase the degree of freedom in stabilization policy. These surpluses make it possible to avoid significant borrowing in a recession when fiscal policy by necessity must be more lax.

Marginal Employment Subsidies

Through labour market policy, expansive firms are relieved of some of the cost of recruiting and upgrading labour. Wage drift is limited and price increases are counterbalanced in sectors with labour shortage and high product demand. Rehn wanted to combine these concealed subsidies from labour market policies with financial supports to expansive firms to obtain an immediate price-depressing effect. He hoped that marginal employment subsidies would increase employment by creating incentives for reducing prices. Thus, these subsidies were considered by Rehn as one stone to kill two birds, unemployment and inflation (arrows 15 and 16, respectively). The proposal assumes that firms act on competitive markets or set their prices on the basis of marginal costs.

Rehn made no original contribution to the theory of marginal employment subsidies, but he did place the subsidies in a stabilization policy context. In fact, marginal employment grants induced Rehn to suggest a modification of the R–M model when unemployment rose in Western Europe in the second half of the 1970s. He recommended the use of marginal employment subsidies together with traditional labour market programmes and measures aimed at *raising* effective demand. This kind of economic policy would have brought the rate of inflation down lower than a purely Keynesian strategy for full employment (Rehn 1982, pp. 3, 8, 18 and 26). Further, Rehn suggested in the 1980s that marginal grants should be offered not only to firms that recruit labour but also to investments and to production increases in general.

The notion of a selective employment policy in the R–M model may give the wrong impression that this policy is always directed towards specific firms, regions, sectors and wage-earner groups. But marginal employment subsidies can be offered to firms in all regions and sectors and for all kinds of labour, as recommended in Rehn's final proposal. It is the conditional character of marginal subsidies – they are offered only to expanding firms – that make them selective and therefore distinct from expansionary monetary measures, public budget deficits or general reductions in pay-roll and profit taxes.[6]

The Uniqueness of the R–M Model

I hope that I have uncovered the radical elements of the R–M model. At the height of the age of Keynesianism, two trade union economists from a country which has been a precursor of the Keynesian revolution were bold enough to recommend a restrictive fiscal policy and placed the priority of price stability on an equal footing with the priority of full employment. The provocative character of their model is illustrated by its conclusion that employment policies must have the smallest, not the largest, positive effects on aggregate demand. The conclusion that the Keynesian model is more applicable in a recession and the R–M model in an overheated economy is a fairly obvious one. The fact that the R–M model was formulated during the early post-war boom determined its character. The intention behind labour market policy, including regional policy, was to eliminate the 'islands of unemployment' resulting from a restrictive general economic policy and a solidaristic wage policy. Rehn and Meidner were not against a traditional Keynesian public-deficit policy in periods of deep recession or a counter-cyclical policy in general.

But the R–M model's advocacy of a tight fiscal policy goes beyond a qualified Keynesian recommendation that expansionary measures should be used cautiously, or even replaced by fiscal and monetary restraints, near full employment. Fiscal policy shall be predominantly restrictive over the business cycle not only to conceive a public saving surplus for distributive and industrial policy reasons but also to set the framework for stabilization policy. Rehn and Meidner wished to replace a pure Keynesian stop–go policy with a policy that permanently kept the rate of inflation under control. They also argued that the struggle against inflation cannot be called off in a recession; expansionary fiscal policies must be complemented or replaced by inflation-dampening measures such as marginal employment subsidies and supply-orientated labour market policies.

The R–M model is unique in terms of its comprehensive view of economic policy. First, one of the model's great advantages is that it embraces all the objectives of post-war economic policy – full employment, price stability, growth and equity. Modern macroeconomic models seldom consider more than two objectives, often price stability and full employment. Second, the R–M model deviates from most macroeconomic models by allotting at least two tasks to each instrument as illustrated by Figure 4.1. For instance, labour market policy has *four* objectives, to achieve full employment, to speed up structural change, to hold back price and wage increases caused by labour market bottlenecks or high profit margins, and to facilitate solidaristic wage policy. And labour market policy has a further redistribution task in the model – full employment should alter functional income distribution in favour of labour by increasing its negotiation strength, both collectively and individually (Rehn 1952a, p. 47 [1948]).

Third, the instruments of the R–M model are complementary. I do not have in mind here that some measures must be introduced in an economic policy model to alleviate the side-effects of other measures; in this case, a restrictive economic policy and a solidaristic wage policy will generate unemployment unless complementary labour market policy measures are introduced. But a partial application of the model is also discouraged by the fact that some measures are effective only when used together with other measures. The trade union movement can only pursue a solidaristic wage policy if labour market policy measures and a restrictive general economic policy are in place to keep wage drift under control. Further, solidaristic wage policy will only put pressure on 'marginal' firms to rationalize if combined with a restrictive general economic policy. Labour market policy might be a necessary condition for a relationship between a solidaristic wage policy and structural change – labour resources can be released through solidaristic wage policy, but labour market policy may be needed to transfer resources to expanding firms and sectors. There are also other complementarities in the R–M model. Fair wages through solidaristic wage policy will not restrain inflation significantly unless a restrictive economic policy and a labour market policy are launched simultaneously. Rehn and Meidner also claim that labour market policy and a restrictive general economic policy are interactive in the fight against inflation and in the attempts to increase wage earners' share of GDP.[7]

Fourth, the R–M model has the advantage of linking together both short- and long-term analyses by assuming that labour market, fiscal and monetary policies all influence growth. Here, the model avoids the one-sided Keynesian view of a positive relationship between profit and demand on the one hand and productivity growth on the other. Rehn did not deny that a restrictive general economic policy might reduce productivity growth if private investments are seriously hampered or if static scale advantages exist (Rehn 1982, pp. 4–5). But according to their model, a restrictive general economic policy may quite simply result in higher productivity levels and growth through rationalization and structural change.

Rehn and Meidner's economic policy model is ingenious in its logic and all-embracing character. Indeed, there is no real counterpart in macroeconomics to their consistently holistic view and the model is easily appreciated in its own right, even by people with other political values or with doubts about its relevance.

THE REHN–MEIDNER THEORY OF INFLATION

Profits and Wage Drift

In the R–M model, the main purpose of tight fiscal policy – foremost an increase in indirect taxes – is to force down companies' profits and profit margins. Rehn and Meidner were convinced that profits are the significant driving force in the process of inflation. High profits lead to a substantial amount of wage drift, in turn triggering demands for corresponding wage increases from groups that have not benefited from the effects of free market forces. The 1951 LO report does not state exactly *why* profits are of central importance in wage formation. Rehn explains himself in an article on the causes of wage drift in Swedish manufacturing written together with Bent Hansen in the mid-1950s (Hansen and Rehn 1956). In that article, changes in nominal wages are profoundly determined by changes in labour demand and supply. Among other things, labour market and solidaristic wage policies are ignored by Hansen and Rehn. Their economy is thus basically one of perfectly competitive labour markets but also one of given prices for individual firms in perfectly competitive product markets or in exposed sectors where foreign firms set prices. In fact, Hansen and Rehn present a marginal productivity theory; wages are determined by the product of prices and physical marginal productivity when labour supply is fixed. However, they make an adjustment for the degree of monopoly in product markets.

Hence, the focus is upon marginal profits in the Hansen–Rehn article. Their fundamental theory simply says that wage drift is determined by the anticipated gain from employing more workers at the initial wage. Erik Lundberg had criticized the Rehn–Meidner wage theory for ignoring the decisive role of labour market rather than profit conditions for nominal wages (Lundberg 1952). Rehn seems to have converged to Lundberg's view in the article he wrote with Hansen. It is true that Hansen and Rehn gave profits an independent position in relation to labour demand when wage drift is determined. But their distinction between profit- and labour-demand determinants within the framework of the marginal productivity theory is a doubtful one (compare Hansen and Rehn 1956, pp. 93–6 with Erixon 2000, pp. 24–5). There is much to indicate, however, that both the LO report and the Hansen–Rehn article made another interpretation of the connection between profits and wages than the one in the marginal productivity theory. Average profits and actual profit margins are not only possible approximations of marginal profits but also important driving forces behind wage drift in and of itself. This interpretation accords with the recommendation in the R–M model that profit margins must be squeezed in the medium term to avoid inflationary wage increases.[8] The Rehn–Meidner wage theory certainly departs from a marginal productivity model adjusted for the degree of monopoly where a rise in actual profit margins, *ceteris paribus*, will curtail labour demand and therefore *reduce* nominal wages.

In fact, Rehn and Meidner must claim that wage drift is primarily induced by high average profits to avoid the awkward conclusion that marginal employment subsidies are inflationary. A marginal subsidy will stimulate marginal rather than average profits. Let us assume that wage drift is primarily determined by marginal profits. Significant wage drift will then occur with a marginal employment subsidy in both competitive markets and in markets in which firms must accept foreign price leadership or set their prices on the basis of marginal costs. A marginal subsidy will also lead to higher wage drift than a general subsidy of the same amount and financed in the same way (if wage drift is primarily due to marginal profits) by the simple fact that the immediate output and employment effects are larger (see Layard 1979; Layard and Nickell 1980; Rehn 1982, pp. 21, 36 and 40; Erixon 2000, pp. 27–30).

There are some ambiguous elements in Rehn and Meidner's explanation for a positive relationship between average profits and actual profit margins on the one hand and wage drift on the other. However, I shall suggest two possible arguments for a relationship, both of which, in the spirit of the R–M model, have firms – and their managers – as the main actors. I shall also put a strong weight on the argument in various work by Rehn and Meidner (including the Hansen-Rehn article) that firms' competition for scarce labour is intensified by high profits (Rehn 1952b, p. 77 [1950]; Meidner and Rehn et al. 1953, pp. 92–3 [1951]).

In the first line of argument, an increase in firms' *self-financing capacity* will stimulate firms' competition for labour. One possible mechanism is that high actual profits lead to more investment and therefore to a stronger demand for labour, since the firms' capital costs will be reduced by self-financing. Similar theories of a relationship between profits, internal saving and investment can be found in the Keynesian literature. But Rehn and Meidner presumably also expected that a stronger financial position would intensify *non-investing* firms' competition for labour. High actual profits improve the financial opportunities of non-investing firms to keep indispensable employees. This allows them to deflect the threat of losing staff to recruiting firms by offering higher wages. Non-investing firms will be particularly anxious to make such offers if their existence literally stands or falls with the loss of valuable employees, that is, no marginal productivity can be attributed to them (the labour demand curve is inelastic). The contribution to wage drift of static firms will speed up the elimination of dynamic firms' gain from investments and labour recruitment.

The second hypothesis about a positive relationship between profits and nominal wages (beyond the marginal productivity theory) is based on the concept of *X-inefficiency*. The theory makes no assumptions about investment costs or non-investing firms' possibilities of competing for labour with investing firms. According to the X-inefficiency theory, efficiency will decline in firms with high historical profitability. Among other things, management will award themselves and certain employees higher wages than their efforts merit. It is assumed that in good times firms will be more careless about offering higher wages, probably both to 'wage drifters' and to wage earners covered by collective agreements.[9] Further, high profits may raise the financial capacity of firms to pay X-inefficient wages to their employees. In the X-inefficiency case, profits are not arguments in a labour demand function as in the first Rehn–Meidner case of a positive relationship between intra-marginal profits and nominal wages. Consequently, both profits and labour market conditions must be included in a wage drift equation representing the R–M model. However, the theory of X-inefficiencies is irreconcilable with an assumption of highly competitive labour *and* product markets.

To summarize, both marginal and average profits seem to matter for wage drift in the R–M model. But the model is shown in a more favourable light if wage drift is caused by high average profits rather than by high marginal profits. In that case, a marginal employment subsidy would initiate less wage drift than a general subsidy. I have suggested two explanations of why wage drift is stimulated by high average profits, both of which remain true to the spirit of the model in their underlying assumption that firms initiate wage increases. First, larger financial endowments will increase the capability of firms to make investments or keep indispensable personnel who threaten to quit; this explanation is compatible with the theory that labour market conditions are decisive for wage drift. Alternatively, high profits may tempt firms to offer high wages without any indication of a higher product demand or a better labour performance (see the X-inefficiency theory).

Galloping Instead of Equilibrium Inflation in the R–M Model

A presentation of the Rehn–Meidner theory of wages and inflation is complicated by some ambiguities in the theory. However, these areas of ambiguity should not be exaggerated. The main weaknesses in the Rehn–Meidner theory are that some of the arguments are implicit, or susceptible to interpretation in various ways, and not that the analysis is inconsistent or based on questionable assumptions.

The Rehn–Meidner(–Hansen) wage-drift theory above, emphasizing the role of both marginal and average profits, is the first component of their inflation theory. Higher product demand, resulting in price increases, or higher physical productivity will induce wage drift in some firms and industries by the stimulation of both marginal and intra-marginal profits; higher product demand will lead to price increases even in the case of imperfect imperfection with sensible assumptions about mark-ups and production conditions (Erixon 2000, pp. 23–4). But the appearance of wage drift will lead to further, centrally negotiated, wage increases. There are two mechanisms for a positive relation between wage drift and central wages in the R–M model. First, wages are not adjusted instantly to market forces. Central wage increases in a specific period are, at least partially, determined by market forces that were not manifested as wage drift in the preceding period. Labour mobility to dynamic firms and sectors is imperfect and wage increases for employees who threaten to quit static firms and industries are delayed. Second, a collective catch-up process in the R–M model can be explained by wage earners' care for relative wages, not for real wages. Wage earners who have gained poorly (or not at all) by wage drift will demand similar wage increases to regain their relative income position. Wage earners compare themselves with wage earners in dissimilar occupations, either within the same firm or in other firms. They may also compare themselves with similar others, for instance with people of the same skill, either in the same or in other firms. However, in this case, the wage norm coincides with the wages determined by market forces (compare with Akerlof and Yellen 1990, pp. 270–71).

In the *General Theory*, and in some efficiency-wage theories (see below), pressures to maintain relativities explain why nominal wages are rigid downward. The R–M model is not directly concerned with the question of absolute wage rigidity. Relative wage preferences are primarily of interest in the phase where 'competitive' wage drift is imitated by collective wage increases. Imitation of wage drift is the basic policy of trade unions in the R–M wage model. Central wage negotiations are elements here in a catch-up process rather than driving forces *per se*. But the possibilities for trade unions to satisfy a relative wage preference depend largely on the power position of labour. This, in turn, is basically determined by the labour market situation. Thus, labour market conditions have a twofold impact on collective wages in the R–M model. They will determine wage drift, which is the guideline of collective wage bargaining, and they will influence the power position of collective labour, which determines the ability to accomplish wage imitation. In the R–M model, the possibilities of wage imitation are also a function of the general position of the trade union movement irrespective of the employment situation. These possibilities are further determined by firms' ability to pass on wage increases to consumers, thus by the degree of monopoly, and by their willingness to accept that labour is rewarded in excess of (marginal) productivity (see the X-inefficiency theory).

The idea that wage–wage–price spirals, inflation in a true sense, will emerge after a positive macroeconomic shock is central in Rehn and Meidner's work. Thus, wages (and prices) will not converge to a new equilibrium level. It is possible to shed light on the Rehn–Meidner view by giving an account of the 1960s Scandinavian model (the Aukrust model in Norway and the EFO model in Sweden). The R–M model allows scope for wage–wage and wage–price spirals, while the similar Scandinavian model is actually a theory of changes in equilibrium wages and prices and of short-run changes in profitability.

In the Scandinavian model, increases in world market prices or productivity generate a short-term upswing in the profit share in the sector exposed to foreign competition. This upswing will lead to higher wages in this sector since higher expected profits and higher self-financing capacity will imply higher investments and more demand for labour.[10] The wage increase in the exposed sector then results in corresponding wage increases in the sheltered sector by virtue of the free market mechanism, relative wage preferences and the solidaristic wage policy – seen here as a phenomenon that reinforces the collective imitation of wage drift. Wage increases in the sheltered sector can be passed on to the consumer through mark-up pricing. (Mark-ups will be constant at a constant price elasticity of demand.[11]) Similarly, the rate of pay increases will self-adjust downward when the profit share is initially reduced. Lower profit margins make it more difficult for firms to self-finance and also make firms more pessimistic which in turn leads to fewer investments and less demand for labour (Edgren et al. 1973; Aukrust 1977).

There are striking similarities between the pictures of the wage process in the Scandinavian and the R–M models. The resemblance becomes even stronger if the R–M model is based on a division into an open and a sheltered sector where the open sector is dominated by wage drift (or by central wage agreements that directly reflect labour market conditions) and the sheltered sector by compensatory, centrally agreed, pay rises; in this perspective, the R–M model must rely on revaluations of the currency rather than on restrictive fiscal policies to prevent the emergence of high profits.[12] But there are also clear differences between the models. The most important difference is that wage–wage and wage–price spirals occur in the R–M model but are prevented in the Scandinavian model. The assumption made in the latter is that prices in the exposed sector are exogenous (at a given exchange rate) and that wages in the sector are determined by these prices (at a given productivity development).[13]

Rehn and Meidner never deal explicitly with the reasons why an economy, when its equilibrium is disturbed, changes from a condition of wage and price rises to a condition of continued wage rises and inflation. A wage–wage spiral will emerge if employees in the open sector wholly or partly succeed in re-establishing the wage lead they initially gained through wage drift. I shall give two possible explanations for this kind of wage development. If these theories are refuted, the R–M model must rely on the economy being exposed to constant disruptions that never allow wages and prices to converge to equilibrium.

A reasonable hypothesis is that mark-up pricing also takes place in the open sector, at least in parts of it. Thus, firms in the exposed sector will accept new wage increases, since they are able to fully pass them on to customers, assuming that the price elasticity of demand is constant. An alternative hypothesis is that firms in the exposed sector are forced to accept or will even initiate wage increases that cannot be passed on. In the first case, indispensable 'wage drifters' manage to enforce further wage increases that maintain their distance to other groups (the labour supply curve in the leading sector shifts upward). In the second case, the behaviour of firms may reflect a lack of information about market conditions, or that the initial profit increase provides scope for 'unearned' rewards for the employees (see the X-inefficiency theory).

It seems, however, that the arguments above offer only a weak case for a sustainable wage–wage–price spiral. The process is easily counterbalanced by monetary restraints unless an accommodating economic policy is pursued. The room for mark-up pricing must also be limited, especially in the open sector. Besides, firms in the open sector will successively require information about market conditions and refuse to give 'unearned' wages to employees when their profits fall. The existence of counteracting forces in the wage–wage–price spiral process does not exclude the possibility of such processes, at least for a while, in a country like Sweden. The Rehn–Meidner assumption of destabilizing macroeconomic shocks should not be rejected without a careful empirical test.

The Failure of Incomes Policy

The R–M inflation model has the advantage of integrating wage theories based on firms' competition for scarce labour, labour strength and relative wage preferences. (I use the notion of labour strength here to cover trade union ability to compensate for wage drift.) Rehn and Meidner's integrated wage theory is also a dynamic one. Wage increases determined by favourable market conditions reproduce themselves in the labour market through employee interest in relative wages and through a strong bargaining position for wage earners covered by collective agreements. Credible explanations are also given for the fact that 'cost crises' often occur in the first phase of a recession. Wage drift eases because of lower labour demand, while the preceding economic boom continues to have a strong influence on wage formation through 'imitating' central agreements, with subsequent individual and local trade union claims to retain a wage advantage. There are similar descriptions of cost crisis in a recession in some (post-)Keynesian theories. The crucial question is why the views on incomes policy differ so greatly between most Keynesians and Rehn–Meidner.

Both neo-Keynesians and 'orthodox' Keynesians (including the post-Keynesians) with some exceptions (see Tobin 1972) exhibit a greater confidence in incomes policy. In textbook IS–LM (investment–savings and liquidity–money supply) versions of Keynesianism, incomes policy is a parameter of action. Price increases induced by higher aggregate demand can be counterbalanced efficiently by incomes policy – represented by a downward shift in the aggregate product supply curve. In Keynesian wage-push models (and also in modern fair-wage, bargaining and trade union models), the extent and performance of incomes policy are a function of wage-earner unity and the degree of wage centralization. Incomes policy is also possible in an economy with high aggregate demand – a strong trade union movement may just as well be party to an incomes policy settlement as to forcing up the level of wages.

The fundamental reason why the potential for incomes policy is limited in the R–M model is the idea that wage increases are initiated by firms' competition for labour. Central trade union organization attempts to introduce wage restraint are effectively counteracted by free market forces and by the unions' demand for compensation for wage drift. A coordination of trade union policy has ambiguous effects on wages in the R–M model. It will facilitate a wage policy of fairness, which will mitigate wage races between trade unions. But it will also raise the potential of wage earners as a group to increase real wages at the expense of profits. The potential of incomes policies is limited, particularly in a boom; it is tempting for trade unions to strive for compensation for significant wage drift when their bargaining position is strengthened. Hence, individual trade unions may resist participating in incomes policy agreements. In addition, any collective wage moderation leading to higher actual profits may increase both company ability and company willingness to offer higher wages to individuals and to trade unions not covered by incomes policy (see Meidner 1952, p. 25 [1948]). Thus, in the R–M model, incomes policy, whether statutory or coordinated by central trade unions, will be undermined by labour market forces and relative wage preferences. These wage preferences are easier to satisfy when unemployment is low and actual profits are high. In addition, even if incomes policy could lead to 'wage moderation', Rehn and Meidner were still critical by claiming that the policy will delay structural change and rationalization.

However, in the end, the creators of the R–M model were open to the idea of incomes policy. They realized that their policy of a general profit-margin squeeze could be too effective – private investments may be seriously hit even if marginal profits are stimulated by mobility-enhancing labour market policies or marginal employment subsidies. Further, Rehn and Meidner recognized that full employment can speed up a wage–wage spiral by increasing the possibilities of fulfilling relative wage preferences and perhaps even by strengthening such preferences *per se*. They emphasized the possibility and desirability of having a central union organization to dampen the general rate of wage increases by means of 'voluntary' incomes policy, at least in normal phases of the business cycle (see, for example, Meidner and Rehn, et al. 1953, pp. 90–91 [1951]; Rehn 1982, p. 8, 1986, p. 76 and 1987, p. 67).

There is an ambiguity between trade union mobilization and the acceptance of 'social responsibility' expressed both in the LO report and in later publications by Rehn and Meidner (compare, for example, Rehn 1982 pp. 8

and 26). The ambiguity reflects a latent dilemma for a reformist labour movement. The LO report avoids the dilemma by declaring that central trade unions have only an *indirect* and *long-run* (rather than medium-term) responsibility for average wage developments. Wage races between trade unions can be prevented indirectly by central wage coordination if a united labour movement pursues a solidaristic wage policy. Furthermore, the LO report avoids the labour reformist dilemma by stating that the trade union movement must *first* force down the profit share and *then* ensure that nominal wages increase in pace with productivity growth. In the first stage, the arguments for income redistribution go hand in hand with the ambition to create more favourable conditions for stabilization policy. In the second stage, the labour movement must take social responsibility to prevent inflationary wage claims and further decreases in the profit share.[14]

The R–M Model and the Modern Wage Theory

Rehn and Bent Hansen saw their wage model of competitive labour markets as an alternative to bargaining and game theories of the time. Analogously, modern bargaining theories are seen as challenges to wage models in which market forces occupy a central position. The focus is here on trade unions or on wage earners with an insider status in labour markets (Layard and Nickell 1990, p. 778; Christofides and Oswald 1992; MacDonald and Suen 1992; Blanchflower et al. 1996, pp. 227–8). An important difference between bargaining models and the R–M model concerns their views of profits in wage formation. In both the R–M model and the bargaining models, wages can be stimulated by marginal profits (thus by a shift upward in the labour-demand curve). Further, in bargaining models, exactly as in the R–M model, high average profits result in high wages. But in bargaining models, a positive relationship between average profits (actual or expected) and wages reflects some form of rent (or risk) sharing.[15] The effects of higher average profits on (real) wages are often illustrated by a shift upward in the wage-setting function. In the R–M model, firms are the only active agents behind a relation between actual profits and wages. High profits result in frivolous wage offers but also in greater possibilities of self-financing investments and of preventing indispensable labour from being attracted away by higher wage offers from expanding firms. In the latter cases, the profit–wage relation derives ultimately from changes in labour demand. In the X-inefficiency case, there is a stable relationship between profits and wages exactly as in bargaining models. However, wage increases are initiated here by companies that are not maximizing profits, they are not the result of a contractual arrangement between employers and employees.[16]

The view on the profit–wage relation in the Rehn–Meidner theory differs from that in the efficiency wage theory as well. The theories share the idea that wage increases are initiated by employers. Another common characteristic, taking the X-inefficiency version of the R–M model into account, is that wages may rise above the competitive equilibrium level (Solow 1979 and 1990; Yellen 1984). Further, in the Rehn–Meidner wage theory and in some efficiency-wage theories, wage earners care for a fair wage distribution (see Summers 1988; Bewley 1998; Agell 1999) and even for a fair functional distribution (see Akerlof and Yellen 1990). Higher average profits will also induce higher nominal wages in both theories (see Akerlof and Yellen 1990, pp. 268–9). Yet the differences between the R–M and the efficiency wage theory are evident. According to Akerlof and Yellen, higher profits accruing to the firms' owners will provoke higher wage claims by wage earners governed by equity concerns. In the R–M model, a positive relationship between independent profits and dependent wages reflects that firms' competition for labour or propensity for X-inefficiencies are raised when profits become higher.[17] Further, there is no analogy in the R–M model to the basic idea in the efficiency-wage literature that higher wages will spur employee efforts or, as in other versions, improve the average quality of job applicants (adverse selection). In the efficiency-wage theory, it is employers' fear that workers otherwise will punish them by putting in less effort which explains why wage claims on equity grounds can be satisfied. With the X-inefficiency interpretation of the R–M model, higher wages are consequences of an inefficient behaviour; they are not means for the firms to raise the productivity of their staff.

The assumption in the R–M model that wage earners care for relative rather than real wages is basic in the *General Theory* and also common in the modern Keynesian literature apart from the neo-Keynesian one (see, for example, Romer 2001). Further, an assumption of relative wage preferences is made in fair-wage models (see the efficiency-wage version above) and in trade union and bargaining models. Like the R–M model, these models claim that concerns for relative wage can induce wage–wage spirals and also that such wage externalities can be internalized by coordinated wage negotiations. Further, trade union and bargaining models agree with the R–M model that coordinated wage bargaining will not necessarily lead to wage restraint. In trade union models, the greater possibilities of internalizing relative wage externalities can be counterbalanced by the mitigation of wage competition between workers who are substitutes in production (Calmfors and Forslund 1990). A similar upward pressure on wages when trade unions cooperate will, *ceteris paribus*, develop in the R–M model even though the model simply assumes, like bargaining models, that unity makes the labour movement stronger. (Modern trade union theories emphasize that positive externalities can be internalized when wage claims are coordinated.)

However, there are some unique features of the Rehn–Meidner analysis of relative wage preferences and a wage policy of fairness. First, this wage policy is not identical to a policy of equal compensation for wage earners with different marginal productivities as in the modern theory of fair wages. The economic arguments for an egalitarian policy that narrows the wage gaps between skilled and unskilled labour (see Akerlof and Yellen 1990, pp. 272–6; Agell and Lommerud 1992; Agell 1999) are thus not really relevant in the case of the R–M model.

Second, the Rehn–Meidner theory of a relationship between aggregate demand and production when wage earners attempt to improve or maintain their relative wages has some original elements. In the *General Theory*, wage earners will provide an increase in the supply of labour after a rise in aggregate demand precisely because of relative wage preferences – that all wage earners' real wages go down when consumer prices go up while relative wages remain unchanged. The R–M model assumes a similar real wage–employment mechanism because of a relative wage preference, but also that wage earners favoured by high labour demand – the 'wage drifters' – will get some nominal wage increases. The *improvement* in the relative pay position of the 'wage drifters' may explain why they accept price increases despite a reduction in real wages (leading to higher employment levels).

Third, in the R–M model, negative (reciprocal) wage externalities from relative wage preferences are not internalized by wage coordination *per se* as in trade union and bargaining models. The importance of central negotiations for wage restraint is indirect only in the R–M model – it is here possible to prevent compensatory wage claims by establishing a consensus on fair wages. In bargaining theories, relative wage preferences go hand in hand with wage restraint at the central level since a unified trade union movement considers that their wage claims will influence other wages and therefore consumer prices. High central pay awards cause substantial wage drift and thus large price increases for consumers. Some bargaining theories state that even key groups in labour markets will reduce their wage claims for similar reasons (Moene et al. 1993, pp. 76–80; Calmfors 1993b, pp. 15–16). In the R–M model, the (expected) negative effects on *real* wages of high wage claims will not lead to wage restraint by trade unions or key groups in labour markets; the assumption that wage earners care for relative wages is basic in the model. Besides, central wage restraint makes financial room for further wage drift in the R–M model, counterbalancing the tendency to internalization of negative wage externalities by wage coordination.

Fourth, the idea that central wage agreements are a positive function of wage drift is a central part of the Rehn–Meidner theory but not in bargaining (or trade union) theories where the relation between wage drift and central wage agreements is taken into account. Wage drift is not a stimulus to central wage increases in bargaining models as in the R–M model. On the contrary, these models assume that wage drift has a negative effect on central wages.[18]

One explanation is that high (anticipated) wage drift is deducted in central wage negotiations. On the other hand, both bargaining models and the R–M model share in common that the relationship may be the converse, that wage drift is determined by collective wage agreements. Besides, the models have in common that the effects of central wage increases on wage drift is ambiguous and that the positive effects are explained by relative wage preferences (Holmlund and Skedinger 1990; Calmfors 1993a, pp. 64–5). The suggested mechanisms behind a negative relationship are different, however. In the bargaining theory, central wage increases are considered in individual negotiations. In the R–M model, high central wages will reduce the financial possibilities for firms to compete for labour or their willingness and financial ability to offer undeserved wage increases to individuals.[19]

Evidence of the Rehn–Meidner Theory of Inflation

I shall now relate the Rehn–Meidner inflation theory to the results of empirical studies that have been carried out, particularly in Sweden in the post-war period. It is beyond the scope of this work to relate all parts of the theory to the empirical literature. A more detailed assessment of whether or not the R–M model has been confirmed by empirical studies can be found in (Erixon 2000).

Profits have a central position in the R–M model as determinants of nominal wages, especially of wage drift. Most studies of wage drift or total wage increases in Sweden up to the 1990s were based on aggregate time-series data. These studies, including Rehn's in cooperation with Bent Hansen, have generally emphasized the importance of labour market conditions and diluted the importance of profits, profit margins or value productivity (see, for instance, Schager 1981, pp. 396–402; Öhman 1982, pp. 52–4; Bosworth and Lawrence 1987, pp. 22–54; Flanagan 1990, p. 408). In some comparative studies of wage developments in the Organisation for Economic Co-operation and Development (OECD) countries (including Sweden) from the early 1960s to the late 1980s, profit variables were simply ignored (Johnson and Layard 1986, pp. 980–85; Poret 1990).

However the R–M model is not really challenged by empirical studies showing that labour market conditions, not profits, are decisive for wage development. The focus on profits and profit margins in the Rehn–Meidner wage theory is explained by its emphasis on labour-demand conditions. Thus, in this perspective, it is not legitimate to include both labour market indicators and profit variables in a wage equation. In a study of wage drift in Swedish manufacturing, labour demand was simply measured by a profit-margin variable; here, profits explained almost all the wage drift (Schager 1988).

The minor (and even insignificant) effects of profits on nominal wages according to time-series analyses where labour market conditions are accounted for could still be critical for the R–M model. First, the X-inefficiency argument justifies the inclusion of a profit variable *per se* in a Rehn–Meidner wage equation. Second, average profits (or actual profit margins) matter for labour demand in the R–M model; in fact, the credibility of the model will increase if average profits are decisive for wage drift. However, a positive relationship between actual profits and nominal wages is probably underestimated in time-series studies where the wage function also includes a labour market indicator. The statistical difficulties in these studies of discriminating between the theories that wage increases are caused by marginal and average profits are monumental.

In any case, the proposition that profits are important for wages in countries like Sweden has not yet been rejected convincingly by aggregate time-series studies. In fact, the emphasis on labour market conditions in many of them supports the Rehn–Meidner theory rather than its rivals in the modern wage literature. But it is too early to declare the survival of the Rehn–Meidner wage model. The model's view of the wage formation process has been questioned in the 1990s by studies of wage differentials between firms and industries.

A long-run correlation, or a direct causality, between profitability (or value productivity) and wages for homogeneous labour in studies of wage differentials between firms and industries shed doubts on the R–M model. This correlation is seen in the empirical literature as a confirmation of the rent-sharing theory or the efficiency wage theory (see, for instance, Christofides and Oswald 1992; Blanchflower et al. 1996). The R–M model leaves room for a stable relation between profits and wages in the case of X-inefficiencies. However, the model is at bottom a competitive wage model or a model of solidaristic wages. Wage gaps between firms and industries because of differences in profitability are avoided here by solidaristic wage policy or eliminated in the long run by labour mobility in competitive markets. On the other hand observations of a short-run relationship between profits (or value productivity) and nominal wages are not rejections of the R–M model. The model emphasizes the importance of market forces even in countries with central wage bargaining, particularly in the short run.

The R–M model is supported by cross-sectional studies in Sweden showing a weak and even insignificant relation between firm performance and wages in the long run (Holmlund and Zetterberg 1991; Forslund 1994a and 1994b; Holmlund 1997). The studies confirm, together with corresponding studies of other countries, that solidaristic wage policy can reinforce or reproduce the tendency towards a weak relation between profits and wages in competitive labour markets. However, a study of wage differences in Sweden based on firm rather than industrial data shows a strong positive relationship in the long run between profits and hourly wages around the 1990s although weaker than shown by analogous studies in the United States (Arai 1999). The R–M model seems seriously hurt by this study, since the role of both competitive forces and solidaristic wage policy is toned down. But these empirical results are compatible with earlier studies in Sweden showing that the relationship between firm performance and wages has been strengthened somewhat since the mid-1980s, when wage bargaining in the country became more decentralized (Holmlund 1997). Further, the study under discussion does not convincingly exclude the possibility that wage differentials between firms reflect transitory rather than permanent profit differentials. Nor does the study (or the similar foreign studies) automatically confirm the rent-sharing or efficiency-wage theories of a long-run relationship between profits and wages. (See the competing Rehn–Meidner theory that high profits result in easygoing wage offers.)

In the R–M model, but not in modern bargaining (and trade union) theories, central wage increases are a positive function of wage drift. The theoretical differences can be used as a reference point for a survey of studies of the relationship between wage drift and central wage increases. Nils Henrik Schager's econometric study of wage formation in Swedish manufacturing shows that the wage increases set out in central agreements are determined by the previous year's wage drift (Schager 1988). The study thus confirms the R–M model's dynamic description of the Swedish labour market. Studies based on bargaining models have produced different conclusions. According to a study by Robert J. Flanagan, wage drift had no effect at all on central agreements in Sweden in 1964–83 (Flanagan 1990). A study very similar to Flanagan's carried out by Douglas A. Hibbs and Håkan Locking even uncovered a negative relationship in 1972–82. Negotiated wage increases in the area covered by LO–SAF agreements were one per cent higher when wage drift fell by one per cent. This relationship was stronger than all other relationships in the central wage equation (Hibbs and Locking 1995).

The Flanagan and Hibbs–Locking studies are not based on a dynamic model like Schager's. The simultaneous occurrence of a low level of wage drift and large central wage increases may reflect that the latter is caused by high wage drift in an earlier period. Besides, the absence of a positive relationship between independent wage drift and dependent central wage increases in the Flanagan and Hibbs–Locking studies can be explained by the inclusion of labour market indicators in the central wage equations (Flanagan 1990, pp. 405–7; Hibbs and Locking 1995, Table 1a). According to the R–M model, the most important cause of wage drift is the labour market situation.

Bertil Holmlund and Per Skedinger's study of regional wage drift in the Swedish wood industry shows that high negotiated wage increases are compensated by moderate wage drift (Holmlund and Skedinger 1990). These results were confirmed by Hibbs and Locking's aggregate study of wage drift in the LO–SAF area (Hibbs and Locking 1995, Table 1b). The R–M model does not preclude that high collective wage increases may reduce the pace of wage drift.[20] But it remains to be investigated whether the underlying mechanism is the one in the model or the one in the bargaining theory.

The econometric studies presented above illustrate the difficulties of discriminating between the bargaining theory and Rehn–Meidner views of wage formation. The difficulties arise from the fact that labour market conditions are important determinants of central wages in bargaining models but of both wage drift, which sets the framework for central wage negotiations, and of collective labour strength in the R–M model. Such difficulties can only be reduced by the use of a dynamic regression model. Schager's study is probably based on less reliable data compared with later studies. But my preliminary assessment is that his dynamic model is the most reasonable one for Sweden and that empirical studies therefore have supported the Rehn–Meidner view of the relationship between wage drift and centrally negotiated wages.

THE REHN–MEIDNER THEORY OF GROWTH

Solidaristic Wage Policy and Structural Change

In the R–M model, economic growth is stimulated by a solidaristic wage policy and a contractionary fiscal policy. The cost pressure from these policies on marginal firms in an industry is illustrated in Figure 4.2. The firms in the industry are listed by their profit margins, that is, the ratio between sales values and wage bills. I assume that there are no other inputs than homogeneous labour and that prices are given and the same for all firms. I further assume, in accordance with the R–M model, that firms have different productivity levels. The number of firms is assumed to be a function of exits only.

The scope of the solidaristic wage policy is represented by the angle of the profit-margin lines in Figure 4.2. Two profit-margin structures are presented. (In the interests of simplicity I assume that the profit-margin structure in the industry can be described in linear terms.) The flatter PM' line shows profit margins in an initial state where wages are more in accordance with firms' ability to pay, which is determined by their value productivity levels. There are thus relatively weak tendencies to solidaristic wage policy or to uniform wages through labour mobility between firms in the initial state.[21] The steeper PM" line shows profit margins at wages that follow the principle of equal pay for comparable work more closely. I have defined the level of solidaristic wages as wages paid by the medium firm (m) in the initial state. The dotted

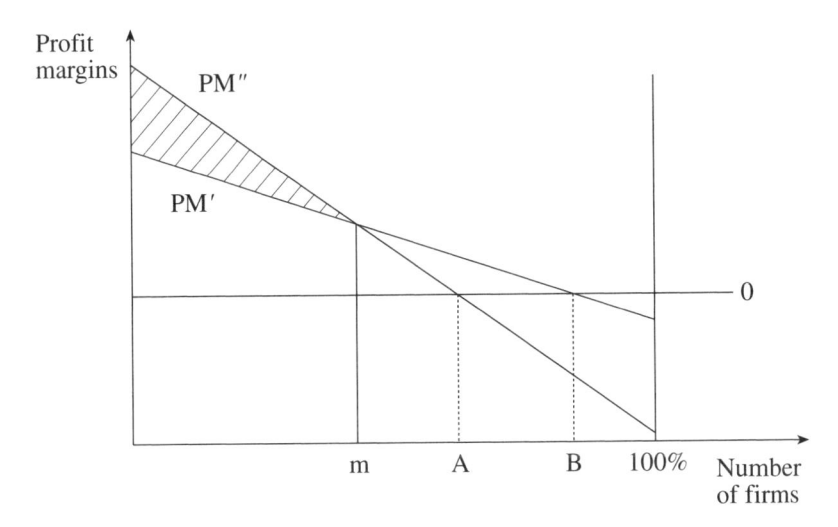

Figure 4.2 Solidaristic wage policy, profit margins and number of firms

lines in Figure 4.2 show the number of firms above the point of break-even (0) where prices are equal to unit wage costs. A smaller number of firms will survive at solidaristic wage policy than at wages that are more adjusted to productivity differences between firms (compare A and B in the figure). But firms with higher productivity levels than the medium ones have larger profit margins if the industry pays solidaristic wages (see the hatched area in Figure 4.2).

Figure 4.2 can also be used to show that a solidaristic wage policy will only lead to closures and a pressure for rationalization if combined with a restrictive general economic policy. Stabilization policy shifts the profit-margin line upward or downward if it results in uniform price changes in the industry under discussion. A downward shift in the profit-margin line will place more firms below the 0 line, the point of break-even, unless they increase productivity.

In both the R–M model and the subsequent vintage models of Salter (1960) and Solow (1964), average productivity is raised by the fact that the oldest plants go to the wall when prices no longer cover their variable costs. One difference between the models is that the pressure on marginal units arises from price competition or new plants' demand for scarce labour in vintage models, not from wage pushes (or stabilization policy) as in the R–M model. Another difference is that the pressure on marginal units in the R–M model will induce, as in the X-inefficiency theory, rationalizations in individual plants. Such units are doomed to die in vintage models in which firms are always maximizing profits and factor substitution is impossible *ex post*.

The R–M model offers an alternative to a neo-classical, Marshallian, model of structural change. This is not to say that there are no similarities between the models. In both of them, relative profitability is the driving force behind structural change. The description of wage formation in a 'free' labour market is also identical – higher pay in expanding sectors attracts labour from other sectors. But the incentives for labour mobility differ between the models. In the neo-classical theory, a change in relative demand causes sector-based wage differentials to emerge. This induces wage earners to change workplaces. Wage equalization is a *result* of this process of adjustment, since wage earners with the same marginal productivity receive the same pay in the new equilibrium. When a solidaristic wage policy is in effect, there can be no transfer of labour because of wage differences. Instead, Rehn and Meidner rely upon a push mechanism, or better, a rationing mechanism in labour markets. Labour mobility is sustained by the threat or appearance of unemployment in unprofitable sectors and also by larger inflows of vacancies in profitable sectors. These flows of job applicants and vacancies at solidaristic wage policy will counterbalance the negative effects on mobility caused by weaker pay incentives. However, a sluggish labour market may hamper structural change; labour market policy measures must therefore be used to oil the mechanism of rationing.

It has often been claimed by Rehn and others that the solidaristic wage policy simulates a perfect market equilibrium for wage earners with the same marginal productivity. But in contrast to the Marshallian model, a solidaristic wage policy *limits* the chances of bringing about a transfer of labour through the wage mechanism. Other motives are needed to create mobility in the labour market. Rehn and Meidner's preference for solidaristic wage policy was based on a conviction that wage differentials must grow large to create a significant labour mobility because of inertia in the labour market (Rehn 1952a, pp. 44–5 [1948]). Large wage differentials are inflationary by causing wage–wage spirals, as well as being unacceptable from an equity point of view.

A solidaristic wage policy will not only create the conditions for structural change by increasing the financial resources of profitable companies and by hastening the stagnation and closure of 'marginal' ones, it will also increase the companies' and the capital market's incentives to facilitate a transfer of resources between sectors by reinforcing differences in profitability. The differences may become so great that any entry barriers and other rigidities (such as sluggish capital markets) that prevent structural change can be overcome. Profit differentials will increase in the R–M model, not only through solidaristic wage policy but also through labour market policy to facilitate dynamic firms' recruitment of labour. The R–M model exchanges large wage differentials and high general profits (see below) for large profit differentials as a positive incentive for economic growth. In addition, the possible growth-dampening effects of low gross profits are counteracted by the access to public capital funds at low interest rates.

Economic Policy and Economic Growth

The theory of transformation pressure developed in Sweden in the 1990s assumes that productivity growth is promoted by cost pressures, intensive competition and low aggregate demand (Erixon 2001a). The Rehn–Meidner theory of a positive relationship between solidaristic wage policy and economic growth is a partial theory of transformation pressure. The policy will eliminate less-profitable firms, freeing resources for the expansion of dynamic firms and industries and also promote productivity within 'marginal' firms since they are forced to rationalize in order to survive. But solidaristic wage policy actually lessens transformation pressure on firms and industries with high historical levels of profitability. In line with the theory of transformation pressure, the Rehn–Meidner model recommends a tight fiscal policy and a selective policy of full employment to generate a hard transformation pressure in general.

A general profit-margin squeeze may stimulate economic growth by (external) structural change – production units, firms and industries with low profitability will shrink or even be eliminated – or by enforced productivity increases in individual plants, firms and industries. In the latter case, the R–M model emphasizes, as does the theory of X-inefficiencies, that firms will reduce slack in productive efficiency. But the R–M model, like the theory of X-inefficiencies, can be extended to a general theory of transformation pressure by considering other sources of productivity increases in firms than rationalizations. A stronger external pressure may stimulate the development of new products, technologies and organizations in firms or mergers to exploit scale advantages in industries (Erixon 2001a, pp. 15–23; Leibenstein 1980, ch. 3).

There is hardly any scope in Keynesian growth theories for such a notion as transformation pressure. Keynesian economists in general deny that economic growth is enhanced by low profits (Erixon 1987, pp. 25–7 and 1991, pp. 247–9). They claim that investment and production growth are stimulated by high profits and high aggregate demand through the importance of self-finance, backward-looking expectations or the accelerator mechanism where investments are a positive function of capacity utilization (or production growth). Productivity will be stimulated as well if static economies of scale prevail or if the accelerator is associated with new techniques (dynamic economies of scale). The Keynesian growth theory has in fact more similarities with the new (neo-classical) growth theory of cumulative processes than with the Rehn–Meidner growth theory (Erixon 2001a, pp. 3–4).

The Relevance of the Rehn–Meidner Growth Theory

Pay equalization between and within industries and plants and between the sexes was more far-reaching in Sweden than in other OECD countries, including the Nordic ones, from the early 1960s until the mid-1970s (Jonsson and Siven 1984, pp. 430–31; Faxén et al. 1988, pp. 54–6; Pissarides and Moghadam 1990; Nilsson 1994; Arai 1994; Hibbs and Locking 1995 and 2000; Edin and Topel 1997). There was a widespread pay equalization not only among blue-collar workers but also, in the 1970s, among white-collar workers. Smaller wage differentials manifested not only the principle of equal pay for equal work as in the R–M model, but also a policy of wage equalization in general. Market forces alone cannot explain the radical reduction of wage gaps in Sweden. Hence, the bargaining system and wage policy must have been important. The trend towards a smaller wage spread slowed down by the middle of the 1970s, and in the mid-1980s wage differences between and within industries and plants increased sharply. Wage gaps grew not only among wage earners with different jobs but also for those with identical jobs and skills, which constituted a real challenge for the R–M model. Swedish economists tend to emphasize the occurrence of a structural shift when wage bargaining became more decentralized in the mid-1980s. But wage relations may also have widened because of strong positive demand shocks, especially in the 1980s, reflecting international recoveries, devaluations (depreciations in the 1990s) and deregulations of the capital market (leading to a loan-based consumption and investment boom) together with growing difficulties for wage earners in the 1990s to compensate for wage drift due to higher unemployment. I shall first survey the empirical literature to ascertain whether the Rehn–Meidner view of the relationship between solidaristic wage policy and economic growth has been confirmed.

The R–M model is often associated with a proposition that structural change is speeded up by solidaristic wage policy. But the proposition is too strong in relation to the R–M model. The model simply says that structural change is possible with solidaristic wage policy and that other adjustment mechanisms are less preferable from the viewpoint of income distribution and price stability (Rehn 1952a, pp. 44–5 [1948]; see, however, Meidner 1969, p. 193 and Rehn 1987, p. 76). But to obtain the same transfer of resources as in a 'free' labour market, the solidaristic wage policy must require the support of labour market policy. The arguments for the Rehn–Meidner growth theory become stronger if the Swedish labour market performed well in the age of solidaristic wage policy.

Labour market mobility in Sweden did not fall in the 1970s despite radical wage equalization. (External labour mobility varied with the business cycle in the 1970s and the 1980s.) Any tendency towards lower labour mobility through smaller wage differences or other factors (double-income households and so on) appear to have been counteracted, *inter alia*, by labour market and educational policy. Flexibility in the labour market was not lower in Sweden compared with other industrialized countries, even though Sweden has a more even wage structure (Nilsson and Zetterberg 1987; Faxén et al. 1988, pp. 248–51). Regional mobility seems to have been higher in the United States than in Western European countries, including Sweden, in the 1970s. But the higher degree of regional mobility in the United States is explained by greater job opportunities, not by the larger wage differentials (Nilsson and Zetterberg 1987, pp. 35–52).

In fact, the Beveridge curve, that is, the mapping between the number of vacancies and the number of unemployed (in relation to the labour force) was more favourable for Sweden than for all other OECD countries in the 1970s and the 1980s. The Beveridge curve did actually shift inward in Sweden during those decades, which was not the case in most other OECD countries. The Swedish shift has been attributed to labour market policy and centralized wage bargaining (Jackman et al. 1990, pp. 477–83). The latter explanation is not compatible with the R–M model unless the wage-moderation effects from solidaristic wage policy are pronounced. However, studies of Sweden have rejected a proposition that a political compression of the wage structure has led to lesser compensatory wage drift (Erixon 2000, pp. 69–71). Besides, the importance of labour market policy for the favourable Swedish Beveridge curve in the 1970s and the 1980s is probably more statistical – the policy reduced the rate of open unemployment – than structural. Further, the role of labour market policy when explaining the relatively high labour market flexibility, and possibly also the compressed wage structure, in Sweden will not be exaggerated (Edin and Topel 1997, pp. 164–7; Erixon 2000, pp. 60–61). In any case, the R–M model does not state that labour market performance is superior in a country with labour market and solidaristic wage policy but rather that this performance is at least as good as in a country in which large wage differentials are more salient for bringing about mobility in the labour market.

The cautious Rehn–Meidner thesis that solidaristic wage policy is neutral where the effects on structural change are concerned is supported by the fact that structural change in Swedish manufacturing in the 1960s and the 1970s, thus in the heyday of solidaristic wage policy, was approximately the same as in other small Western European countries. The extent of structural change is calculated here as an index of movements in employment between industries. Inter-industrial change in Swedish manufacturing was in fact speeded up in the latter part of the 1960s and the early 1970s (Fries 1983, pp. 143–7; Nilsson and Zetterberg 1987, pp. 17–19; Andersson et al. 2000).

It is difficult to give a clear picture of Swedish structural change in the 1980s and also to relate it to solidaristic wage policy. From 1978 to 1988, structural change in manufacturing became more rapid in Sweden than in other OECD countries, including the Nordic ones but excluding Canada and the United States (Hansson and Lundberg 1995, pp. 146–8). At the same time there are indications of a slower transformation of resources to research and development (R&D) and human-capital-intensive industries in Sweden compared with other OECD countries in the 1980s (Edquist 1991; Hansson and Lundberg 1995, pp. 79–82). In addition, there are difficulties in deciding whether these indications of a relatively slow structural change in Sweden in the 1980s are arguments for or against the R–M model. In fact, they can be seen as support for the model since wage differentials became larger and wage bargaining more decentralized during the decade. But Swedish wage gaps were still small and the relation between changes in wage spread and structural change are hardly immediate. Besides, it seems that the allocation of resources to R&D and human-capital-intensive industries accelerated in Sweden in the 1990s, thus during a decade when wage differentials in Sweden returned to the state of the mid-1970s (Hibbs and Locking 2000, pp. 755–9).

The relationship between solidaristic wage policy and structural change has been addressed directly by two Swedish studies. Both studies are based on the bold hypothesis that structural change is speeded up by solidaristic wage policy, thus not on the cautious hypothesis in the R–M model that structural change is possible with solidaristic wage policy. In one cross-sectional study of wage and employment developments in Sweden, the bold hypothesis was accepted if employment had risen more in industries with higher initial wage rates and lower wage increases. The hypothesis was actually confirmed in the study which covered all two-digit sectors of the economy, including the public sector, from the early 1960s to the mid-1980s (Edin and Topel 1997). In manufacturing, both the correlations were stronger in 1963–75, thus in the period of smaller wage gaps, than in 1975–85. Industries in manufacturing with high wage growth experienced low employment growth in 1963–75 in the United States as well, but the correlation was stronger in Sweden. Besides, in the United States, there was no evidence at all of a positive relation between initial wages and employment growth. The conclusion drawn was that solidaristic wage policy has led to Swedish restructuring (Edin and Topel 1997, pp. 175–84 and 197).

The weaker positive correlation between initial wages and employment growth in 1975–85 does not constitute a strong case against a bold hypothesis about the relationship between solidaristic wage policy and structural change. The theory was suggested in Erixon (1985) that solidaristic wage policy had facilitated the contraction of high-wage industries hit by harder competition from Japan and the newly industrialized countries in the 1970s and the early 1980s (mainly mining, steel and shipbuilding). The compressed wage differences in Sweden due to solidaristic wage policy made it easier for wage earners to accept employment in other industries (Erixon 1985, p. 27; see also Rehn 1987, pp. 76–7). This view is compatible with Lawrence Summers's theory of frictional unemployment. Small inter-firm differences in wages of equally skilled labour, for institutional or other reasons, will lead to low transitional unemployment; workers who lose attractive high-wage jobs are less reluctant to accept other jobs if pay differentials are relatively small (Summers 1986, pp. 370–80).

The bold hypothesis about the structural effects of solidaristic wage policy was also confirmed by a production-function-based study of the effects of wage dispersion on output and productivity in the Swedish private business sector. The contention is that solidaristic wage policy led to a significant increase in aggregate output and blue-collar labour productivity by speeding up the transformation of resources between plants and industries (Hibbs and Locking 2000). The limitations of the stylized theoretical approach of Hibbs and Locking (2000) are admitted in the study, one obvious weakness being that the effects of wage distribution on structural change are not related to other factors such as international competition and macroeconomic policies. In addition, a study of Nordic countries similar to Edin and Topel (1997) gave solidaristic wage policy a more modest role as a cause of changes in industrial composition and plant closures in manufacturing. The decline in relative production and the number of production units in industries with initially lower wages than the average (textile and garment, wood products) was no stronger in Sweden than in other Nordic countries in 1960–73. The study also questions the contention that wage pressure on 'marginal' plants and stagnating sectors was brought about by wage policy and not by free market forces (thus by wage and job opportunities in other plants and sectors), possibly in conjunction with relative wage preferences. The cost pressure on stagnating industries was not systematically higher in countries with a more solidaristic wage policy (Erixon 1984, pp. 27–37). The study confirms the conclusions of other studies that the extent of solidaristic wage policy has not been decisive for differences in structural changes and wage developments between the Nordic countries. (See the studies above of changes in the employment composition of manufacturing, and also Holmlund and Zetterberg 1991, pp. 1023–5). Hence, several studies support Rehn and Meidner's cautious view of the relationship between solidaristic wage policy and structural change.

An influential argument in the Swedish debate is that solidaristic wage policy has prevented a renewal of Swedish industry. Dynamic new firms have died at an early age because of solidaristic wage policy without having reached their potential profit levels. Further, solidaristic wage policy is said to have favoured large, established firms with a limited growth potential. In total, solidaristic wage policy has been accused of having preserved an outdated industrial structure with negative consequences for Sweden's growth performance (Davis and Henrekson 1997, pp. 354 and 376–7).

The argument that solidaristic wage policy has made Swedish industry obsolete seems reasonable. In the mid-1970s, non-agricultural self-employment as a proportion of total civilian employment in Sweden fell below the level of all other OECD countries. Swedish production (in manufacturing) and export were, and still are, dominated by large, established firms, even by international standards (Erixon 1997b, pp. 17 and 83). It seems, however, that the 'mature' industrial structure of Sweden was formed already in the interwar period, thus before the age of solidaristic wage policy (Erixon 1997b, pp. 25–8). This policy may have reinforced the large-firm character of Swedish industry in the 1960s and 1970s. But the strong concentration of firms in Sweden in the post-war years is probably better explained by the openness of the economy, the character of risk-capital markets, profit taxes and public sector growth. Further, equal wages for similar jobs will also emerge in competitive labour markets. Finally, large corporations in the export sector have had a wage-leading role in Sweden in the post-war period (Erixon 1997b, p. 35).

My tentative conclusion is that empirical studies have not rejected a cautious Rehn–Meidner hypothesis that structural change is possible with a solidaristic wage policy. However, I cannot decide with certainty whether solidaristic wage policy has speeded up structural change, whether the policy's positive and negative effects on structural change have cancelled each other out (as expected in the R–M model), or whether in fact wage equalization has had no significant effect at all on sector and company composition in Sweden. Let us now focus on empirical studies testing the Rehn–Meidner hypothesis that economic growth is promoted by general reductions in profits and profit margins.

A proposition that economic growth is stimulated by low profit levels has been rejected by many time-series and cross-country studies showing – in accordance with the Keynesian view – that high aggregate demand and profits have a positive effect on investments as well as on productivity growth, at least on aggregate levels (Michl 1985; Erixon 1987, pp. 202–10 and 1994, pp. 42–52; Maddison 1987). But the low productivity growth in most OECD countries during the boom of the 1980s cannot be explained in terms of low demand and profits. Further, growth studies are often too aggregate, concealing that some industries may rather confirm a theory of transformation pressure. Besides, a positive (Keynesian) relationship between profits and demand on the one hand and growth on the other is often overestimated in time-series analyses because of simultaneity problems – high growth may result in high profits and activity levels. A theory of transformation pressure is also not confirmed by the fact that a negative relationship is probably more delayed than a positive relationship and therefore more difficult to capture in quantitative terms.

There is some empirical support for a hypothesis that Swedish growth has been stimulated by transformation pressure. High productivity growth in manufacturing in the 1960s is explained largely by mergers and, in raw materials industries, by the fact that plants with low productivity growth were eliminated (Wohlin 1970; Rydén 1971). These mergers and closures in raw materials industries were primarily caused by harder international competition and recessions. The potential for mergers and the differences in productivity between marginal and best plants were large in the 1960s due to a weak transformation pressure in the preceding decade (Wohlin 1970, p. 109; Rydén 1971, pp. 198–206).

The importance of economic policy (and solidaristic wage policy) for transformation pressure was toned down in the Swedish studies above. Yet, explaining the country's relatively low productivity growth in the 1980s in terms of a weak transformation pressure, some Swedish economists focused on economic policy. Devaluation policies were accused of having delayed structural change, rationalizations and the introduction of new organizations, technologies and products in manufacturing (Erixon 1991; Swedish Productivity Commission 1992). The conclusions were based on some approximate evidence, but also on the results of time-series analysis. Profit variables were here included as determinants (together with other variables) of labour productivity in Swedish manufacturing in 1957–87. It was possible to demonstrate for manufacturing as a whole that profits had a (delayed) negative effect on labour productivity in accordance with a theory of transformation pressure. Several industries on the two- and three-digit levels, particularly the machine, pulp and paper industries, showed a similar negative relationship between profits and productivity (Erixon 1991, pp. 349–56).

The theory of transformation pressure is partly confirmed by labour (and total factor) productivity developments in Swedish manufacturing in the 1990s. Sweden performed better than most other OECD countries during this decade. The exceptional labour productivity growth in Sweden in the first half of the 1990s is largely explained by rationalizations, although often in conjunction with labour substitution and the introduction of new work organizations, and – although to a lesser degree – by the elimination of 'marginal' production units. Rationalizations and organizational changes in manufacturing were induced by the deep Swedish recession and high real rates of interest in the early 1990s and due to the weak transformation pressure in the 1980s, much room was also provided for productivity gains. The high productivity growth in Sweden in the 1990s cannot fully be explained by a theory of transformation pressure. Fiscal policy was mainly tight but there was a strong depreciation of the Swedish krona and high rates of unemployment in the first half of the

1990s leading to exceptionally high profit shares in Swedish manufacturing for the rest of the decade. (Sweden changed to a system of flexible exchange rates in 1992.) On the other hand, statistics do not confirm a competing theory that Swedish productivity was stimulated by high profits in the 1990s. The major part of labour (and total factor) productivity growth in the Swedish business sector in 1995–2000 reflected a favourable productivity development in one sector – telecommunications (Edquist and Henrekson 2001).

In any case, empirical studies offer no general support to a hypothesis that economic growth is promoted by profit squeezes. But a categorical proposition that growth is enhanced by low profitability levels gives no representative picture of Rehn and Meidner's view. They realized that an extreme pressure on profitability could seriously curb private investments, particularly by restricting the possibilities of self-finance (see above). This view is in fact compatible with that in modern industrial economics that the optimal transformation pressure is moderate rather than maximal (Erixon 2001a, pp. 26–30).

THE VALIDITY OF THE R–M MODEL – SOME FINAL COMMENTS

The Swedish model, synonymous here with the R–M model, represents a unique policy in combining full employment and equity with growth and price stability. The combination is achieved by a wage policy of solidarity and the use of selective instruments – primarily labour market policies and marginal employment subsidies – within the framework of a restrictive fiscal policy.

My main aim behind this chapter was to show the compound and unique character of the R–M model and to relate its underlying economic theory about inflation and growth to modern economics. The model is in harmony with modern growth theories of transformation pressure and with social theories of fair wages. Further, its description of wage formation is, by its dynamic and comprehensive character, a serious challenge to current bargaining and trade union theories, giving room for competitive forces, X-inefficient firms, relative wage preferences, labour market policies and a wage policy of fairness.

The main argument today against the R–M model is that internationalization has narrowed the scope for an economic policy that aims to keep down the general level of profits. The model was conceived for an economy with small movements of financial capital over national borders. Furthermore, overseas production by companies was less extensive and less interchangeable with domestic production than is the case today. Internationalization is also said to have narrowed the scope for solidaristic wage policy. Wage earners in high demand who are hit by the fair-wage principle have greater opportunities today of moving to other countries.

Internationalization has undeniably limited the possibilities for any single country to apply the R–M model. But marginal employment grants (or similar subsidies) will increase the incentives for dynamic companies to locate expansion within their own countries. Non-subsidized companies will suffer a profit loss, particularly if the subsidies are financed by increases in average pay-roll taxes. But these companies are hardly the ones that make large contributions to a country's economic growth.

International labour mobility is still limited in scope but certainly a real challenge for solidaristic wage policy. The road is long to coordinated wage policy actions on the European Union (EU) level. But the R–M model does not rule out wage differences between individuals based on differences in job content, competence and education. Further, Rehn and Meidner would probably have claimed that high wage levels for key groups in labour markets must be met by extensive educational and labour market programmes to eliminate excess demand, not by an acceptance of larger wage differentials.

Swedish labour market policy programmes were appreciated by foreign economists for having prevented large cyclical swings and protracted spells of unemployment up until the 1990s (Blanchflower et al. 1995). But labour market policies were criticized by both foreign and Swedish economists for being insufficient and ineffective instruments to combat massive unemployment in the 1990s (see, for instance, Ackum Agell 1995 and Forslund and Krueger 1997). The argument that the R–M model is not relevant in a situation of high unemployment has been made by a heterogeneous group of economists. The group consists of mainstream economists who advocate reductions of real wages by structural reforms in labour markets or reductions in corporate and pay-roll taxes, and also of post-Keynesians who favour coordinated or individual actions among EU member states to raise effective demand. But it can be argued that the founders of the model were not against expansionary general measures in a situation with high unemployment. In fact, Rehn recommended measures aimed at raising effective demand when unemployment is high, though in combination with marginal employment subsidies and labour market programmes. Without referring to the R–M model, Swedish governments generally adopted the means of the R–M model in the 1990s. In particular, extensive labour market programmes were pursued whether the governments were led by Social Democrats or non-socialist parties. But the governments were nevertheless unable to combine low inflation with full employment.

In 1999, the Social Democrats adopted a medium-term target for fiscal policy that public saving should show a surplus over the business cycle. The target agrees with the R–M model even though the ultimate of aim is not as in the model to squeeze profits and give priority to public saving as a source of private investments at the expense of company self-financing. The relation between the R–M model and the EU project is equally ambiguous. Official declarations by the EU since the late 1990s that full employment and active employment policy measures must be prioritized once again (see the Luxembourg process) but within a stable macroeconomic policy framework are clearly in the Rehn–Meidner spirit. By its emphasis on selective interventionism and supply-orientated measures in labour and product markets to achieve full employment without giving up the restriction of price stability, the R–M model has silently sneaked in by the back door in the 1990s, both in Sweden and in the EU. In addition, when joining the Economic and Monetary Union (EMU), fiscal policy will once again become the prime instrument of stabilization policy in countries with flexible exchange rates in the 1990s. Further, a strategy to avoid unemployment in a single EMU country during a recession by an expansionary fiscal policy demands public saving over the business cycle as advocated by the R–M model. The recommendations of the Stability and Growth Pact for positive public budget surpluses over the entire business cycle accord with the R–M model even though the Pact gives no priority to lower profit shares and public saving.

The EU idea of a macroeconomic dialogue with social partners seems to accord with the R–M model, but the emphasis on wage restraint to achieve price stability and competitiveness is not anchored in it. Rehn and Meidner had a sceptical view of 'incomes policy' as a means of controlling wage developments and also providing high economic growth, as they presumed that productivity is stimulated by pressures on profit margins. Further, the prohibition of public budget deficits above 3 per cent of GDP in the Stability and Growth Pact is certainly not compatible with the high ambitions of full employment in the R–M model. A fiscal policy obeying the rules of the Pact must be *contractive* during a recession in countries with a large public sector like Sweden because of built-in stabilizers. However, a referendum in September 2003 clearly rejected a Swedish participation in the EMU.

This chapter shows the R–M model in a favourable light. But it has also raised some fundamental objections to the model's underpinning economic theory. It may seem inconsistent to give market forces a decisive role in wage formation that, for example, makes incomes policy impossible, and to expect at the same time that wages can be regulated by solidaristic wage policy. From the angle of the R–M model, it seems difficult to control market forces by such regulations even if they have the aim of simulating a competitive labour market in equilibrium. There is definitely some truth in these objections. But again, it is necessary to emphasize the coherent nature of the model. It is impossible to lift out some parts of the model and keep the rest. A solidaristic wage policy cannot be applied or be non-inflationary without a restrictive general economic policy and a mobility-enhancing labour market policy. It is too early to pronounce the R–M model dead. The model may still be a possible lodestar for economic policy, particularly on the EU level, but it will collapse like a house of cards if only partially applied.

NOTES

1. Rudolf Meidner (1914–) was the head of the Economics Research Department of the LO (Landsorganisationen i Sverige) and Gösta Rehn (1913–96) the department's most outstanding economist. Rehn had served as an expert on the committee that formulated the Swedish labour movement's post-war programme in 1944. Both Rehn and Meidner had academic qualifications and were well-respected participators in the contemporary macroeconomic discussion.
2. The importance of central wage agreements for recorded total wage increases in Sweden has sometimes been overstated in the foreign literature; central agreements are reached either for a particular industry or by a process of coordinated negotiations for all industries. Wage drift has accounted for about half the total increase in blue-collar workers' wages in Sweden in the post-war period (Nilsson 1994).
3. In the Swedish case, statutory incomes policy is a threat to the 'Saltsjöbaden spirit'. According to the 1938 Saltsjöbaden agreement between the LO and the Swedish Employers' Federation (the SAF, Svenska Arbetsgivareföreningen), labour market conflicts should be resolved through negotiated agreements and not by legislation.
4. Low-paid groups were favoured in coordinated negotiations in Sweden from the mid-1960s to the early 1980s. This policy of wage equalization did not follow directly from the principle of fairness in the R–M model. But the LO (and Meidner) argued that the policy indirectly satisfied the ideal of solidaristic wage policy – wage differentials were too large to be explained or justified by 'objective' differences in work content or worker productivity.
5. Labour market policy would prevent wage adjustments downward for two reasons. First, the tendency to wage reductions in competitive labour markets is counterbalanced by the fact that potentially unemployed people are placed in various labour market programmes. Second, trade unions are in a better negotiating position if open unemployment is kept low.
6. A similar condition can justify seeing public employment services as selective policy instruments. The services reduce information and transaction costs for firms recruiting labour.
7. It is not obvious why a cost–push policy established through labour market policy measures must be complemented with a tight general economic policy to guarantee a profit margin decline. There are clear limitations on the possibilities of marking up cost increases in models of imperfect competition when the price elasticity of demand is a negative function of output. A shift upward of the marginal cost curve will reduce markups, for instance in the case of a linear demand curve, since demand becomes more elastic at lower output levels. The relationship probably characterizes an open economy with some scope for independent price policies by domestic firms. Here, profit margins are likely to be reduced by unilateral labour market policy measures to achieve full employment, since foreign competition prevents all wage increases from being passed on to prices. Further, Rehn and Meidner did not weigh the possibility that in the long run, a profit fall in the analysed sector (or country) is counteracted by exits. They could have assumed that entry barriers would prevent firm flight to other sectors (Erixon 2000, pp. 38–43).
8. In the controversy with Lundberg, Rehn claimed that the relative importance of labour market and profit effects on nominal-wage increases is of minor interest within the

framework of the R–M model; the labour market effects of a restrictive fiscal policy are always neutralized by a selective policy of full employment (Rehn 1952b, pp. 72–3 [1950] and 1987, pp. 67–8).

9. Labour market conditions may influence collective wages, especially on the level of the firm. But I shall treat collective wage increases on the company level as wage drift in accordance with the practice of Swedish statistics (see Nilsson 1994, pp. 8–9).

10. Higher profits will also lead to higher wage claims and a weaker resistance to such claims in central wage negotiations (Aukrust 1977, p. 115). The first argument is similar to the one in the efficiency wage theory (see further above) while the second argument has been attributed to the R–M model in this chapter.

11. The average rise in prices in the whole economy will probably be higher than in the competitive sector because of a lower rate of productivity growth in the sheltered sector.

12. In fact, the R–M model's hypothesis that profitability will fall when domestic demand is curbed is challenged by the assumption that export is stimulated by an accompanying reduction in the rate of price and wage increases. The challenge was accepted early by Rehn (see Rehn 1952b, pp. 78–9 [1950]).

13. The Keynesian theory of 'equilibrium inflation' was inspired by the Scandinavian model, which in turn exhibits similarities with the R–M model (Jackson et al. 1975). But a strategy of 'equilibrium' (or moderate) inflation was already criticized by Rehn and Meidner in the 1951 LO report by references to the possibility of wage–wage–price spirals at macroeconomic shocks.

14. The Rehn–Meidner theory of functional income distribution is similar to Michal Kalecki's. Kalecki refers to the 'degree of monopoly' determined by market-structure conditions, the extent of means of competition other than prices, 'tacit' agreements between producers, and the power of trade unions. Strong trade unions will push for high nominal wages that are difficult to mark up due to restraints from competition in commodity markets (Kalecki 1965, pp. 17–18 and 30–31 [1954]). The main difference between the theories concerns the cyclical pattern of profit shares. In the R–M model, profit shares are pro-cyclical since nominal wages react more slowly than prices to changes in aggregate demand (Erixon 2000, pp. 35–8). In Kalecki's theory, nominal wages are exogenous while mark-ups are countercyclical, *inter alia* as firms try to protect profits by 'tacit agreements' in a slump. If overhead labour and material costs are ignored, profit shares will then vary countercyclically in Kalecki's model.

15. In one bargaining model, a positive relationship between profits and wages is explained by the fact that the position of trade unions is strengthened (weakened) by high (low) profits (see Christofides and Oswald 1992, p. 988).

16. Rehn and Hansen discuss some wage-drift mechanisms that are similar to the ones in bargaining theory. Wage drift will emerge irrespective of labour market conditions at higher intensity of work or through technical improvements which benefit employees as an 'institutional habit' (Hansen and Rehn 1956, pp. 89–90 and 96–7). The hypothesis induced Rehn and Hansen to consider average physical labour productivity as a third wage-drift determinant beside profit margins and labour shortage. However, there is difficulty, both in theory and practice, in separating this hypothesis from one that says that wage drift is stimulated by higher average profits or higher actual profit margins.

17. The X-inefficiency interpretation of the R–M model is supported by Rehn and Hansen's statement that high profits make employers more careless with regard to wage payments (Hansen and Rehn 1956, p. 89). A complicating circumstance is that Rehn–Meidner, and also Hansen–Rehn, support a hypothesis that high profits and dividends may induce wage claims on equity grounds. Hansen and Rehn's thesis that high profits make individual employees more eager to exploit the wage-paying capacity of companies is similar to the one in the efficiency-wage theory above (Hansen and Rehn 1956, p. 89; Rehn 1982, pp. 2 and 1987, pp. 65 and 68). However, I still claim that the fundamental idea in the R–M model is that companies and their managers are the main actors behind a positive relationship between average profits and wage drift.

18. It is true that key groups in labour markets are wage leaders in some bargaining theories

(see above). But their wages are in turn determined by negotiation strength, not directly by market forces.
19. Bargaining theorists have also suggested that wage drift is the market's correction of central agreements of 'fair wages'. Significant central wage increases will, at least partially, be compensated by lower wage drift since excess demand situations become less likely. A similar argument can, in fact, be found in the R–M model itself. The model emphasizes that dynamic firms have incentives for circumventing a policy of solidarity wages.
20. But the model is not confirmed by the conclusion in the Hibbs–Locking study that collective wage increases have a stronger effect on wage drift than labour market conditions. However, the impact of labour market conditions on wage drift is probably underestimated in the Hibbs–Locking study by their inclusion of a central-wage variable. Besides, the study may have captured a correlation rather than a causality (see the comments on the central-wage functions above).
21. I have not considered the extreme case of a horizontal PM line where productivity differences are completely matched by wage differences. If the number of firms is large, the profit-margin line will be identical to the 0 line in Figure 4.2.

REFERENCES

Ackum Agell, Susanne (1995), 'Swedish labour market programs: efficiency and timing', *Swedish Economic Policy Review*, **2** (1), 65–98.
Agell, J. (1999), 'On the benefits from rigid labour markets: norms, market failures, and social insurance', *Economic Journal*, **109** (453), F143–F164.
Agell, J. and K.E. Lommerud (1992), 'Union egalitarianism as income insurance', *Economica*, **59** (236), 295–310.
Akerlof, G.A. and J.L. Yellen (1990), 'The fair wage-effort hypothesis and unemployment', *Quarterly Journal of Economics*, **105** (2), 255–83.
Andersson, L., O. Gustafsson and L. Lundberg (2000), 'Structual change, competition, and job turnover in Swedish manufacturing, 1964–96', *Review of International Economics*, **8** (3), 566–82.
Arai, M. (1994), 'An empirical analysis of wage dispersion and efficiency wages', *Scandinavian Journal of Economics*, **96** (1), 31–50.
Arai, M. (1999), 'Wages, profits and capital intensity: evidence from matched worker–firm data', Research Papers in Economics 1999:3, Stockholm: Department of Economics.
Aukrust, O. (1977), 'Inflation in the open economy: a Norwegian model', in L.B. Krause and W.S. Sâlant (eds), *Worldwide Inflation: Theory and Recent Experience*, Washington, DC: Brookings Institution, pp. 107–53.
Bewley, T. (1998), 'Why not cut pay?', *European Economic Review*, **42** (3–5), 459–90.
Blanchflower, D.G., R. Jackman and G. Saint-Paul (1995), 'Some reflections on Swedish labour market policy', Report to the Committee on Swedish Labour Market Policy, SOU 1995:39E, Stockholm: Fritzes.
Blanchflower, D.G., A.J. Oswald and P. Sanfey (1996), 'Wages, profits and rent-sharing', *Quarterly Journal of Economics*, **111** (1), 227–51.
Bosworth, B.P. and R.Z. Lawrence (1987), 'Adjusting to slower economic growth: the domestic economy', in B.P. Bosworth and A.M. Rivlin (eds), *The Swedish Economy*, Washington, DC: Brookings Institution, pp. 22–54.

Calmfors, L. (1993a), 'Lessons from the macroeconomic experience of Sweden', *European Journal of Political Economy*, **9** (1), 25–72.
Calmfors, L. (1993b), 'Centralisation of wage bargaining and macroeconomic performance – a survey', Working Paper no. 131, OECD Economics Department, Paris: OECD.
Calmfors, L. and A. Forslund (1990), 'Wage formation in Sweden', in L. Calmfors (ed.), *Wage Formation and Macroeconomic Policy in the Nordic Countries*, Oxford: Industrial Council for Social and Economic Studies (SNS Förlag) and Oxford University Press, pp. 63–130.
Christofides, L.N. and A.J. Oswald (1992), 'Real wage determination and rent-sharing in collective bargaining agreements', *Quarterly Journal of Economics*, **107** (3), 985–1002.
Davis, J.S. and M. Henrekson (1997), 'Industrial policy, employer size, and economic performance', in R.B. Freeman, R. Topel and B. Swedenborg (eds), *The Welfare State in Transition – Reforming the Swedish Model*, Chicago and London: University of Chicago Press, pp. 353–97.
Edgren, G., K.O. Faxén and C.E. Odhner (1973), *Wage Formation and the Economy*, London: Allen & Unwin.
Edin, P.-A. and R. Topel (1997), 'Wage policy and restructuring: the Swedish labor market since 1960', in R.B. Freeman, R. Topel and B. Swedenborg (eds), *The Welfare State in Transition – Reforming the Swedish Model*, Chicago and London: University of Chicago Press, pp. 155–201.
Edquist, C. (1991), 'Högteknologiska produkter och produktivitet i svensk industri' (High-tech products and productivity in Swedish manufacturing), in *Forskning, teknikspridning och produktivitet* (Research, Diffusion of Technology and Productivity), Expert report no. 10 to the Swedish Productivity Commission, Stockholm: Allmänna Förlaget.
Edquist, H. and M. Henrekson (2001), 'Solowparadoxen och den nya ekonomin' (The Solow paradox and the new economy), *Ekonomisk Debatt*, **29** (6), 409–19.
Erixon, L. (1984), 'Den svenska modellen i medgång. En analys av dess innehåll och effekter under perioden 1960–1974' (The success of the Swedish Model – An analysis of its content and effects in the 1960–74 period), Stockholm: Swedish Institute for Social Research (SOFI), mimeo.
Erixon, L. (1985), 'What's wrong with the Swedish model? An analysis of its effects and changed conditions 1974–1985', Working Paper no. 12/1985, Stockholm: Swedish Institute for Social Research.
Erixon, L. (1987), *Profitability in Swedish Manufacturing – Trends and Explanations*, Stockholm: Almqvist & Wiksell International.
Erixon, L. (1991), 'Omvandlingstryck och produktivitet' (Transformation pressure and productivity), in *Konkurrens, regleringar och produktivitet* (Competition, Regulations and Productivity), Expert report no. 7 to the Swedish Productivity Commission, Stockholm: Allmänna Förlaget.
Erixon, L. (1994), *Investeringar och lönsamhet* (Investments and profitability), Expert report no. 7 to the Medium Term Survey, Stockholm: Fritzes.
Erixon, L. (1997a), 'The father of the Swedish model', *Economic and Industrial Democracy*, **18** (4), 635–50.
Erixon, L. (1997b), 'The golden age of the Swedish model', Report 97:9, Oslo: Institute for Social Research.
Erixon, L. (2000), *The 'Third Way' Revisited. A Revaluation of the Swedish Model*

in the *Light of Modern Economics*, Stockholm: Trade Union Institute for Economic Research (FIEF).
Erixon, L. (2001a), 'Transformation pressure and growth – a missing link in macroeconomics', Working Papers in Economics 2001:3, Stockholm: Department of Economics, Stockholm University.
Erixon L. (2001b), 'A Swedish economic policy – the theory, application and validity of the Rehn–Meidner model', in H. Milner and E. Wadensjö (eds), *Gösta Rehn – At Home and Abroad*, London: Ashgate, pp. 12–49.
Faxén, K.O., C.-E. Odhner and R. Spånt (1988), *Lönebildningen i 90-talets samhällsekonomi* (Wage Formation in the Economy of the 90s), Stockholm: Rabén & Sjögren.
Flanagan, R.J. (1990), 'Centralized and decentralized pay determination in Nordic countries', in L. Calmfors (ed.), *Wage Formation and Macroeconomic Policy in the Nordic Countries*, Oxford: Industrial Council for Social and Economic Studies (SNS Förlag) and Oxford University Press, pp. 395–414.
Forslund, A. (1994a), 'Wage setting at the firm level – insider versus outsider forces', *Oxford Economic Papers*, **46** (2), 245–61.
Forslund, A. (1994b), 'Labour market policies and wage setting: a study of Swedish unemployment insurance funds', in B. Holmlund (ed.), *Pay, Productivity, and Policy – Essays on Wage Behavior in Sweden*, Stockholm: Trade Union Institute for Economic Research (FIEF).
Forslund, A. and A.B. Krueger (1997), 'An evaluation of the Swedish active labor market policy: new and received wisdom', in R.B. Freeman, R. Topel and B. Swedenborg (eds), *The Welfare State in Transition – Reforming the Swedish Model*, Chicago and London: University of Chicago Press, pp. 267–98.
Fries, H. (1983), 'Structural change and industry performance in four Western European countries', in G. Eliasson, M. Sharefkin and B.C. Ysander (eds), *Policy Making in a Disorderly World Economy*, Stockholm: Industrial Institute for Economic and Social Research (IUI), pp. 111–67.
Hansen, B. and G. Rehn (1956), 'On wage-drift. A problem of money-wage dynamics', in *25 Economic Essays in Honour of Erik Lindahl*, Stockholm: Ekonomisk Tidskrift, pp. 87–133.
Hansson, P. and L. Lundberg (1995), *Från basindustri till högteknologi? Svensk näringsstruktur och strukturpolitik* (From Basic to High Technological Industries? Industrial Composition and Structural Policy of Sweden), Stockholm: Industrial Council for Social and Economic Studies (SNS Förlag).
Hibbs, D.A. Jr. and H. Locking (1995), 'Wage compression, wage drift, and wage inflation in Sweden', *Journal of Labor Economics*, **14** (1), 109–41.
Hibbs, D.A. Jr. and H. Locking (2000), 'Wage dispersion and productive efficiency: evidence for Sweden', *Journal of Labor Economics*, **18** (4), 755–82.
Holmlund, B. (1997), 'Some new evidence on wage behaviour in Sweden', in N. Elvander and B. Holmlund (eds), *The Swedish Bargaining System in the Melting Pot – Institutions, Norms and Outcomes in the 1990s*, Stockholm: Swedish Center for Work Life Research, pp. 91–107.
Holmlund, B. and P. Skedinger (1990), 'Wage bargaining and wage drift: evidence from the Swedish wood industry', in L. Calmfors (ed.), *Wage Formation and Macroeconomic Policy in the Nordic Countries*, Stockholm and Oxford: Industrial Council for Social and Economic Studies (SNS Förlag) and Oxford University Press, pp. 363–88.

Holmlund, B. and J. Zetterberg (1991), 'Insider effects in wage determination – evidence from five countries', *European Economic Review*, **35** (5), 1009–34.
Jackman, R., C. Pissarides and S. Savouri (1990), 'Labour market policies and unemployment in the OECD', *Economic Policy*, no. 11, October, 450–90.
Jackson, D., H.A. Turner and F. Wilkinson (1975), *Do Trade Unions Cause Inflation?*, London: Cambridge University Press.
Johnson, G.E. and R. Layard (1986), 'The natural rate of unemployment: explanation and policy', in O. Ashenfelter and R. Layard (eds), *Handbook of Labor Economics*, Vol II, Amsterdam: North-Holland, pp. 921–99.
Jonsson, L. and C.-H. Siven (1984), 'Löneutjämningens mekanismer' (The mechanisms of wage equality), *Ekonomisk Debatt*, **2** (7), 429–41.
Kalecki, M. ([1954] 1965), *Theory of Economic Dynamics*, New York and London: MR Modern Reader.
Keynes, J.M. (1936), *The General Theory of Employment, Interest and Money*, London: Macmillan, St Martin's Press.
Layard, R. (1979), 'The costs and benefits of selective employment measures: the British case', *British Journal of Industrial Relations*, **90** (1), 187–204.
Layard, R. and S. Nickell (1980), 'The case for subsidising extra jobs', *Economic Journal*, **90** (357), 51–73.
Layard, R. and S. Nickell (1990), 'Is unemployment lower if unions bargain over employment?', *Quarterly Journal of Economics*, **105** (3), 773–87.
Leibenstein, H. (1980), *Beyond Economic Man – A New Foundation for Microeconomics*, Cambridge MA: Harvard University Press.
Lindbeck, A. (1997), 'The Swedish experiment', *Journal of Economic Literature*, **35** (3), 1273–319.
Lundberg, E. (1952), 'A critique of Rehn's approach', in R. Turvey (ed.), *Wages Policy Under Full Employment*, London: William Hodge, pp. 55–71.
Maddison, A. (1987), 'Growth and slowdown in advanced capitalist economies: techniques of quantitative assessment', *Journal of Economic Literature*, **25** (2), 649–98.
MacDonald, I.A. and A. Suen (1992), 'On the measurement and determination of trade union power', *Oxford Bulletin of Economics and Statistics*, **54** (2), 209–24.
Meidner, R. (1952), 'The dilemma of wages policy under full employment', in R. Turvey (ed.), *Wages Policy Under Full Employment*, London: William Hodge, pp. 16–30. Revised version of 'Lönepolitikens dilemma vid full sysselsättning', *Tiden*, **40** (9), 1948.
Meidner, R. (1969), 'The goals of labour market policy', in *On Incomes Policy*, Papers and Proceedings from a Conference in Honour of Erik Lundberg, Stockholm: SNS Förlag, pp. 189–98.
Meidner, R. (1974), *Samordning och solidarisk lönepolitik* (Co-ordination and Solidaristic Wage Policy), Stockholm: Swedish Confederation of Trade Unions (LO).
Meidner, R., G. Rehn et al. (1953), *Trade Unions and Full Employment*, report to the LO Congress 1951, Stockholm: Swedish Confederation of Trade Unions (LO), first published in Swedish in 1951.
Michl, T.R. (1985), 'International comparisons of productivity growth', *Journal of Post Keynesian Economics*, **7** (4), 474–92.
Moene, K.O., M. Wallerstein and M. Hoel (1993), 'Wage demands by unions and employers', in R.J. Flanagan, R.O. Moene and M. Wallerstein (eds), *Trade Union Behaviour – Pay Bargaining and Economic Performance*, Oxford: Clarendon.

Nilsson, C. (1994), 'Negotiated wages and wage drift: a study of the Swedish pulp and paper industry', in B. Holmlund (ed.), *Pay, Productivity, and Policy*, Stockholm: Trade Union Institute for Economic Research (FIEF), pp. 1–32.

Nilsson, C. and J. Zetterberg (1987), *Lönestruktur och strukturella arbetsmarknadsproblem* (Wage Structure and Structural Problems in Labour Markets), Appendix to the Medium Term Survey 1987, Stockholm: Allmänna Förlaget.

Öhman, B. (1982), 'Solidarisk lönepolitik och löntagarfonder' (Solidaristic wage policy and wage earner funds), Expert report from *Utredningen om löntagarna och kapitaltillväxten SOU 1982:47*, Stockholm: Allmänna Förlaget.

Pissarides, C. and R. Moghadam (1990), 'Relative wage flexibility in four countries', in L. Calmfors (ed.), *Wage Formation and Macroeconomic Policy in the Nordic Countries*, Oxford: Oxford University Press and Industrial Council for Social and Economic Studies (SNS Förlag), pp. 417–42.

Poret, P. (1990), 'The "puzzle" of wage moderation in the 1980s', Working Paper no. 87, OECD Department of Economics and Statistics, Paris: Organisation for Economic Co-operation and Development.

Rehn, G. (1952a), 'The problem of stability: an analysis and some policy proposals', in R. Turvey (ed.), *Wages Policy Under Full Employment*, London: William Hodge, revised version of 'Ekonomisk politik under full sysselsättning', *Tiden*, **40** (3), 1948.

Rehn, G. (1952b), 'A reply to Professor Lundberg', in R. Turvey (ed.), *Wages Policy Under Full Employment*, London: William Hodge, revised version of 'Lönepolitiken och fullsysselsättningen. Replik till professor Lundberg', *Ekonomisk Tidskrift*, **52**(1), 1950.

Rehn, G. (1969), 'Labour market policy and the "Rehn model"' and 'The relationship between productivity development and the state of overall demand', in *On Incomes Policy*, Papers and Proceedings from a Conference in Honour of Erik Lundberg (chairman introductions by Rehn), Stockholm: Industrial Council for Social and Economic Studies (SNS Förlag), pp. 163–70.

Rehn, G. (1977), 'Finansministrarna, LO-ekonomerna och arbetsmarknadspolitiken' (Finance ministers, LO economists and labour market policies), in *Ekonomisk Debatt och ekonomisk politik – Nationalekonomiska föreningen 100 år* (Economic Debate and Economic Policy. The Swedish Economic Association 100 Years), Stockholm: Norstedts.

Rehn, G. (1980), 'Idéutvecklingen' (Developments of the ideas), in *Lönepolitik och solidaritet* (Wage Policy and Solidarity), Stockholm: Swedish Confederation of Trade Unions (LO).

Rehn, G. (1982), 'Anti-inflationary expansion policies (with special reference to marginal employment premiums)', Report to the Commission of the European Communities. Occasional Paper No. 4, Brussels: Commission of the European Communities.

Rehn, G. (1986), 'Hur bädda för en antiinflatorisk inkomstpolitik?' (How do you create stable conditions for an anti-inflationary incomes policy?), in *Förhandlad inkomstpolitik?* (Negotiated Incomes Policy), Stockholm: Trade Union Institute for Economic Research (FIEF), pp. 71–89.

Rehn, G. (1987), 'State, economic policy and industrial relations in the 1980s', *Journal of Economic and Industrial Democracy*, **8** (1), 61–79.

Romer, D. (2001), *Advanced Macroeconomics – Second Edition*, Berkeley: McGraw-Hill Companies.

Rydén, B. (1971), *Fusioner i svensk industri* (Mergers in Swedish Industries), Stockholm: Industrial Institute for Economic and Social Research (IUI).

Salter, W.E.G. (1960), *Productivity and Technical Change*, Cambridge: Cambridge University Press.

Schager, N.H. (1981), 'The duration of vacancies as a measure of the state of demand in the labour market. The Swedish wage drift equation reconsidered', in G. Eliasson (ed.), *Studies in Labour Market Behaviour: Sweden and the United States*, Stockholm: Industrial Institute for Economic and Social Research (IUI), pp. 393–442.

Schager, N.H. (1988), 'Causes of wage increases in Swedish manufacturing: a remarkable case of regular behaviour', Working Paper no. 195, Stockholm: Industrial Institute for Economic and Social Research (IUI).

Solow, R. (1964), *Capital Theory and the Rate of Return*, Amsterdam: North-Holland.

Solow, R. (1979), 'Another possible source of wage stickiness', *Journal of Macroeconomics*, **1** (1), 79–82.

Solow, R. (1990), *The Labour Market as a Social Institution*, Cambridge, MA and Oxford, Basil Blackwell.

Summers, L.H. (1986), 'Why is the unemployment rate so very high near full employment?', *Brookings Paper on Economic Activity*, no. 2, 339–83.

Summers, L.H. (1988), 'Relative wages, efficiency wages, and Keynesian unemployment', *American Economic Review*, **78** (2), 383–8.

Swedish Productivity Commission (1992), *Forces of Productivity and Prosperity*, Summary of SOU 1991:92, Stockholm: Allmänna Förlaget.

Tobin, J. (1972), 'Inflation and unemployment', *American Economic Review*, **62** (2), 1–18.

Wohlin, L. (1970), 'Strukturomvandling inom skogsindustrin' (Structural change in wood industries), *Skandinaviska Banken Kvartalsskrift*, **51** (4), 104–9.

Yellen, J.L. (1984), 'Efficiency wage models of unemployment', *American Economic Review*, **74** (2), 200–205.

5. The economic policy in Spain during the decades of the 1980s and the 1990s

Jesus Ferreiro and Felipe Serrano

INTRODUCTION

The government of the Socialist Party (Partido Socialista Obrero Español, PSOE) came to office in November 1982 and left in March 1996, when the elections were won by the Partido Popular, a right-wing Christian democratic party. During those 14 years, the economic policy of the different Felipe González administrations focused on two objectives. From a macroeconomic point of view, the entire strategy focused on the control of inflation. The problem of mass unemployment was subordinated to this main objective. Such a strategy was coincidental with the dominant strategies implemented in other Western economies. In this chapter we shall not analyse whether the adoption of this strategy was due to an ideological change within the Socialist Party which took place after they came to power or because it was the only strategy that could be implemented effectively. It is likely that both explanations have some validity. It should not be forgotten that during this period the Socialist Party suffered serious internal conflicts because of the strategy of economic policy supported by members of the government.

From a long-term perspective, the general orientation of its economic policy was a response to two objectives: one with an ambiguous definition and difficult to measure and the other deeply rooted in the classic European social democratic tradition. The former was related to the idea of modernization, that is, of social and economic adaptation to the changes which arose as a result of the structural crisis that Western countries had been suffering since the late 1960s. The latter was the construction and consolidation of the welfare state. In the Spanish case, this process involved not only a coherent set of forms of public intervention but also a growth in social public expenditures with the declared purpose of achieving a more egalitarian distribution of income.

Throughout the period of Socialist government, these objectives underwent several phases depending on the constituency's support or rejection, the changes in the international economic situation, and the contradictions existing among such objectives. Our purpose is not to make a deep analysis of those phases or to make a personal and subjective interpretation of the general outcomes of those 14 years of Socialist administration. Instead, we shall examine various elements of the debate showing which, in our opinion, were the outstanding features of those years.

THEORETICAL FRAMEWORK

During the early years of Socialist government, economic policy was constrained by both economic and political elements. We must bear in mind that the Socialist Party came to office during the 'political transition', when the democratic system was not fully consolidated, and there was a severe economic crisis: during the period from 1979 to 1982, real GDP grew at the following rates: 0.04 per cent (1979), 1.3 per cent (1980), –0.2 per cent (1981) and 1.6 per cent (1982). Furthermore, the changes that were taking place in the economic, social and political structures inherited from the Franco era, involved a radical change in the instruments of public intervention. On the one hand, as we shall see later, the basis for implementing demand-side policies was consolidated only in the mid-1980s (after the tax reform in 1981, the changes in the financing of public budget deficits and, finally, the changes in the banking system that took place after the deep crisis of the late 1970s). On the other hand, the possibility of implementing proactive supply-side policies (for example, industrial policy) had to wait until the late 1980s: until then all industrial policy decisions had a defensive nature focusing on the restructuring and reconversion, started in 1981, of those manufacturing industries affected by the economic crisis.

Consequently, the use of incomes policy as the main instrument of economic policy from 1977 until 1986 can be explained by the problems of adopting other supply- or demand-side policies. Voluntary wage moderation was used to reduce the inflation rate (at least that part of inflation explained by a wage-costs push) and the unemployment rate (wage moderation should increase corporate profits and, subsequently, private investments and, finally, employment). As we shall see below, although incomes policy had positive effects on inflation its outcome in terms of unemployment was poor.

In fact, from the early years the labour market reforms were the cornerstone of the Socialist economic policy. The French experience in 1981–82 led the Spanish Socialist government to refuse to implement an expansionary economic policy based on loose monetary and/or fiscal policy. Getting the right rate of wage growth became the key instrument to correct both internal (inflation and unemployment) and external (trade deficit) disequilibria.

Despite the importance given to wage moderation in this first stage, this did not mean that for the Socialist government the labour market, or even wage growth, were the main reasons for the economic crisis and the problems of inflation and unemployment. In fact, there was a consensus about the origin of the structural problems suffered by the Spanish economy: the combination of the economic crisis suffered by all Western economies and the inaccurate forecast for the productive structure of the Spanish manufacturing sector. None the less, it was argued that an appropriate wage growth (that is, below productivity growth) could help to reduce those disequilibria, could make the implementation of loose (or, at least, less tight) demand-side policies easier, and, in some cases, could reduce the negative effects generated by a necessarily tight monetary policy. However, incomes policy was abandoned in 1986, when the trade unions (mainly the Unión General de Trabajadores (UGT) (General Union of Workers), a union historically linked to the Socialist Party) and the government itself valued their involvement in incomes policy as a net cost in political terms.

Monetary policy and labour market reforms increased their importance after 1986, when incomes policies ceased. This policy mix of tight monetary policy and institutional reforms in the labour market was justified by the assumed existence in the Spanish economy of a vertical Phillips curve: excessive wage growth led to an increase in the inflation rate, which should be curbed with a tight monetary policy if wages did not fall. In this reasoning, the high rates of unemployment and the high non-accelerating inflation rate of unemployment (NAIRU) were explained not by the wage growth but by a set of institutional elements of the labour market which led to excessive wage increases and which, consequently, halted the creation of employment and the fall in the unemployment rates, exerting an upward pressure on the inflation rate. Therefore, the only way to accelerate the creation of employment (without raising the inflation rate) was to increase the elasticity of the creation of employment relative to economic growth, which involved the reform of the labour market.

In this situation, there were two alternatives to reduce the inflation rate: to halt the wage growth or to implement a tight monetary policy. In both cases, the short-run Phillips curve would move downwards, reaching the price stability consistent with the current NAIRU, which would be determined by institutional elements. To reduce the unemployment rate permanently, that is, to move the vertical Phillips curve to the left, supply-side policies should be implemented. These policies should be focused on reforming those institutional elements of the labour market that led to higher employment rates of growth consistent with a halt in the wage growth and in the inflation rates.

This strategy of economic policy lasted until 1995, just one year before the defeat of the Socialist Party in the 1996 elections, when the Socialist government was beginning to accept its failure in the matters of inflation and employment. In fact, the main weakness of the economic strategy was the incorrect analysis of both the economic disequilibrium and the effectiveness of the measures of economic policy adopted. As we mentioned above, the high inflation and unemployment rates were thought to be explained by an excessive wage growth generated by an inaccurate labour market model. However, as we shall see later, wage growth plays only a minor part in both disequilibria. In fact, the main reason for inflation must be found in the lack of true competition in some areas, especially in the services sector, which allowed high mark-ups.

Furthermore, the implementation of the general strategy of economic policy was highly segmented. Every instrument was implemented bearing in mind only its direct and short-run effects. The potential indirect effects generated on other variables, or even their negative consequences on the effectiveness of other instruments of economic policy, were never considered. Thus, we can understand the contradictions generated by this economic policy strategy, for instance, the depressive effect of the 1994 labour market reform on household consumption; the adoption of a model of competitiveness that was extremely harmful from a long-run perspective because of the proliferation of fixed-term employment contracts; the negative impact of the high interest rate on the inflation rate; or the upward pull generated by the fall in real wages and the increase in temporary employment contracts on social protection expenditure and, subsequently, on the budget deficit.

THE GENERAL STRATEGY OF THE ECONOMIC POLICY OF THE SOCIALIST GOVERNMENTS: THE FIGHT AGAINST INFLATION

When the Socialist Party came to power, the political situation was the central concern not only of the entire population but also of all the social, economic and political agents. The collapse of the dictatorship in the second half of the 1970s heralded an intense cycle of political change that only came to an end when Spain became a member of the European Economic Community in 1986. Entry into the EEC signalled the ultimate international support to the political change that had started in 1975 with the death of the Dictator, General Francisco Franco. Furthermore, entry into the EEC helped to put an end to the putschist tendency existing in Spain (which had led to a failed *coup d'état* in February 1981). The Socialist administration ended such a political cycle, starting a phase of democratic consolidation in which economic problems ultimately became the dominant concern of the people.

The legacy inherited by the Socialist government was very complicated. Two crises emerged during the process of political transition. First, the general crisis that affected all Western economies. Whether the origin of such a crisis was in the increase of oil prices or, as we believe, in the contradictions themselves which arose from the growth model generalized after the Second World War, is not important here. Second, there was a crisis in the economic regulation model dominant during the Franco era, whose foremost characteristics were a high degree of public intervention and strong foreign protection. The Socialist governments faced the need to manage a deep economic crisis by designing and implementing new forms of intervention, which involved breaking down the prevailing inertia and privileges – a process that the most directly affected sectors and agents would find difficult to accept.

During the early years of the Socialist administration, and from a microeconomic perspective, the supply-side policy of the Socialist government focused on the reconversion of the manufacturing industries that had been most seriously damaged in the crisis. Those sectors, shipbuilding, iron and steel and so on, suffered from a number of problems: fall in demand, new foreign competitors, and an inaccurate forecast of the evolution of world demand made by the last Francoist governments. The political transition was an obstacle to the implementation of the measures needed to adapt those sectors to the new market conditions (in fact, the only measure adopted was the generalized nationalization of many firms and sectors), and the first measures promoting the reconversion of those sectors had to wait until 1981. Indeed, the first Reconversion Act was not enacted by the first Socialist government until 1983. Its main objective was to accommodate the productive capacity of those industries to the size of the demand, which led to the closure of many firms and the loss of thousands of jobs in the surviving firms. The manufacturing reconversion was at the core of industrial and regional policies, because those sectors in crisis were located in specific regions. Since the mid-1980s, when the reconversion was completed, active state intervention in the field of industrial policy has ceased. Subsequently, the modernization of productive organization has been left in the hands of private investors, both domestic and foreign (Recio and Roca 1998).

From a macroeconomic perspective, the control of the inflation rates was the main objective of the economic policy implemented by all the Socialist governments, starting during the first mandate. As Solchaga (1997), Minister of the Economy during that period, wrote some years later,

> [The fight against inflation] was the previous requirement to lay the foundations to reduce unemployment in Spain. The search for short cuts was in vain. To trust the old strategy of expansionary policies was dangerous. The point was the cost of disinflation. During the whole time I was leading the coordination of the economic policy of the Spanish government, I was under the opinion that such a cost would be smaller if the halt to inflation was reached through wage moderation than if it were obtained by a restrictive monetary policy, which I had wanted to avoid at any price. (p. 201)

The Role of Incomes Policy (1977–1986)

During the first ten years of democracy, incomes policy was the pillar of the economic policy both for the centrist governments of the Unión del Centro Democrático (UCD) and for the first Socialist government. The political consensus among all the social and political agents to consolidate the political transition moved to the economic arena, leading to the implementation of a voluntary incomes policy. The main objective was to provide a brake to the inflationary process and to increase the profit margins through voluntary wage moderation. Five social pacts were signed during this period: the *Pactos de la Moncloa* (Pacts of Moncloa) (signed in 1977 and with validity for 1978), the *Acuerdo Marco Interconfederal* (Interconfederative Frame Agreement) (signed in 1980 and with validity for 1980 and 1981), the *Acuerdo Nacional de Empleo* (National Employment Agreement) (signed in 1981 and with validity for 1982), the *Acuerdo Interconfederal* (Interconfederative Agreement) (signed in 1983 and with validity for 1983), and the *Acuerdo Económico y Social* (Economic and Social Agreement) (signed in 1984 and with validity for 1985 and 1986).[1]

Incomes policy was an effective tool to reduce inflation rates. The inflation rate fell from 24.5 per cent in 1977 to 8.6 per cent in 1986 thanks to a fall of 9 per cent in real wages (Comisiones Obreras 1989). Despite the fall in the inflation rate, which can be seen in Figure 5.1, incomes policy replaced the

Source: Instituto Nacional de Estadística (INE), www.ine.es.

Figure 5.1 Unemployment and inflation rates (%)

labour market reforms in the fight against inflation and unemployment for two reasons. First, there were economic considerations, such as the poor outcomes in the matter of unemployment; instrumental considerations, arising from the fact that incomes policy could not affect the non-wage costs directly (for example, firing costs, social security contributions and so on); and political considerations, arising from the difficulty in maintaining a consensus between social agents and the government on wage moderation, mainly when the fiscal policy adopted a restrictive position that curtailed the growth of social expenditures, the chief means of offsetting wage moderation (Ferreiro and Gómez 1995). However, the main reason for the change was the theoretical assumptions according to which the macroeconomic disequilibria (unemployment and inflation) were due to a set of institutional features in the labour market that generated an excessive rigidity in that market. According to those assumptions, inflation and unemployment rates could only fall through a greater flexibility in the labour market. In order to reach this flexibility, the social democratic labour market that allowed the implementation of incomes policy should be reformed (Recio and Roca 1998).

As we argued above, incomes policy halted the inflationary process. This effectiveness can be explained because, to a large extent, during this period the origin of the inflation can be found in wage growth. Either because of the need to legitimate the new democratic regime or because of a wage reaction of wage earners after the end of the dictatorship, until 1977 the growth in inflation rates (from 8.3 per cent in 1971 to 24.5 per cent in 1977) had been accompanied by a strong growth in real wages: from 1971 until 1976, the accumulated growth in real average earnings was 63.2 per cent (Argandoña and García-Durán 1985). Since then, as can be seen in Figure 5.2, where the data related to the evolution of the rate of inflation and the wage growth approved in collective bargaining agreements are shown, in the ten years of validity of incomes policy the wage growth was below the actual rate of inflation, helping to control the inflationary process.

The New Strategy of the Macroeconomic Policy: The Significance of Monetary Policy

Although implementation of the anti-inflationary monetary policy began in the late 1970s, its effectiveness was limited, largely because of the finance mechanisms of the government budget deficit that had been generated since 1975. The growth in public expenditure generated since 1975, which concentrated on social expenditure, led to an increase in the budget deficit which grew from 0.5 per cent of GDP in 1975 to 6.4 per cent GDP in 1982 and 6.9 per cent GDP in 1985. Until 1980, the main mechanism for financing the budget deficit was the credit from the Banco de España. From 1980 until

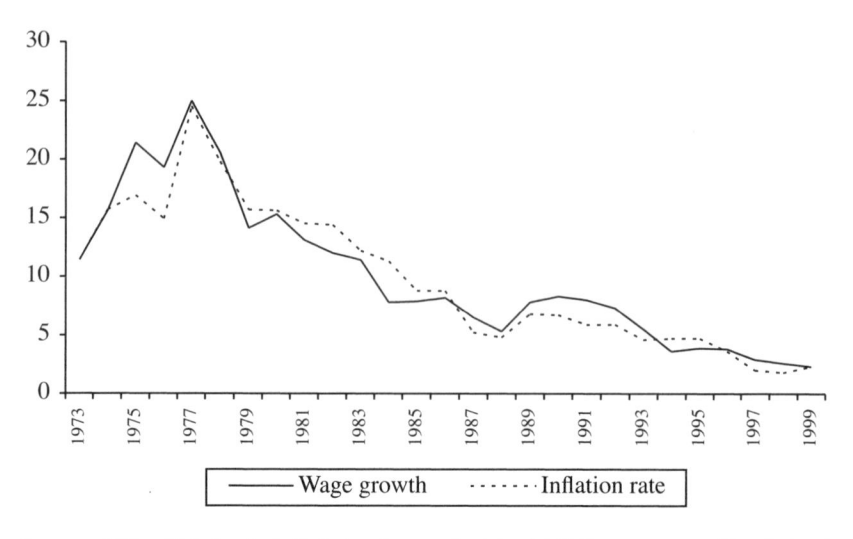

Source: INE and Ministerio de Trabajo y Asuntos Sociales (MTAS), www.mtas.es/Estadisticas/ BE.

Figure 5.2   Wage growth approved in collective bargaining agreements and rate of inflation (%)

1990, the financing of the budget deficit was complemented with a mechanism of privileged finance: very low interest rates for public debt issues was guaranteed because banking institutions had to observe high minimum investment ratios (Hernández 1996). Only after 1985, when the orthodox mechanism to finance the budget deficit (issuing public debt securities in market conditions) was implemented, did monetary policy become the main instrument in the fight against inflation. In sum, until 1985 the impact of the monetary policy in the control of inflation was small due to three reasons: first, because of the importance given to incomes policy; second because monetary policy had until then focused only on the sterilization of the monetary effects of the public deficit; and third because of the limitations generated by the working of excessive intervention in the financial system (Marín and Peñalosa 1997). Until 1985, the financing of the budget deficit via legal investment ratios, in addition to the high bank reserves ratios, prevented the Banco de España from adopting monetary measures via short-term interventions such as, for instance, interbank loans or open market interventions using public debt issues in the hands of commercial banks. We must bear in mind that in 1985 nearly 50 per cent of total assets in the banking system were affected because of the different legal investment ratios (Marín and Peñalosa 1997).

Since 1987, after the changes in the mechanism to finance the budget deficit and the measures adopted to liberalize the financial system and the foreign capital inflows, and coinciding with a phase of strong economic growth, monetary policy focused upon fighting inflation, as can be confirmed when the evolution of real interest rates is analysed. After several years of decline, which led to those rates reaching 2.9 per cent in 1986, real interest rates began to increase, peaking during the economic recession of the early 1990s. Since 1987, Spain has had the highest real interest rates in Europe; in fact, only the United Kingdom had higher rates than Spain, for a couple of years during the late 1980s. Between 1987 and 1993 the average real interest rate in Spain was 9 per cent. For the government, this tight monetary policy was explained by the combination of three elements (Solchaga 1997): first, an excessive wage growth that pushed the inflation rates upwards; second, a budget policy that had generated an upward pressure both on domestic demand and on monetary aggregates; and finally, the inward flows of capital that offset the credit restraints induced by the restrictive monetary policy.

The high real interest rates caused the Spanish currency to appreciate strongly, which, jointly with the pressure on domestic demand, led to a deficit of 6.9 per cent of GDP in 1992 in the current balance account. From 1985 until the first devaluation in 1992, the real effective exchange rate of the Spanish peseta, in relation to the currencies of the developed countries, appreciated by around 30 per cent. The change in the economic cycle that began in 1992, in addition to the subsequent devaluations and the wider fluctuation bands within the European Monetary System, allowed the relaxation of monetary policy and the subsequent fall of the real interest rate.

The tight monetary policy created a vicious circle that seriously damaged the fight against unemployment. In 1977, the rate of unemployment was 5.7 per cent. In 1985, it increased up to 21.6 per cent, fell to 16 per cent at the peak of the boom of the late 1980s, and rose again reaching 24.1 per cent in 1994. However, the relation between disinflation and unemployment is alone not enough to explain the high rates of unemployment in Spain. It is true that the high interest rates and the appreciation of the Spanish peseta could have contributed to the slowdown in the rates of economic growth (which, in any case, were really high during the second half of the 1980s, as we shall see later) but the increase in unemployment registered during the first years of the 1980s was mainly due to the severe adjustment in the productive capacity of the economy. Actually, the increase in unemployment rates in the first half of the 1980s took place simultaneously with a significant fall in real interest rates, which were 2.9 per cent in 1986 (when the rate of unemployment reached 21 per cent). During the boom of the late 1980s, however, the rate of unemployment fell while monetary policy tightened. The entry into the labour market of a new population, mainly female, made it impossible for the economic growth in the second half of the 1980s to generate a more intense fall in the unemployment rates.[2]

However, we are not the only ones to make these points. On the contrary, we shall focus on the economic policy options available to the PSOE to shed light on the gaps existing, in our opinion, between its statements and practice. As Minister Solchaga stated above, the strategy of the Socialist government was to control the inflation rate and allow private initiative to do the rest, that is, to increase private investment in order to create employment and thereby reduce unemployment.[3] Regarding the origin of inflation, successive Socialist governments always thought that it was to be found in the wage determination process, and therefore they insisted on presenting the restrictive monetary policy as the only alternative to wage moderation. The reform of the labour market, enacted in 1994, which will be analysed below, was the logical outcome of the Socialist governments' economic analysis.

In our opinion, however, the core of this economic policy strategy was flawed. The thesis held by the government was built on the assumption that the inflation process was the direct outcome of excessive wage growth, taken as given that business profits were not responsible for the inflationary process. It was assumed that the rate of profits remained stable and that it was not influenced by investment decisions, the existence of monopolies in some relevant branches of the economy or the consequence of the economic policy measures that had been implemented. If wage costs were held steady, the inflation rate could also be curbed and, therefore, monetary policy could be relaxed, competitiveness could be improved through the exchange rate, and demand (mainly, foreign demand) and employment could be increased. The working of such a strategy could involve either the re-implementation of an incomes policy[4] or the modification of the wage-setting processes through a new labour market reform (as occurred in 1994). The labour market reform had other advantages that the government did not ignore: limiting the political and social influence of the trade unions (which had increased after the success of the 1988 general strike) and contributing, even slightly, to increasing employment by removing some rigidities that were blamed by the employers as the main reason for the high rate of unemployment.

However, such debate failed to grasp the correct nature of the inflation problem suffered by the Spanish economy. Consequently, the effectiveness of the different strategies and economic policy measures that were implemented with the aim of reducing the inflation rates was limited. As can be seen in Figure 5.2, since the end of the incomes policy era, and coinciding with the beginning of the tightening of monetary policy, wage growth began to rise after 1987. It could be argued that the acceleration in the inflationary process was explained and fuelled by a wage push, in other words by a nominal wage growth above the increases in the expected rate of inflation and the growth of productivity; that is, the cause of the inflation was a presumed growth in the real unit labour costs. However, the evolution of sectorial prices was not directly related to the evolution of wage costs, especially in the case of the services sector. During these years, the Spanish economy suffered, and still currently suffers although with a lower intensity, a dual inflation which was not directly related to a presumed process of wage imitation and different sectorial productivities.[5] Let us analyse this point more deeply.

As can be seen in Figure 5.3, there was a wide gap between the evolution of prices in the services sector and those in the manufacturing sector during the years of restrictive monetary policy: namely, between 1987 and the beginning of the crisis in 1993. Since 1986, prices in the manufacturing sector have shown a clear downward trend, despite some temporary increases; also, the rate of growth of prices in the manufacturing sector was always below that in the services sector. Indeed, the turning point of the growth rate in the services sector prices did not take place until 1993, in the trough of the crisis of the early 1990s. During the previous years, the prices in the services sector grew above the general rate of inflation and, especially, well above the rate of growth of manufacturing prices. In fact, the trend of services sector prices changes only when there is a halt in the general rate of inflation in the late 1990s, although there are still, albeit less marked, differences in the evolution of prices in both sectors.

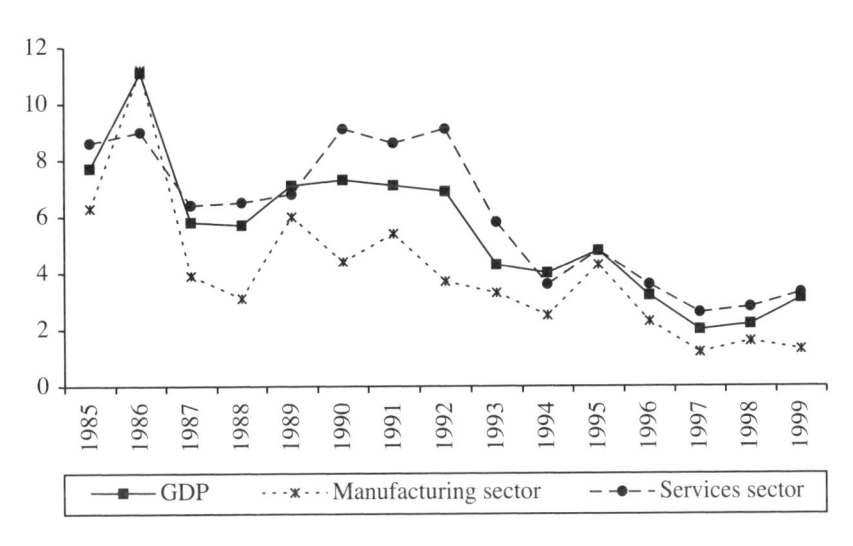

Source: INE.

Figure 5.3 Evolution of implicit deflators (%)

According to the 'orthodox' view held by the Socialist government, and shared by the Banco de España, the Spanish inflation could be explained by the Scandinavian model of inflation[6] (Calmfors 1990). That is, the high rates of inflation were a result of the different behaviour of sectorial prices, where the closed sectors (mainly, the services sector) pushed the general rate of inflation upwards. The higher increases in the services sector prices were due to a wage growth in the services sector based on imitation of the wage growth in the manufacturing sector, despite the fact that the latter enjoyed a higher productivity than the former. Consequently, in order to curb the inflationary process, a labour market reform should work as an effective instrument to eliminate the imitation effect and, therefore, to make wage growth keep pace with productivity growth.

When we analyse the data on collective bargaining, it is easy to reach a conclusion similar to that mentioned above. The wage increases passed on by the collective bargaining agreements are similar in both sectors. None the less, when sectorial wage costs are analysed in depth and compared with the evolution of sectorial prices, we can raise objections to the logic of the dominant strategy. Figures 5.4 and 5.5 show the sectorial evolution of labour costs and prices in both the services and manufacturing sectors. Data about

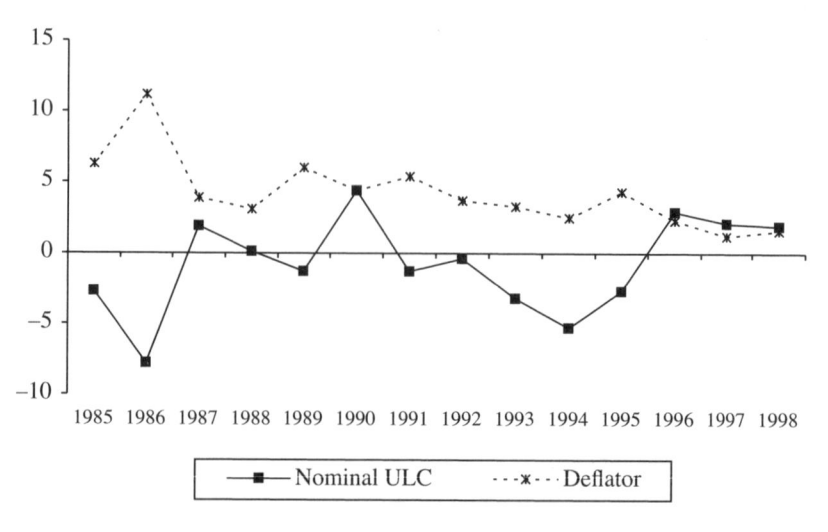

Source: Our calculations from INE and MTAS.

Figure 5.4 Rates of growth (%) of costs and prices in the manufacturing sector

Figure 5.5 Rates of growth (%) of costs and prices in the services sector

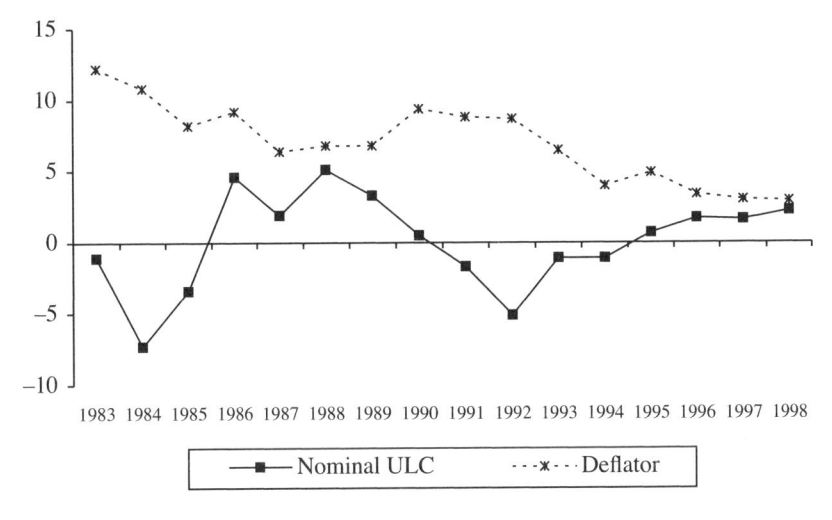

labour costs are calculated using the real total earnings per worker. The behaviour of the services sector shows a wide gap between the series of prices and labour costs. The nominal unit labour costs (ULC) grew at positive rates from 1986 to 1990, but since 1990 they show negative rates of growth. If the thesis held by the government were true, the evolution of the services sector prices should be according to the evolution of such costs. However, during the period of restrictive monetary policy (1987–93), the accumulated growth of nominal labour costs was 2.58 per cent, whereas the accumulated growth of the services sector deflator was 67.2 per cent. Therefore, the wage growth would have been responsible for only 3.8 per cent of the price growth registered in the services sector. On the contrary, in the manufacturing sector, the gap between both series is narrower. The nominal unit labour costs in the manufacturing sector show positive rates of growth in 1987, 1988 and 1990, years of strong economic growth and, therefore, strong demand for employment. From 1987 to 1993, the manufacturing nominal unit labour costs grew 0.01 per cent in accumulated terms, while the manufacturing sector deflator grew 33.84 per cent. There was no clear correlation between the evolution of prices and wage costs in the manufacturing sector, although the gap between such variables is narrower than in the services sector.

The data shown in Figures 5.4 and 5.5 demonstrate that wage growth has little bearing on price evolution. This fact makes it necessary to search for an explanation to the two following questions:[7] what causes price growth and why is such an increase higher in the services than in the manufacturing sector?

Regarding the first question, we should highlight certain points for the analysis. The first one is related to the problems of blaming the inflationary strains in the Spanish economy on the increase in the price of imported goods. During this period, the peseta appreciated as a result of the restrictive monetary policy, which should have helped to restrain the price increases. In fact, the appreciation of the peseta was used as part of the general anti-inflationary strategy of the economic policy. In our opinion, the reason is to be found in the consequences generated by the monetary policy itself on the business profit margin.

During the years of tight monetary policy (1985–90) there was a strong growth of private investment: the average annual rate of real growth of investment was 12.2 per cent.[8] The estimated profitability of those investments had to take into account the cost of borrowing in addition to future profit expectations. The cost of borrowing in the case of the Spanish companies was very high due to an excessive dependence on external finance. Despite the lack of significant statistical data about the evolution of business profitability during those years, there are indirect data that allow us to speculate on the significance of this fact (Banco de España, various years). During the years of rising investment, the profitability of the net assets of those companies for which there is available information was higher than the real rates of interest. When the rates of profitability fell, the rates of investment growth slowed down and eventually became negative. High rates of profitability could be maintained because of low labour costs so that prices could be contained within the limits imposed by increasing competition, mainly in the case of the manufacturing sector. However, any small increase in the labour costs exerted an upward pressure either on the rates of profitability or on prices, since the increase in costs could not be passed on to prices; business profits were squeezed and investment halted. Therefore, a less restrictive monetary policy could have allowed lower rates of profitability and, subsequently, for the same labour costs, a slowdown in the rate of inflation.

The differences registered in the evolution of sectorial prices are due to the monopolistic positions existing in the services sector. In order to study this point in depth, we must analyse the structural reforms adopted (and also those which were not) by the Socialist governments, whose declared objective was to modernize productive organization.

During Franco's dictatorship, the model of productive organization was characterized by strong public intervention and a high level of protection against foreign competition. The degree of protection was gradually reduced after the arrival of democracy in 1977. It was commonly accepted that the entry of Spain into the EEC, besides being a widely accepted objective for political reasons, could act as a powerful instrument to adapt and modernize the obsolete productive organizations. According to this logic, the competition that would arise from entry into the EEC would have a salutary effect on the recently modernized Spanish companies. The increased competition would force firms to learn to survive in a new environment where rules were dictated by a market defined by the existence of a large number of competitors. Initially, such an external way of adaptation should have been complemented by the needed reforms to remove the inherited ties to the old regime. The degree of foreign opening of the Spanish economy during the Socialist administrations was very high. When Spain joined the EEC in January 1986, the sum of exports and imports was 37.6 per cent of GDP; in 1996, it was 48.6 per cent and in real terms (in terms of 1986 prices) the degree of opening was even higher: 63.6 per cent of national production. This helped to accelerate the process of adaptation mainly in the manufacturing industry, whose foreign opening had already begun in the early 1970s. However, in the services sector the effects were much smaller due to, among other reasons, the difficulty of opening it to foreign competition.

Among the criticisms usually made of the Socialist governments, one is often mentioned: not enough attention was paid to some of the structural transformations that economic integration in the world markets was generating in the Spanish economy. The first criticism is focused on the lack of an industrial policy that could have helped to alleviate the costs (that is, unemployment) generated by the fierce competition arising from foreign opening. None the less, this criticism must be attenuated when we take two circumstances into account: first, the restrictions imposed by entry into the EEC on the implementation of an autonomous industrial policy and; second, the fact that the responsibility for industrial policy had been transferred from the central government to the regional governments during the first years of the Socialist administration. In any case, for the Socialist governments, the industrial policy was identified with the maintenance of an 'institutional and macroeconomic environment competitive enough to benefit all companies' (Espina 1995, p. 45).

A change in industrial policy was initiated during Felipe González's last government. However, the guidelines (of a microeconomic nature) of the industrial policy designed in the *Libro Blanco de la Industria* (Industry White Paper) (Ministerio de Industria y Energía 1995), had no real consequences due to the change of administration that took place in 1996 when the Partido Popular of José María Aznar won the election.

The smaller foreign competition in the services sector, which allowed a larger market fragmentation, involved a more acute need for reform. However, the Socialist government interventions in this sector were much less pronounced, leading to a slower adaptation of the sector and to the maintenance of monopolistic situations that, despite a policy of imposing a price ceiling in some areas, delayed the processes of innovation needed to increase the sector's productivity. The outcome was that the services sector acted as a bottleneck that restrained the growth and development of the manufacturing sector because of their ineffective services and their high prices (Cuadrado and Del Río 1993). This situation lasted until the mid-1990s when some industries, telecommunications and air transport for instance, opened to domestic and foreign competition. The liberalization in the financial sector, although intense in some specific activities, kept consumers captive in some segments of business of vital importance to the public, for instance, in the mortgage market (in 1995 the legislation was modified, allowing customers to make a low-cost transfer to other financial firms). In the energy sector, there are still entry barriers of an administrative nature, with negative consequences for energy prices, despite the existence of a policy of price ceilings which limits the influence of the oligopoly that dominates the sector. In the liberalization and opening to foreign competition, the privatization of the public-owned companies played a key role.

THE ROLE OF LABOUR MARKET REFORMS[9]

The process of modernization of the productive organization of the Spanish economy generated a strong increase in the unemployment rates as a consequence of the severe cutback in jobs. It was clear that the enormous increase in the unemployment figures was not related to the working *per se* of the labour market. The existence of an inefficient productive organization (an obsolete productive organization concentrated in low demand and low technological intensity sectors), the fall in domestic and foreign demand and, finally, the massive entry into the active population of youngsters and women, were the main reasons for the increase in the rates of unemployment. However, the lack of an active supply-side policy, mainly of an industrial policy, and the lack of an expansionary demand-side policy,[10] led the government to consider the adoption of measures to increase the flexibility of labour turnover as an effective tool to reduce the high rate of unemployment. As we saw above, those measures did not redress the causes of unemployment, but at least they could help to alleviate the problem of mass unemployment. This reasoning led to the first labour market reform which was introduced in 1984.

Ten years later, due to reasons related to the labour market model arising from the 1984 labour market reforms and to the induced consequences generated by the economic policy strategy as explained above, it was thought necessary to introduce a new labour market reform. This second labour market reform, which was adopted in 1994, had a different objective – to reduce the rate of inflation, which had increased since the early 1990s.

Only a few years after this second reform, both social agents and government became aware of the negative consequences generated by the labour market. The negative micro- and macroeconomic effects of both reforms led to a third labour market reform, adopted by the Partido Popular in 1997, whose purpose was to reintroduce the principle of causation that had been paramount in the labour law in the early 1980s. Its aim was to remove the constraints that excessive labour segmentation placed on economic growth, to reduce unemployment rates, and to change the dominant pattern of competitiveness in Spanish companies.

The First Labour Market Reform

The first labour market reform was introduced in 1984, only four years after the enactment of the *Estatuto de los Trabajadores* (Workers' Statute), which had been the basic labour relations law since 1980. In the matter of hiring workers, the *Estatuto* was based on the causation principle, according to which, permanent labour contracts had to be used for permanent jobs while fixed-term labour contracts could be used only for those temporary jobs linked to the needs of productive organizations or to temporary increases in demand. This principle was violated in the reform of 1984, which allowed the use of fixed term employment contracts (with a legal duration limited to three years, both in the case of a single employment contract and in the case of a renewal of a temporary employment contract) for permanent jobs. Thus, the 1984 reforms changed the entry procedure for new workers into the companies: workers could initially be hired under a fixed-term contract, which would subsequently be transformed into a permanent one.

The objective of this first labour market reform was to increase the flexibility in labour turnover. Since 1977 most of the measures implemented to increase the flexibility in the labour market focused on wage evolution. However, after experiencing five different income policies, it was thought that wage moderation alone was not enough to reduce the high rates of unemployment, which reached 21.3 per cent in 1984. The employers' associations argued that the main reason for the poor creation of employment was the excessive rigidity of the Spanish labour market, both in the hiring and firing of workers. The employers claimed that free dismissal was the most effective tool to create employment. The Socialist government sanctioned the generalized use of fixed-term employment contracts as an alternative to free dismissal. This alternative was accepted several months later by the employers' associations Confederación Española de Organizaciones Empresariales (CEOE) (Spanish Confederation of Business Organizations) and Confederación

Española de Pequeñas y Medianas Empresas (CEPYME) (Spanish Confederation of Small and Medium Enterprises) and the Socialist UGT. In fact, those organizations included the acceptance of the generalized use of temporary employment contracts in the last incomes policy pact: the *Acuerdo Económico y Social* (Flórez 1994). Initially, the labour market reform was a complementary tool to incomes policy. The *Acuerdo Económico y Social*, signed in October, included the signatories' acceptance of the labour reform introduced by the government in August. Although the wage moderation adopted in the pact was focused on the objectives of reducing the inflation rate (from 12.2 per cent in 1983 to the target of 6 per cent in 1986) and expanding domestic demand, for the Socialist government the control of the inflationary process and the budget deficit was a necessary but not a sufficient condition to foster the creation of employment – hence the need to implement structural reforms also in the labour market (Ministerio de Trabajo y Seguridad Social 1985).

The ultimate objective of the reform, to increase the elasticity in the labour demand, was actually achieved, as shown in Figure 5.6. After the 1984 reform, employment and GDP evolved as highly correlated variables. Employment, at least salaried employment, lost its role as economic stabilizer. As we shall see later, although this change could be positive during the boom of the late 1990s, it showed its negative face during the crisis of the early 1990s. The elasticity of salaried employment relative to real GDP increased

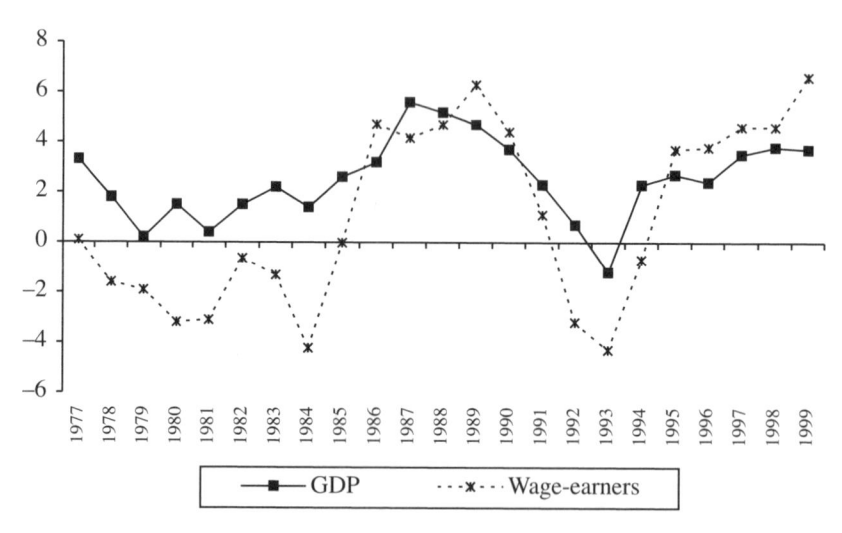

Source: INE.

Figure 5.6 Evolution of real GDP and wage earners' rates of growth (%)

Economic policy in Spain during the 1980s and 1990s 135

from −1.2 in 1974–84 up to 0.6 in 1985–91, due to the creation of 2 063 640 salaried jobs in the latter period (+28.2 per cent) that offset the loss of 1 283 260 salaried jobs from 1976 to 1985 (−15 per cent). The strong creation of salaried employment allowed a reduction in the rate of unemployment from 21.6 per cent in 1985 to 16.2 per cent in 1990.

The creation of employment, however, was not homogeneously distributed. In the private sector, it was concentrated only on temporary employment. From 1987 to 1994, in the private sector 1 239 500 new temporary jobs were created, whereas 913 300 permanent jobs were lost. The result was an enormous increase in the rate of temporary employment, as Figure 5.7 shows, due to the termination of permanent employment (which lasted until 1995) and the high rate of growth of temporary workers: in 1995 more than 40 per cent of the salaried workers in the private sector 'enjoyed' a fixed-term employment contract.

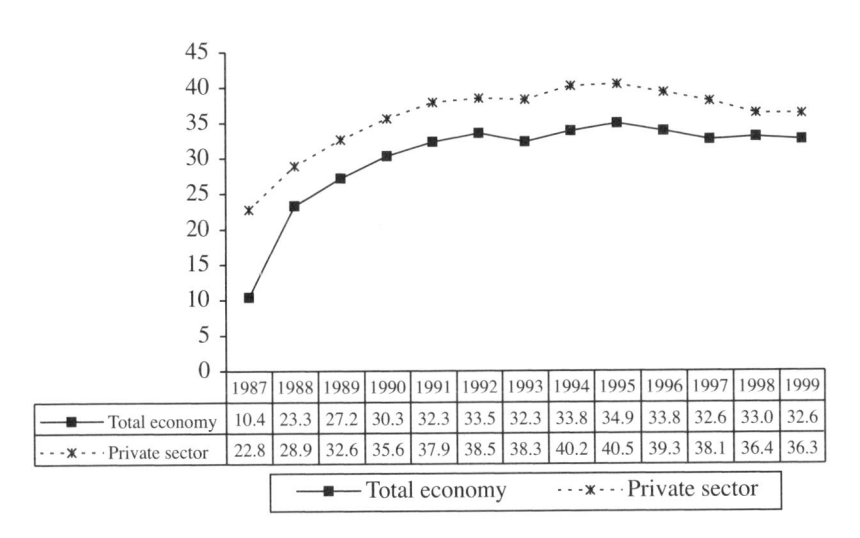

	1987	1988	1989	1990	1991	1992	1993	1994	1995	1996	1997	1998	1999
Total economy	10.4	23.3	27.2	30.3	32.3	33.5	32.3	33.8	34.9	33.8	32.6	33.0	32.6
Private sector	22.8	28.9	32.6	35.6	37.9	38.5	38.3	40.2	40.5	39.3	38.1	36.4	36.3

Source: INE.

Figure 5.7 Employment rates of temporary workers (%)

The evolution of fixed-term employment contracts was totally unexpected for the Socialist government and the UGT, who initially supported them, and even for the employers' organizations. According to the initial plans of the Socialist government, the fixed-term employment contracts should have worked as a complementary tool to a consensual wage moderation. Wage moderation (that is, real wage growth below the growth of productivity) should have been the main tool to moderate the inflation rates (offsetting the negative effects generated by a restrictive monetary policy) and to promote the creation of employment. On the other hand, the fixed-term employment contracts would correct those institutional restrictions (for example, firing costs) that curbed the creation of new employment. This low creation of employment was explained by the employers' fear of engaging in new contracts that would be very costly to renegotiate in the case of a future recession.

However, in reality, the expansion of fixed-term contracts worked as a substitute for an incomes policy. The reason must be found in the impact on wage evolution generated by the temporary employment contracts, due to the lower wages of temporary workers. Information on wage distribution is available only from official surveys made by the Instituto Nacional de Estadística for the years 1988, 1992 and 1995 (INE 1992, 1995, 1997). These surveys clearly show the earnings gap between temporary and permanent wage earners: in 1988 the average total earnings (including wages fixed in collective bargaining agreements and wage drifts) of a temporary worker were only 57.7 per cent of a permanent one, 59.4 per cent in 1992 and 44.8 per cent in 1995. This earnings gap helps to explain how and why, in a context defined by high rates of growth of real GDP and an intense creation of employment, permanent employment was subjected to severe cutbacks. Many permanent workers were replaced by temporary ones, not only because of the cheaper firing costs of the latter (with the sole exception of one category of fixed-term employment contracts, which involved a compensation payment of 12 days' salary per year worked, the fixed-term contracts had no compensation provision when the contract ended) but, mainly, because of the lower wages of the temporary workers.

The above explanation helps us to understand how the replacement of permanent workers by temporary ones led to cost reductions. None the less, it does not explain the need for companies to reduce labour costs, as stated above. In our opinion, the growth in the number of temporary workers was, to a large extent, the logical answer of the employers to a strategy of economic policy which was harmful for productive activity (mainly in the case of the manufacturing sector) and which, because of the high real interest rates, promoted financial and speculative activity.

On the one hand, the manufacturing companies were constrained by a policy of high interest rates that raised the cost of bank credit and, therefore, the financial cost of productive investments. This price constraint in the access to external borrowing led those companies to finance their investments through undistributed profits. On the other hand, the high prices in some branches of the services sector involved a transfer of resources from open sectors (mainly, manufacturing ones) to the sheltered ones (basically, services sectors). If we consider the limits that foreign competition imposed on price increases, the only way for the open sectors to, first, increase their profits and, second, offset such a transfer of resources was by reducing their labour costs, that is, by increasing their share of temporary workers.

Despite the positive effect exerted by the 1984 reform on the creation of employment, the excessive use of fixed-term employment contracts generated a set of latent problems that surfaced during the recession of the early 1990s. First, the high elasticity in labour demand involved not only a more intense creation of employment during the expansions but also a more severe process of termination of employment during the slumps. In fact, during the 1991–94 recession, 630 200 permanent jobs and 139 600 temporary jobs were lost.

The second problem was related to the effects of labour segmentation on the evolution of wages. Although the extension of temporary employment helped to moderate wage growth during the late 1980s, this effect was exhausted by the early 1990s. From 1990 until 1993, real earnings in the private sector grew 7.7 percentage points, which affected, although it did not explain fully, the acceleration in inflation rates. From 1988 to 1992, the earnings of both temporary and permanent wage earners grew in real terms at similar rates: 24.3 per cent for permanent workers and 28.9 per cent for temporary ones. It could be assumed that this growth was the normal result of economic expansion. However, we must bear in mind that during that period, temporary employment grew by 951 000 new jobs while permanent employment decreased by 535 900 jobs. The insider–outsider theory can help to explain such wage behaviour (Lindbeck and Snower 1988; Lindbeck 1993): bargaining power was concentrated in permanent workers (insiders), who could set high wage increases regardless of the general economic situation and the size of the insider worker group. Only under such assumptions can the evolution of wages during the recession of the early 1980s be understood. Again, according to the available data (as above), from 1992 to 1995, average earnings in the private sector increased by one point. None the less, while real earnings for temporary workers decreased by 25.2 per cent, real earnings for permanent workers increased by 2.9 per cent.

In 1991 and 1992, the Socialist government, facing the problem of the acceleration of inflation rates and the loss of foreign competitiveness, offered the trade unions two new incomes policy pacts, which were both rejected. These pacts were based on a proposal of positive real wage growth below the growth of productivity. The main difference between them was that the pact proposed in 1992 (the *Programa de Convergencia*) insisted on the need to reform the labour market, in line with the 1984 reform, not only to promote the creation of employment but also to slow down the inflation rate. In this sense, the *Programa de Convergencia* opted for developing the set of measures designed in the 1984 reform, for promoting functional and geographical mobility, for promoting the substitution of the *Ordenanzas Laborales* (legal norms that regulated labour relations within firms) for rules arising from collective bargaining, and for restricting the conditions of access to unemployment compensations in addition to their reduction.

The Second Labour Market Reform

The unions' rejection of the incomes policy led the government to introduce the second labour market reform in 1994, a reform that was directly opposed by the trade unions. Unlike the 1984 reform, the objective of the 1994 reform was not to foster the creation of employment but to reduce the inflation rate through wage growth moderation. Whereas the 1984 reform was based on the assumption that the unemployment was due to an excessive rigidity in the labour market, the 1994 reform was based on the assumption that the Spanish inflation was due to excessive wage growth explained by the institutional framework of wage setting, which favoured wage growth above productivity growth.

The excessive wage growth was explained by two factors. First, the inordinate bargaining power of insiders meant that insiders could set their wages regardless of the actual economic situation not only of the whole economy or the labour market but also of the situation of their own companies. Behind such bargaining power there was a legal system of labour relations that explicitly favoured those workers and prevented companies from adopting measures to reduce their power (and, consequently, to stop their wage claims) and to increase productivity (which, if the wages were constant, would reduce unit labour costs and increase profits). Second, a generalized imitation effect led to similar wage growth in the collective bargaining agreements regardless of the economic situation or the levels and growth of productivity of the firms involved. Behind this imitation effect would be an intermediate structure of collective bargaining whose content was limited in most cases to setting the wage growth.

The 1994 reform included measures to increase labour productivity through a more flexible use by companies of the yearly working hours. Among these measures was the possibility of an irregular distribution throughout the year of annual working hours. Before the 1994 reform, collective bargaining could decide the annual working hours, but there was a legal ceiling to the daily working hours (9 hours) and to the weekly working hours (40 hours). The 1994 reform removed those legal daily and weekly limits. Since then, firms can concentrate the annual working hours set in the collective bargaining agreements during the weeks or months that coincide with the peaks of production and demand, and, conversely, they can concentrate and distribute the days off during the rest of the year. Another measure was related to the professional categories and the functional mobility of workers. Until 1994, issues such as working hours, job content, geographical and/or functional mobility and so on, were regulated by legal norms inherited from the Franco era. The employers criticized these *Ordenanzas del Trabajo* (In-House Labour Rules) as one of the most significant sources of rigidity in the Spanish labour market. The fixed-term employment contracts had been used as a mechanism to generate some flexibility in the workforce, adapting them to changes in demand and the productive needs of companies by hiring and firing temporary workers. The 1994 reform provided a more flexible definition of jobs, which would arise from collective bargaining, promoting the internal mobility of workers among different jobs within the firm. Finally, the reform promoted the geographical mobility of workers as a consequence of productive, technological or economic changes in the companies.

Other measures focused on the wage-setting process. First, the reform tried to give more importance to the variable part of salaries, in order to link earnings to the economic circumstances of the companies or the individual characteristics of workers. Since the 1994 reform, the variable part of earnings has to be agreed in collective bargaining, and, therefore, agreed by employers and workers/unions. However, the approval of such rates of pay does not involve consolidation for future years and, consequently, they must be renegotiated in the following collective bargaining agreements. The aim of this reform was to remove the imitation effect in the wage-setting processes, individualizing wage evolution by adapting it to the specific conditions of every agent involved (firms and workers).

Second, in order to eliminate the imitation effect, the 1994 reform promoted a decentralized collective bargaining. Thus the economic situation of individual companies would settle the wage growth, relating wage to productivity growth. If this were the case, the 'right' wage growth would help to reduce inflation and the unemployment rates (Jimeno 1992; Blanchard and Jimeno 1994; Milner and Metcalf 1995). Since the last incomes policy pact, signed in 1984, the degree of coordination and decentralization in Spanish collective bargaining had been reduced (Revenga 1994). The dominant structure of collective bargaining was an intermediate one, formed by provincial- and interprovincial-industry collective bargaining agreements, where wage increases were well above those passed at the firm- or national-industry levels. The 1994 reform promoted firm-level collective bargaining agreements. With this aim, the reform adopted two measures. First, the so-called 'let-down clause'. Until 1994, according to the *Estatuto de los Trabajadores*, the lower-level collective bargaining agreements (firm level, for instance) could not impose worse conditions than those in the higher-level ones (for example, industry level). The 'let-down clause' allowed firms to abrogate those collective bargaining agreements that permitted wage increases in excess of what a company could afford, that is, when those wage increases could endanger the economic situation of the firm. Second, the reform

Table 5.1 Real rate of growth of monthly average earnings (%)

	1989	1990	1991	1992	1993	1994	1995	1996	1997	1998	1999
Total economy	−1.1	1.8	1.9	1.6	1.8	0.0	−0.2	0.9	1.4	0.5	0.0
Manufacturing	−2.1	1.8	2.9	2.1	1.9	0.0	0.2	1.9	2.6	1.8	−0.3
Services	2.5	1.9	0.8	1.1	1.5	−0.6	−0.9	−0.3	0.8	−0.2	−0.2

Source: Our calculations from INE.

Economic policy in Spain during the 1980s and 1990s 141

removed the 'ultra-activity of the expired collective bargaining agreement', that is, it prevented the consolidation of the benefits gained by workers in every collective bargaining agreement, so that every agreement (basically, labour and wage conditions) should reflect the current economic situation of the companies and, obviously, the workers' (trade unions') and employers' bargaining power.

As Table 5.1 shows, since 1994 wage growth moderation has been clear, affecting every economic sector although especially the services sector, where average earnings have decreased since 1994 by 1.4 per cent in real terms. This wage moderation has taken place in a context characterized by high rates of economic growth (an average rate of growth of 3.2 per cent of real GDP in 1995–99 and an average rate of growth of salaried employment in that period of 4.6 per cent), which should have involved positive real growth in earnings for wage earners.

The 1994 reform, among several other elements, had a positive consequence on inflation, shown in Figure 5.8. Since 1994, the current phase of economic expansion has been accompanied by a stable low rate of inflation, despite the increase registered since 1999.

In spite of the effects on the inflation rate, the segmentation of the labour market also generated a set of negative consequences, as a result of excessive temporary employment, that led three years later, in 1997, to the third labour market reform whose objective was to correct these negative consequences.

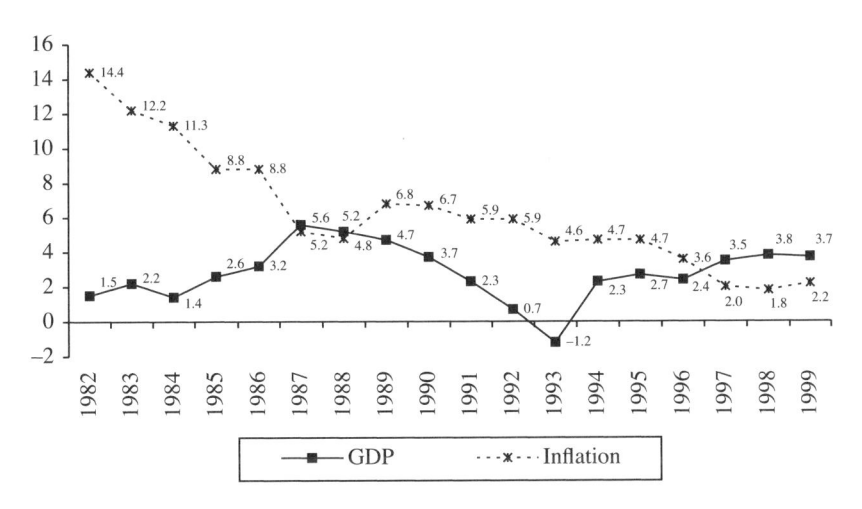

Source: INE.

Figure 5.8 Inflation and real GDP rates of growth (%)

As Figure 5.7 showed, the employment rate of temporary workers reached 40.5 per cent in the private sector and 34.9 per cent in the whole economy. The segmentation between temporary and permanent workers is even greater when two new elements are taken into account. The first one is the extension of part-time employment. The 1994 reform promoted the use of part-time employment contracts as a tool to increase the flexibility in the labour market, which, in turn, was expected to involve higher productivity through better management of the workforce. The result was that in 1999, 18.8 per cent (2 412 283) of the total new employment contracts signed were part-time ones and 7.9 per cent of wage earners were part-timers, with temporary workers comprising 57.1 per cent of this group. We must consider the fact that, according to the official surveys, in 1999 the average hourly earnings of a part-timer was only 56.1 per cent of that of a full-time worker. Furthermore, until 1998, when an agreement between the government and the unions UGT and Comisiones Obreras (CC.OO) was signed, the social protection to which part-timers were entitled was less than that of full-time workers.

The second element increasing the segmentation in the labour market is the high labour turnover, which is the result of the reduction in the length of the fixed-term employment contracts. According to the employment contracts statistics from the Instituto Nacional de Empleo (National Employment Institute, www.inem.es), 12 017 000 new fixed-term contracts were signed in 1999. Taking into account that in 1999 there were 3 554 850 temporary wage earners, a simple calculation shows that on average, temporary workers stayed in their job for 3.5 months. This conclusion agrees with the data relative to the length of those fixed-term contracts: in 1999, 45.72 per cent of the new temporary contracts were for less than three months, 39.95 per cent had an indeterminate length, and only 0.19 (24 100 contracts) were for more than one year.

The extension of temporary contracts meant that most Spanish companies adopted a pattern of competitiveness based on low costs and salaries, achieved by the intensive use of temporary workers, as several empirical studies have shown (Banco de España 1998; Serrano et al. 1998). The growth of fixed-term contracts had negative effects on labour productivity and, therefore, on labour competitiveness and also on the possibility of companies adopting a model of value-added competitiveness. This model requires a high percentage of highly skilled and permanent workers, where the key elements for competitiveness are not low wages but innovation, knowledge, research and development (R&D), productivity and so on. Opting for a pattern of competitiveness based on low wages reinforces the need to use temporary workers in order to maintain the required level of competitiveness, as demonstrated by the fact that most competitive Spanish companies, those that increase their market share, keep their permanent employment levels almost constant, while clearly increasing their temporary employment levels.

None the less, the most evident macroeconomic consequence of the 1994 labour market reform was the change generated in the pattern of private consumption and saving. This change was the outcome of excessive use of temporary workers, low wages for temporary and part-time workers and a regressive distribution of income, which will be analysed in the following section. At the very onset of the economic upswing, several official studies noted that the economic growth was not accompanied by the expected acceleration in private consumption (Consejo Económico y Social 1995, 1996; Dirección General de Previsión y Coyuntura 1995; Secretaría General Técnica 1995). This slowdown in private consumption constrained the growth in aggregate demand and in the creation of employment.

Figure 5.9 shows the evolution of household consumption and saving. From 1993 to 1997 the real rate of growth of household consumption fell below that of real GDP. This trend has changed since 1998, but in that year the differential between both series was very narrow: the real rate of growth of GDP was 4 per cent in 1998 and 3.7 per cent in 1999, but the real rate of growth of household consumption was 4.1 per cent in 1998 and 4.5 per cent in 1999. More interestingly, since 1993 the rate of household gross saving (measured by the household gross saving as a percentage of the household disposable gross income) was higher than that registered during the boom of the late 1980s. During the 1985–91 period, the average rate of household saving was 10.7 per cent whereas in 1994–98 this rate was 13 per cent. In

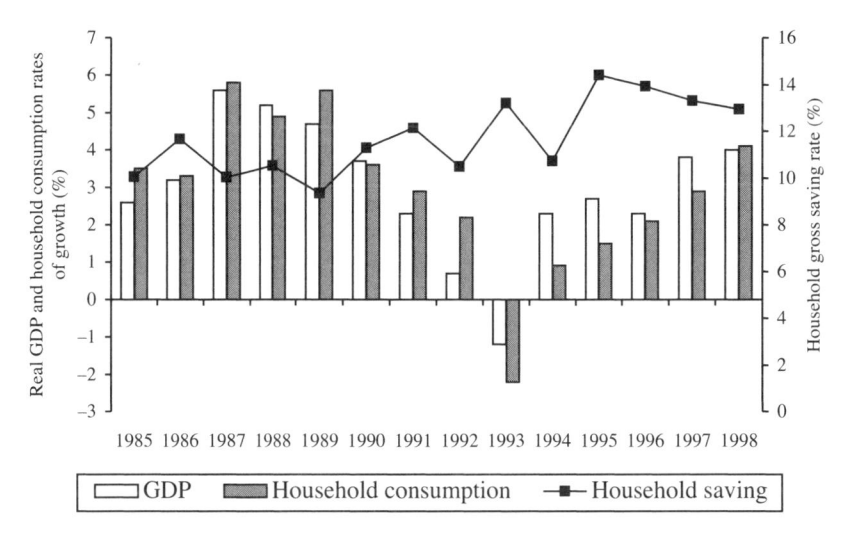

Source: Our calculations from Banco de España, www.bde.es.

Figure 5.9 Evolution of household consumption and saving

addition, the small fall in the rate of saving in the latter period is surprising, barely 1.4 percentage points: from 1986 to 1989 the rate of household gross saving fell 2.3 percentage points. This evolution of consumption and saving could be explained by an increase in precautionary saving, generated as a consequence of the increasing uncertainty that wage earners suffered as a result of a highly segmented labour market.

The Third Labour Market Reform

With the aim of correcting the undesired effects of the previous labour market reforms, the Partido Popular government agreed the third labour reform with employers' associations and the unions UGT and CC.OO. It was accepted that the excessive use of fixed-term employment contracts had generated both macroeconomic and microeconomic problems. Therefore, the promotion of permanent employment was considered to be a needed strategy in order, first, to reduce the uncertainty suffered by wage earners, and, consequently, to accelerate private consumption and economic growth; and, second, to promote the change to a different pattern of competitiveness in Spanish firms.

In order to reduce the rates of temporary employment, a new permanent employment contract with a lower severance pay was created.[11] The severance pay for these new permanent contracts was 33 days' salary per year worked to a maximum of 24 monthly salaries. Severance pay in the case of null and unfair dismissal was smaller than that applied in previous permanent contracts: 45 days' salary per year worked to a maximum of 42 monthly salaries. Furthermore, the 1997 reform tried to clarify the reasons that define an individual or wholesale dismissal (which has lower severance pay) as a fair dismissal. In 1980 the *Estatuto de los Trabajadores* defined a dismissal as 'fair' when there were economic and technological reasons that justified it. In the 1994 reform, those reasons included organizational and productive ones: when the dismissal could help to solve a negative situation within the company or when it could guarantee the future viability of the company and the level of employment with a better organization of (human) resources. However, such a definition of 'fair' dismissals included a large degree of discretion. The outcome was that generally the Labour courts decided on the nature of the dismissals, in most cases determining them as unfair ones. Thus, the 1997 reform clarified the reasons that defined a dismissal as fair, transferring the control and monitoring of the fair dismissals to collective bargaining (Consejo Económico y Social 1998). On the other hand, the 1997 reform deepened the process (begun in 1994) of reducing public intervention in labour relations, substituting law norms for rules arising from collective bargaining. Since then, some points such as employment contracts, hours of work, wage structure, professional categories and so on, must be defined in the collective bargaining agreements.

To conclude, and under the assumption that the collective bargaining structure was harmful to the objective of linking wage evolution to increases in productivity, the 1997 reform tried to rationalize such a structure by reducing the excessive atomism in collective bargaining, defining the contents of each level of bargaining, and allowing the modernization of the content of the collective bargaining agreements.

WELFARE STATE AND INCOME DISTRIBUTION

European social democracy has always been closely related to the development and consolidation of the welfare state, perhaps the most important feature of the European strategy of management of capitalism. The Spanish Socialist Party has always participated in that tradition, so we shall examine what achievements the Socialist governments have made in this field. Next we shall make a twofold, and complementary, analysis: first, we shall analyse the constraints operating on the development of the welfare state in Spain; and second, we shall focus on the effects generated by the welfare state on income redistribution. In relation to the last point, we should note that there are problems arising from the lack of relevant statistical data.

The fiscal policy of the Socialist governments was constrained by the problem of the budget deficit and the link between the needs of budget deficit finance and the restrictive monetary policy. Figure 5.10 shows the evolution of public administration expenditure from the early 1980s until 1996, showing also the evolution of the interest payments on public debt. Throughout this period, once the interest payments on the public debt have been excluded, public expenditure showed a slight upward trend. Most of this growth was concentrated in the first half of the 1980s. From 1980 until 1985, the weight of public expenditure in relation to GDP increased by 8 percentage points. During the second half of the 1980s, there was a downward trend and later, during the decade of the 1990s, the trend was upward again, due to, among other reasons, not only the crisis of the early 1980s but also the unions' claims after the 1988 general strike (Recio and Roca 1998).

Considerations about the optimal size of the public sector aside, the evolution of social expenditure was constrained by the problem, faced by all the Socialist governments, of the government budget deficit. After several years of growth, in 1982 the deficit reached 5.6 per cent of GDP. None the less, as noted above, the privileged finance of the budget deficit transferred the problem to inflation and the management of monetary policy. The compulsory purchase of public debt issues by the banking system and the finance of the budget deficit by the credits from the Bank of Spain (Banco de España) generated monetary and financial strains because of the increase in the price

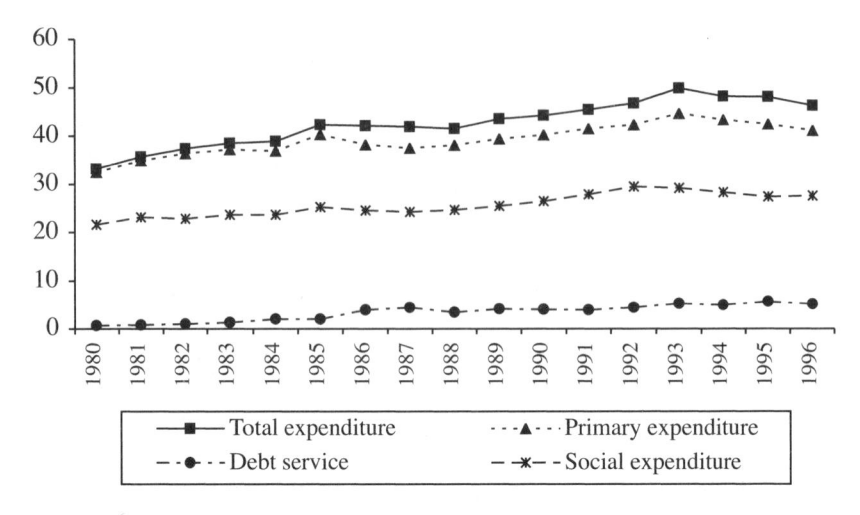

[Figure: line chart showing Total expenditure, Primary expenditure, Debt service, and Social expenditure as % of GDP from 1980 to 1996]

Source: Our calculations from Banco de España.

Figure 5.10 Evolution of public administration expenditure (% GDP)

of the banking credit (due to the privileged finance of the budget deficit) and the upward pressure exerted on the banking credit and the money supply because of the finance from the Bank of Spain. The high budget deficits constrained the effectiveness of the monetary policy. On the one hand, the latter had to sterilize the liquidity created by the credits from the Bank of Spain. On the other, the implementation of a tight monetary policy was constrained because of the high interest rates that private agents had to pay for the bank credits and loans as a consequence of the privileged finance of budget deficits. Therefore, because inflation was the main target of economic policy, the objectives of the fiscal policy became, first, the change to an orthodox budget deficit finance in order to help monetary policy to reduce inflation rates, and, second, to reduce the budget deficit by increasing the tax pressure and curbing the growth rates of public expenditure.

Since 1985 the orthodox finance of the budget deficit has gained significance, and therefore the interest rates of public debt issues jumped, which increased the debt burden. Figure 5.10 showed that since 1985 a gap opened between primary and overall public expenditure. Between 1986 and 1996, the average debt service was 4.4 per cent of GDP, a figure similar to public education expenditure and more than twice that of unemployment compensation (during a period when rates of unemployment oscillated between 16 and 24 per cent). Debt service acted as a brake on the growth of social expenditure, which was increased, first, by the lack of more intense measures against

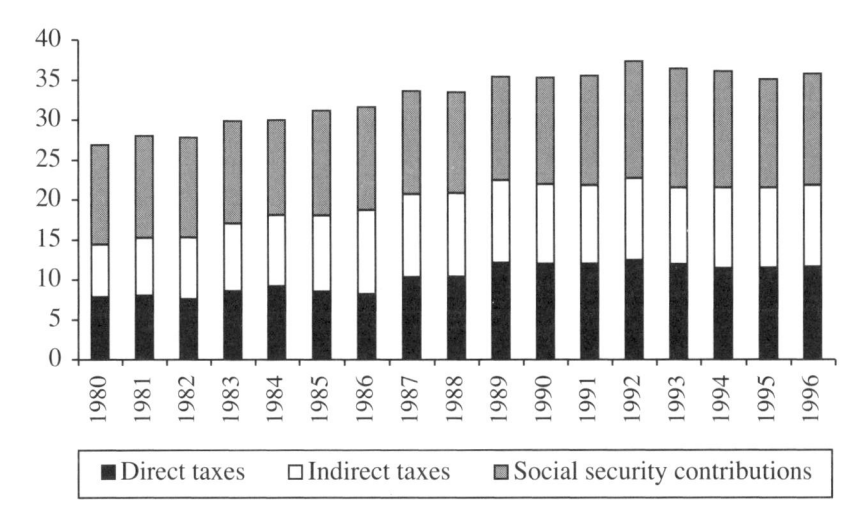

```
  40
  35
  30
  25
  20
  15
  10
   5
   0
```
1980 1981 1982 1983 1984 1985 1986 1987 1988 1989 1990 1991 1992 1993 1994 1995 1996

■ Direct taxes   □ Indirect taxes   ▨ Social security contributions

Source: Our calculations from Banco de España.

Figure 5.11   Evolution of fiscal pressure (% GDP)

tax evasion, then by the fiscal requirements of the Maastricht Treaty and later by the Growth and Stability Pact.

Figure 5.11 shows the evolution and structure of fiscal revenues in Spain since the early 1980s. In 1982, fiscal pressure was 28 per cent of GDP. In 1996, the year of the last Socialist government, this ratio was 35.8 per cent of GDP, a figure below the highest one reached in 1992 (37.3 per cent of GDP). The growth in fiscal pressure was concentrated on direct taxes, whose share in GDP increased by 5 points, and on indirect taxes, whose weight increased by 3 points after the implementation of value-added tax (VAT) in 1986. Social security contributions increased their share in GDP by only 1 point during this period. On the other hand, the Socialist fiscal policy did try to promote the progressive nature of direct taxation, even though the high fiscal evasion weakened the real progressiveness of direct taxes and, therefore, the intended redistribution of income by the tax system.

The financial problems generated by debt service, in addition to a political option not to increase fiscal pressure and a clear incapability to reduce fiscal evasion, reduced the capacity of subsequent governments to develop the welfare state. As seen in Figure 5.10, social expenditure shows a stable tendency. In 1982, overall social spending reached 22.8 per cent of GDP. In 1996 this share had risen to 27.5 per cent of GDP, peaking at 29 per cent during the recession of the early 1990s. Despite the small size in relation to all the social needs that required attention, by itself the growth in social expenditure does not fully explain the task faced by the Socialist governments and their efforts undertaken in the field of social welfare.

During the Franco era, a form of welfare state had been developed. This model, with a clear legitimating logic, reached its limit during the years of the political transition when the economic crisis started.[12] From 1977 until the first Socialist government in 1982, total social expenditure grew at a high rate, but without a plan or, what it is most important, a reference to its permanence in the future. It is in the last two areas that the task of the Socialist governments appears to have been more positive. Their plans for the welfare state involved a set of reforms, some completed during their term of office and others during the first year of the Partido Popular administration, whose objective was to lay a new basis for the welfare state.

The public pension scheme was at the core of those measures. Committed to its maintenance during the years of fierce conservative criticism to the pay-as-you-go (PAYG) systems, the Socialist governments undertook a first reform in 1984 and a subsequent one in 1996, whose objective was to rationalize the rate of growth of the expenditure by tightening the links between, first, the time, and second, the amount of contributions and the entitlement and amount of benefits. Both reforms also aimed to rationalize the claims for an intergenerational redistribution on which the PAYG systems are based. On the other hand, both reforms went hand in hand with active policies to increase the minimum benefits, to add pension supplements to the lowest pensions, and to maintain the purchasing power of all pensions. In fact, 54 per cent of the growth registered in the public spending on pensions from 1982 (6.7 per cent of GDP) to 1996 (9.1 per cent of GDP), was due to the increase in pensions, according to the evolution of the consumer price index.

The evolution of expenditure in unemployment compensation was related to the evolution of the unemployment figures. None the less, this insurance coverage is brought about by the entitlement to unemployment compensation. The Spanish system of unemployment benefits has never had universal coverage. The entitlement to benefits has always been limited to those salaried workers who have worked for a minimum period. Under these legislative constraints, the Socialist governments made an effort to increase the coverage rate of unemployment benefits, although this declined in the last years of the Socialist administration. In 1982, the share of unemployed workers who received unemployment benefits was 33.6 per cent: this rate increased up to a peak of 76 per cent in 1993. There were three reasons for this evolution: first, the maintenance of and slight increase in the expenditure in this budget item, which was always above 2.5 per cent of GDP; second, the fall in the rates of unemployment during the late 1980s; and third, as a consequence of the extension of fixed-term employment contracts, the increase in the number of unemployed workers entitled to unemployment benefits. However, during their final years in office, the last Socialist government reformed unemployment insurance by hardening the requirements for getting those benefits.[13] The outcome of this reform, introduced in 1992, was a fall in the coverage rate to 58 per cent in 1998.[14]

The social expenditure on health and education also grew at a very high rate during the 13 years of the Socialist administration: from 7.3 per cent of GDP in 1982 to 10.4 per cent of GDP in 1996. This increase was the outcome, first, of the extension of those benefits to the whole population by making their coverage universal, and, second, of an increase in per capita expenditure. When the Socialists left office, the public health system had universal coverage, the real per capita expenditure in health had doubled since 1982, and the public education system covered all levels, from primary to university education.

Finally, we shall analyse the distributive consequences of the Spanish welfare state. We have mentioned above the problems caused by the lack of statistical information and the problems relating to the methodology of existing studies. Nevertheless, any analysis about the redistributive consequences of the welfare state must focus on both expenditure and revenue.

However, before starting this analysis, we must note the negative consequences of the labour market reforms on the personal distribution of income. The previous section discussed the earnings gap among permanent salaried workers, temporary salaried workers and part-timers. This gap had increased considerably from 1988 to 1995. Unfortunately, more recent data about such a gap are not available. However, data do exist about the earnings gap between full- and part-time workers, showing that it is currently widening. If we take into account this data and the fact of the small real earnings growth, seen in Table 5.1, we can pose the hypothesis of a rising inequality in the income distribution, not only between capital and wage earners, but also within the salaried population itself, where temporary and part-time workers would have been at a disadvantage.

In this case, a good proxy for the analysis of the income distribution in Spain is supplied by the personal income tax statistics compiled by the Instituto de Estudios Fiscales (Tax Studies Institute)[15] (which is affiliated to the Ministry of Economics and Finance). In 1996, of a total of 12 068 827 salaried workers, 3 793 592 of them (31.4 per cent) earned less than the yearly minimum wage, receiving only 5.6 per cent of total salaries.

When we analyse the redistributive effect of the welfare state on household income (measured by the income distribution among deciles), we see that the taxation system (the sum of direct taxes, indirect taxes and social security contributions) has a neutral redistributive effect. Direct taxation has a progressive effect in terms of income redistribution, social security contributions have a neutral, if not a small regressive impact, and indirect

Table 5.2 Distribution of salaried workers according to their labour revenues (%)

	1992		1993		1994		1995		1996	
	<AMW	>5AMW	<AMW	>5AMW	<AMW	>5AMW	<AMW	>5AMW	<AMW	>5AMW
Total salaried employment	27.2	8.3	27.4	8.8	28.7	8.3	29.3	8.2	31.4	8.1
Total wage revenues	5.0	27.0	4.5	28.5	5.1	27.2	5.1	27.3	5.6	27.8

Note: AMW: annual minimum wage.

Source: Our calculations from Instituto de Estudios Fiscales, www.ief.es/estadistica/estabasetribu.htm#salarios.

taxes have a regressive impact. The sum of all these effects generates a neutral effect of the taxation system on income redistribution. On the contrary, social expenditure does have a clear redistributive impact, although that impact is not the same for all the expenditure items. Cash benefits (public pensions and unemployment benefits) have a higher redistributive effect than benefits in kind (health, education and housing), with expenditure in education and health having the smaller redistributive impact. Thus with regard to revenue and expenditure, the welfare state as consolidated by the Socialist Party, does have net redistributive consequences (Calonge and Manresa 1997[16]).

During its first term (1996–2000), the Partido Popular government has not adopted any measures to reduce social expenditure. However, it has introduced some measures in relation to taxation that can erode, in the medium and long terms, not only the redistributive capacity of the welfare state but also the maintenance at the current levels of the main items of social expenditure.

In aggregate terms, and focusing only on central government (social security excluded), the share of direct taxes has fallen from 46.7 per cent of total revenues (9.4 per cent of GDP) in 1996 to the 42.9 per cent of total revenues (8.3 per cent of GDP) forecast for 2000. This fall has been concentrated on personal income tax, which has decreased from 36.3 per cent of total revenues to 27.3 per cent (from 7.3 to 5.3 per cent of GDP). Indirect taxes, mainly VAT, have worked during this period as an offsetting mechanism of the smaller relative revenues from the direct taxes. However, such offset has been only partial, and since 1996 to 2000 the share of total revenues has fallen from 20 to 19.4 per cent[17] (García and Martín 1999).

This financing of the Spanish welfare state, based mainly on revenues from VAT and social security contributions, faces the problem that welfare state financial sufficiency depends on the evolution of economic activity, because the taxes which have increased their share in public expenditure finance (business tax, VAT and social security contributions) are those that are more sensitive to the business cycle – hence, the problem that can arise in the case of a change in the business cycle. Public revenues can fall if such a change takes place, which can lead to adjustments in public expenditure, and cuts in social expenditure, a likelihood increased as a result of the added budget constraint arising from the Stability and Growth Pact.

This change in the taxation system has clear redistributive effects. As we stated previously, all the redistributive effects from taxation are concentrated in personal income tax. Therefore, the regressive nature of indirect taxes and social security contributions, in addition to their higher share of total revenues registered during the first Partido Popular government, may involve the loss of the neutrality of the taxation system, making this system a regressive one.

Furthermore, the conservative government introduced a regressive reform in personal income tax in 1998. This reform included, among other measures, the reduction of the maximum marginal income tax rate from 56 to 48 per cent, the reduction of the minimum marginal income tax rate from 20 to 18 per cent, and the setting of a single tax rate of 20 per cent for the surpluses generated in the investment funds (García and Martín 1998; Consejo Económico y Social 1999). As a result of that reform, it is estimated that the government did not collect 670 000 million pesetas in 1999 and 2000. Of that amount, 20 per cent would have come from the 1 per cent of taxpayers. The outcome of the reform has been a fall in the redistributive capacity of personal income tax (García and Martín 1999). In sum, as a consequence of the above changes, since 1996, during the term of the Partido Popular, the redistributive capacity of the Spanish welfare state has diminished.

Since the mid-1980s, the welfare state has played the role of an offsetting mechanism of the negative effects generated by the labour market reforms on income distribution. Largely because of social expenditure, that is, thanks to the current welfare state model (with the current kind and level of benefits), low-income households have been able to balance their diminishing earnings from temporary and part-time employment contracts. If the Partido Popular government during its second term had insisted on the taxation reforms explained above, the only way to avoid and reduce the current inequality on income distribution is via a new labour market reform. This new labour market reform, promoting permanent employment contracts, should lead to an increase in the earnings of temporary and part-time salaried workers and, therefore, to a more egalitarian income distribution, at least within the collective of salaried workers.

CONCLUSION

The general strategy of economic policy followed by the Socialist governments has been conditioned by a mistaken diagnosis of the core objective of Spanish economic policy (inflation) and by the implementation, first, of a tight monetary policy joined to a hard currency policy, and, second, of a set of institutional reforms focused on the labour market to solve a structural problem. However, the inflation must be explained by the existence of a degree of monopoly and small domestic and foreign competition in some branches (mainly, within the services sector), which, in addition to a restrictive monetary policy, generated high inflation rates.

The extreme flexibility generated by the two labour market reforms introduced by the Socialist governments generated a set of induced problems on the demand, supply and distribution sides, which led to the adoption of offsetting measures. In this sense, the problems generated by wage earners' uncertainty and consumption, and the perverse competitiveness model adopted by most Spanish companies, in both cases as a result of the excessive segmentation existing in the labour market, led the Conservative government to introduce, with the agreement of the trade unions and employers' organizations, the third labour market reform in 1997. The objectives of this reform were to generate certainty in the workers (and, consequently, to increase private consumption) and to facilitate the change to a value-added competitiveness model.

On the other hand, the current labour market model led to the necessary consolidation and maintenance of the current welfare state, which explains the commitment of both the past Socialist governments and the first Partido Popular government to maintain and secure in the long run the current levels of social expenditure. None the less, we should mention the shadows cast by the fiscal measures passed by the Partido Popular government. These measures could lead to a future fall in fiscal revenues, which would endanger the current welfare state model. In this case, the Spanish welfare state would lose its role as a cushion against the undesired consequences of the current labour market model.

NOTES

1. For a deeper analysis of the content of the social pacts, see De la Villa (1985), Zaragoza (1988) and Roca (1993).
2. Despite the creation of 1 964 000 new jobs between 1985 and 1991, the rate of unemployment fell only 4.8 percentage points, from 21.1 to 16.3 per cent. The reason is the increase in the active population, which grew to 1 286 000 workers (+9.3 per cent): 95.6 per cent of this increase was explained by the increase in the active female population.
3. We should mention the role played by foreign investment in the modernization of Spanish productive organization, mainly in the case of the manufacturing sector. Since 1986, and as a result of a proactive policy developed by the Socialist government to promote inward foreign direct investment (FDI), foreign investors became key actors in the process of modernizing the manufacturing sector through either the creation of new companies or the acquisition of local firms. In the 1990–95 period, Spain became the fourth OECD country to receive FDI inflows, behind the United States, the United Kingdom and France (OECD 1996), and in the year 1991 the FDI inflows amounted 3 per cent of GDP and 16.7 per cent of gross capital formation (Ferreiro et al. 1997b; Muñoz 1999). For a deeper analysis of inward FDI in Spain, see Ferreiro et al. (1997a, 1997b) and Muñoz (1999).
4. In fact, the Socialist government offered social agents two new social pacts in 1991 and 1992. Both pacts were rejected by the unions, who did not accept the government proposal of a real wage growth under the productivity growth in spite of the offsetting measures included in both pacts. None the less, while the 1991 proposal could have been advantageous for the unions, the 1992 proposal was clearly negative for them. In fact, this pact included the acceptance by the unions of the guidelines of the labour market reform introduced by the government two years later, in 1994, a reform which was rejected by the unions.
5. The dual nature of Spanish inflation and the role played by profit margins has only

recently been recognized by the economic authorities (Estrada and López-Salido 2001 and 2002; Banco de España 2003).
6. The Scandinavian model of inflation is based on the sectorial models of inflation, in which inflation is the outcome of: (i) the homogeneity in the wage growth in the manufacturing and services sectors, (ii) the differences in the respective productivity growths (higher in the manufacturing sector), and (iii) the opening of the manufacturing sector to foreign competition whereas the services sector is closed to such competition (Baumol 1967; Frisch 1983). Based on these models, and under the additional assumptions of fixed exchange rates, growth of domestic industrial prices similar to the foreign growth of those prices, and a model of price setting based on the existence of mark-ups (where the conditions of domestic and foreign competition determine the mark-up), for the Scandinavian model the source of inflation must be found in the services (closed) sector because of its lower productivity, the homogeneity in the sectorial wage growth and the higher mark-up. Therefore, the level of the inflation rates will depend on the relative weight of the services sector in the whole economy (Aukrust 1970; Edgren et al. 1973).
7. In the next section we shall show how the labour market reform, which facilitated external labour flexibility within the companies through the use of fixed-term employment contracts, helps to explain the slowdown in labour costs registered during this period.
8. The Spanish case is a good example of the endogenous nature of money. Despite the permanent adjustments in the money supply, and the consequent increase in the real interest rates, the heightened expectations expanded bank credit. Optimism about the strength of the economic growth led companies to maintain high levels of investment (in many cases devoted not only to the modernization of productive capacities but also to an enlargement of such capacities). These investments were mostly financed by resource to banking borrowing, despite the high real rates of interest. This behaviour was based on the high level of profits and on the expectation of the maintenance in the long run of the strong economic growth. The credit expansion led the Banco de España to adopt legal limits to the growth of bank credit, compelling the domestic agents that were borrowing in foreign capital markets (to avoid credit limits) to maintain a deposit in pesetas with no interest (a share of the amount borrowed) in the Banco de España (Ayuso and Escrivá 1997).
9. For a deeper analysis of the labour market reforms implemented in Spain, see Ferreiro and Serrano (2001).
10. There are several reasons that help to explain the lack of an expansionary demand policy. On the one hand, the need to reduce inflation removed the possibility of implementing a loose monetary policy; furthermore, the fear of an acceleration of inflation and the need to reduce the high public deficit removed the possibility of implementing an expansionary fiscal policy. On the other hand, and perhaps one of the key reasons, the Socialist government did not want to repeat the failure of the French Socialist government when it tried to implement an expansionary economic policy in 1981, ignoring the situation in the rest of the world (Solchaga 1997).
11. The reform established that the new permanent employment contract could be used for three years. During this period, the government and the social agents should analyse the outcome of the reform in terms of reducing the rate of temporary workers and deciding whether to retain the new employment contract. In 2001, the Partido Popular government decided, without the consensus of the trade unions, to extend the permanent contract arising from the 1997 reform, widening the groups of workers that could benefit from it. In addition, this new fourth labour market reform adopted other measures affecting, for instance, part-time employment and establishing compensation payments for some temporary contracts, once concluded.
12. The Francoist dictatorship lacked a true fiscal policy, which was created only during the democratic regime. This lack generated a fiscal crisis during the first years of democracy, due to the increase in public expenditure as a consequence of the economic crisis which could not be financed through an increase in public revenues. In addition, and most importantly, during the dictatorship the social policy, mainly the social security system, was used as a tool to finance economic development. Despite the low social security

contributions, the low individual pensions generated a permanent surplus in the social security system. This surplus was not consolidated, however, and therefore could not be earmarked to finance future higher expenditure; on the contrary it was used (and, therefore, exhausted) to finance public investment (Serrano 1989).
13. To be entitled to get an unemployment benefit, a wage earner must have paid contributions for at least 360 days (one year) during the previous six years, which would entitle him/her to receive benefits for four months. The maximum length of such benefits is for those wage earners who have paid contributions for at least 720 days (two years), entitling them to receive unemployment benefits for 2160 days (six years).
14. The reform in unemployment insurance was linked to the assumption according to which a generous unemployment benefit system discourages job seeking and, therefore, promotes the maintenance of high rates of unemployment. When the reform in unemployment insurance was passed, the economic growth rates slowed and, consequently, the unemployment rates increased to 24 per cent.
15. Information taken from their website: www.ief.es.
16. This analysis is made using data referring to the year 1991.
17. When social security is included, the share of direct taxes (social security contributions included) in relation to GDP falls from 9.4 to 8.2 per cent, social security contributions increase from 11.7 to 12 per cent, and indirect taxes increase from 7.7 to 8.7 per cent. In sum, fiscal pressure falls from 33.5 in 1996 to 32.4 per cent in 2000 (García and Martín 1999).

REFERENCES

Argandoña, A. and J.A. García-Durán (1985), *La Economía Española en Cifras* (The Spanish Economy in Figures), Barcelona: Ediciones Orbis.
Aukrust, O. (1970), 'Prim I: a model of the price and income distribution mechanism of an open economy', *Review of Income and Wealth*, **16** (1), March, 51–78.
Ayuso, J. and J.L. Escrivá (1997), 'La Evolución de la Estrategia de Control Monetario en España' (The evolution of the strategy of monetary control in Spain), in Servicio de Estudios del Banco de España, *La Política Monetaria y la Inflación en España* (Monetary Policy and Inflation in Spain), Madrid: Alianza Editorial, pp. 89–120.
Banco de España (2003), *Informe anual 2002* (Yearly Report 2002), Madrid: Banco de España.
Banco de España (various years), *Central de Balances del Banco de España* (Commercial Performance Information Bureau of the Bank of Spain), Madrid: Banco de España.
Baumol, W. (1967), 'Macroeconomics of unbalanced growth: the anatomy of urban economy', *American Economic Review*, **57**, June, 415–26.
Blanchard, O. and J.F. Jimeno (eds) (1994), *El Paro en España: Tiene Solución?* (The Unemployment in Spain: Does it have a Solution?), Madrid: CEPR.
Calmfors, L. (ed.) (1990), *Wage Formation and Macroeconomic Policy in the Nordic Countries*, Stockholm: SNS Förlag.
Calonge, S. and A. Manresa (1997), 'Consecuencias Redistributivas del Estado del Bienestar en España: un Análisis Empírico Desagregado' (Redistributive consequences of welfare state in Spain: A desegregated empirical analysis), *Moneda y Crédito*, **204**, 13–65.
Comisiones Obreras (1989), *De los Pactos de la Moncloa al AES* (From the Pacts of Moncloa to AES), Madrid: Comisiones Obreras.

Consejo Económico y Social (various years), *Report on the Socio-Economic and Labour Situation in Spain*, Madrid: Consejo Económico y Social.
Cuadrado, J.R. and C. Del Río (1993), *Los servicios en España* (The Services Sector in Spain), Madrid: Pirámide.
De la Villa, L.E. (1985), *Los Grandes Pactos Colectivos a partir de la Transición Democrática* (The Great Collective Pacts Since Democratic Transition), Madrid: Ministerio de Economía y Hacienda.
Dirección General de Previsión y Coyuntura (1995), *Informe de Coyuntura Económica* (Report of Economic Situation), October, Madrid: Secretaría General Técnica, Ministerio de Economía y Hacienda.
Edgren, G., K.O. Faren and C.L. Ohdner (1973), *Wage Formation and the Economy*, London: Allen & Unwin.
Espina, A. (1995), *Hacia una Estrategia Española de Competitividad* (To a Competitive Spanish Strategy), Madrid: Fundación Argentaria.
Estrada, A. and J.D. López-Salido (2001), 'La inflación dual en la economía española' (Dual inflation in Spain), *Boletín Económico del Banco de España*, May, 1–5.
Estrada, A. and J.D. López-Salido (2002), 'Understanding Spanish dual inflation', Documento de Trabajo, Banco de España, no. 0205.
Ferreiro, J., C. Gálvez and C. Rodríguez (1997a), *La Inversión Directa Extranjera en la Industria Vasca durante la Década de los Noventa* (Foreign Direct Investment in the Basque Manufacturing Sectors in the Decade of the 1990s), Bilbao: Círculo de Empresarios Vascos.
Ferreiro, J. and M.C. Gómez (1995), 'Sobre la Posibilidad Actual de un Acuerdo de Política de Rentas en España' (On the current possibility of an incomes policy pact in Spain), *Cuadernos Europeos de Deusto*, **12**, 31–50.
Ferreiro, J., C. Rodríguez and F. Serrano (1997b), 'The role of foreign direct investment in an old industrial region: the case of the Basque country and Japanese FDI', *European Planning Studies*, **5** (5), 637–57.
Ferreiro, J. and F. Serrano (2001), 'The Spanish labour market: reforms and consequences', *International Review of Applied Economics*, **15** (1), 31–53.
Flórez, I. (1994), *La Contratación Laboral como Medida de Política de Empleo en España* (Labour Contracts as a Measure of Employment Policy in Spain), Madrid: Consejo Económico y Social.
Frisch, H. (1983), *Theories of Inflation*, Cambridge: Cambridge University Press.
García, M.A. and C. Martín (1998), *Situación de la Economía Española y Presupuestos del Estado 1999* (Situation of the Spanish Economy and Public Budget 1999), Madrid: Confederación Sindical de CC.OO.
García, M.A. and C. Martín (1999), *Situación de la Economía Española y Presupuestos del Estado 2000* (Situation of the Spanish Economy and Public Budget 2000), Madrid: Confederación Sindical de CC.OO.
Hernández, G. (1996), 'La Deuda Pública en la Democracia' (Public debt in the democracy), *Papeles de Economía Española*, **68**, 214–26.
Instituto Nacional de Estadística (INE) (1992), *Distribución Salarial en España* (Wage Distribution in Spain), Madrid: Instituto Nacional de Estadística.
Instituto Nacional de Estadística (INE) (1995), *Encuesta sobre la Distribución Salarial en España 1992* (Survey on Wage Distribution in Spain), Madrid: Instituto Nacional de Estadística.
Instituto Nacional de Estadística (INE) (1997), *Encuesta de Estructura Salarial 1995* (Survey of Wage Structure 1995), Madrid: Instituto Nacional de Estadística.
Jimeno, J.F. (1992), 'Las Implicaciones Macroeconómicas de la Negociación Colectiva:

el Caso Español' (Macroeconomic consequences of collective bargaining. The Spanish case), *Moneda y Crédito*, **195**, 223–81.

Lindbeck, A. (1993), *Unemployment and Macroeconomics*, Cambridge: MIT Press.

Lindbeck, A. and D.J. Snower (1988), *The Insider–Outsider Theory of Employment and Unemployment*, Cambridge, MA: MIT Press.

Marín, J. and J. Peñalosa (1997), 'Implicaciones del Marco Institucional y de la política Presupuestaria para la Política Monetaria en España' (Implications of institutional frame and the fiscal policy for the Spanish monetary policy), in Servicio de Estudios del Banco de España, *La Política Monetaria y la Inflacíon en España*, Madrid: Alianza Editorial, pp. 181–221.

Milner, S. and D. Metcalf (1995), 'Relaciones Laborales y Resultados Económicos en España' (Labour relations and economic outcomes in Spain), *Moneda y Crédito*, **201**, 11–48.

Ministerio de Industria y Energía (1995), *Libro Blanco de la Industria. Una Política Industrial para España* (White Paper of Manufacturing Sector. An Industrial Policy for Spain), Madrid: Ministerio de Industria y Energía.

Ministerio de Trabajo y Seguridad Social (1985), *Acuerdo Económico y Social 1985–1986* (Economic and Social Agreement 1985–1986), Barcelona: Ministerio de Trabajo y Seguridad Social.

Muñoz, M. (1999), *La Inversión Directa Extranjera en España. Factores Determinantes* (Foreign Direct Investment in Spain. Determinant Factors), Madrid: Civitas.

Organisation for Economic Co-operation and Development (OECD) (1996), *International Direct Investment Statistics Yearbook 1996*, Paris: OECD.

Recio, A. and J. Roca (1998), 'The Spanish Socialists in power: thirteen years of economic policy', *Oxford Review of Economic Policy*, **14** (1), 139–58.

Revenga, A. (1994), 'Aspectos Microeconómicos del Mercado de Trabajo español' (Macroeconomic elements of the Spanish labour market), in Blanchard and Jimeno (eds), pp. 133–56.

Roca, J. (1993), *Pactos Sociales y Políticas de Rentas* (Social Pacts and Incomes Policies), Madrid: Ministerio de Trabajo y Seguridad Social.

Secretaría General Técnica (1995), 'Algunas Reflexiones en torno a la Recuperación del Consumo Privado en España' (Some reflections on the recovery of household consumption in Spain), *Boletín Económico de ICE*, **2454**, 3–6.

Serrano, F. (1989), 'Crisis Económica y Crisis de la Seguridad Social' (Economic crisis and the crisis of social security), *Información Comercial Española*, **665**, 70–81.

Serrano, F. et al. (1998), *La demanda de trabajo de la industria manufacturera vasca* (The Labour Demand of the Manufacturing Sector in the Basque Country), Vitoria-Gasteiz: Gobierno Vasco.

Solchaga, C. (1997), *El Final de la Edad Dorada* (The End of the Golden Age), Madrid: Taurus.

Zaragoza, A. (ed.) (1988), *Pactos Sociales, Sindicatos y Patronal en España* (Social Pacts, Unions and Employers Associations in Spain), Madrid: Siglo XXI de España.

6. The costs of neomonetarism: the Brazilian economy in the 1990s

Alfredo Saad-Filho and Lecio Morais*

INTRODUCTION

At the turn of the millennium, the Brazilian economy was the largest in Latin America, and one of the ten largest in the world. It was also one of the fastest growing economies in the second half of the twentieth century. Between 1949 and 1980, annual GDP growth in Brazil averaged 7.3 per cent (3.8 per cent per capita). This impressive performance deteriorated sharply after 1980, while inflation rates accelerated almost relentlessly, from under 20 per cent in 1972 to around 5000 per cent (annual rate) in mid-1994.

After several failed stabilization attempts, the 'Real Plan' successfully reduced annual inflation rates to less than 10 per cent. However, the elimination of high inflation did not lead to the resumption of rapid growth. In fact, in the 1990s the Brazilian economy had the worst economic performance on record. Whereas in 1981–89 (the so-called 'lost decade') Brazilian annual average GDP growth was 2.0 per cent, in the 1990s these rates were only 1.7 per cent (per capita growth rates were approximately zero in both decades, due to the rapid decline in the population growth rate).

In spite of the poor performance of most aggregate indicators, in the 1990s the Brazilian economy experienced more substantial changes than in any decade in the post-war period. The most important change was the abandonment of import-substituting industrialization (ISI). ISI, and the corresponding industrial structure, were replaced by another system of accumulation based on the microeconomic integration of Brazilian industry and finance within transnational capital.[1] The new accumulation strategy was inspired by the Washington Consensus and by similar experiences in Argentina, Mexico, South Korea and elsewhere. The strategic shift in the accumulation process, and the ensuing productive changes, has been imposed primarily through the shift of government policies towards neomonetarism. In contrast, ISI developed largely 'spontaneously', that is, initially in the absence of stimulating industrial policies (Silva 1976; Suzigan 1986; Suzigan and Villela 1997).

The viability of the neomonetarist policies implemented in the 1990s, and the corresponding changes in the productive system, were contingent on substantial inflows of foreign goods, services and finance. Not at all by coincidence, the early 1990s were a period of abundant liquidity in the international markets and growing internationalization of production, what is usually (if superficially and often wrongly) called 'globalization' (see Fine 1999b). In other words, the transition presumed that high domestic interest rates and trade and capital account liberalization would provide the real and financial inflows of foreign resources required to support the new system of accumulation. In reality, however, the transition has been far from smooth. The neomonetarist policy shift has increased the vulnerability of the Brazilian economy to fluctuations in international liquidity and in the cost of foreign finance, which has made the costs of transition to the new system of accumulation much higher than had been anticipated.

This chapter reviews the nature, impact and costs of neomonetarism in Brazil.[2] These policies were implemented incrementally but unevenly across the decade, and they were motivated by internal as well as external factors. We show that the costs of neomonetarism were high, and argue that there is no reason to expect that they will decline in the near future, leading to the desired resumption of sustained growth. In spite of this dismal perspective, the ideological climate in Brazil and elsewhere has prevented policy alternatives from being considered seriously. Instead, neomonetarist policies have been imposed by force, and then justified by their purported inevitability.

The balance sheet of a decade of neomonetarism can be summarized as follows. Between 1992 (when the liberalization of the capital account was completed) and 1998 (the last year of the Real Plan), Brazil received financial transfers from the rest of the world worth US$58.2 billion, including mainly foreign direct investment (FDI) and portfolio capital inflows (net of profit remittances) and new loans (net of foreign debt repayments). These inflows were used to finance a trade (visibles and invisibles) deficit of US$22.9 billion, and to accumulate US$35.2 billion in new foreign reserves. The 1999 crisis has shown that these reserves were unable to defend the currency, and this chapter argues that their stockpiling may have been counterproductive.

The post-1994 trade deficit, the overvaluation of the domestic currency (the real) and the policy-induced pressure for industrial restructuring had lasting effects on the Brazilian economy. Financial difficulties and intense foreign competition reduced productive capacity in several important sectors, especially the capital goods industry, leading to a loss of one million manufacturing jobs during the decade. Total (open and hidden) unemployment reached 20 per cent in the larger metropolitan areas, swelling the ranks of the self-employed and the informal sector. Industrial restructuring and the internationalization of the manufacturing base reduced the economy's employment generating capacity and increased Brazil's dependence on imports and foreign finance. As a result, the balance of payments constraint became increasingly severe. In spite of these shortcomings, there were substantial productivity gains in agriculture and in certain manufacturing industries, especially through the use of foreign technology, shifts in the composition of the output and the elimination of the less efficient producers.

The potential welfare impact of these productivity gains was partly cancelled out by the high domestic interest rates, which were required to attract foreign capital. On average, Brazilian real (overnight) interest rates doubled from 12 per cent per annum, between June 1990 and December 1991 (when the degree of liberalization was small), to 24 per cent between 1992 and 1998. The ensuing financial costs were the main cause of the explosive growth of the domestic public debt (DPD).[3] Between 1991 and 1998, the DPD increased by US$257.7 billion, in spite of the fiscal surplus (non-financial revenues minus expenditures) of US$48.7 billion.

In the light of these costs, it is not surprising that the government found it difficult to defend and implement its preferred policies. More importantly, this chapter shows that the poor macroeconomic performance of the Brazilian economy in the 1990s is due to both internal and external causes but, increasingly, it derives from the attempt to implement an accumulation strategy that, until now, has been stable only exceptionally.[4]

This chapter includes this introduction, six substantive sections, and the conclusion. The next section defines neomonetarism and briefly explains neomonetarist economic policies. The third section reviews the transition to neomonetarism in Brazil. The fourth section reviews the Real Plan, and shows that it was the pretext for the implementation of a neomonetarist economic strategy under the guise of stabilization. The fifth section analyses the impact of neomonetarism on the Brazilian manufacturing sector, and the sixth section shows why this strategy led to an industrial, fiscal and financial crisis. The seventh section reviews the events leading to the (largely inevitable) *dénouement*, the currency crisis of January 1999. The conclusion draws the main implications and lessons from the Brazilian economic policies in the 1990s.

NEOMONETARIST PERSPECTIVES

Neomonetarism is the hegemonic economic policy in Brazil and in the world today.[5] It can be analysed at two levels. At the microeconomic level neomonetarism, like all mainstream approaches, presumes that in a decentralized and deregulated economy free competition leads to full employment equilibrium. Consequently, the market rather than the state should address such economic problems as industrial development, international competitiveness and employment creation. By the same token, policy-orientated shifts in relative prices and in the allocation of resources (for example, through industrial policy, see Chang 1994) should be avoided. At the macroeconomic level, neomonetarism argues that the world economy is characterized by the relentless advance of 'globalization' and international capital mobility. They offer the possibility of rapid growth through the attraction of productive and financial foreign capital ('foreign savings'). However, this growth strategy can be successful only if domestic policies conform to the short-term interests of the financial markets. This policy guideline implies that interventionist state policies are unfeasible, because any policy deemed undesirable or unsustainable by the financial markets would lead to capital flight, a balance of payments crisis and, inevitably, economic collapse. 'Credibility' is essential and, in practice, policy credibility derives from the preferences of the international financial conglomerates, the US government and the International Monetary Fund (IMF). In sum, neomonetarism is presumably optimal because it offers the best, and the only viable, set of economic policies, and these policies are taken to be viable and optimal because they are in the interests of the international financial institutions.[6] The most important neomonetarist policy tool is the interest rate. Presumably, the 'correct' interest rate can deliver balance of payments equilibrium, low inflation and sustainable levels of investment and consumption and, therefore, high growth rates in the long term (Arestis and Sawyer 1998). The implementation of neomonetarist policies can be analysed from two angles.

On the one hand, it implies that domestic interest rates are generally higher than they would be under an alternative regime, where similar objectives may be pursued using a larger set of tools. Higher interest rates tend to reduce the levels of employment, investment, output and income relative to what they would be in an alternative scenario, in the short and in the long runs. More specifically, long-term unemployment tends to increase because capacity tends to become fully utilized, and the balance of payments constraint becomes binding, before unemployment declines substantially.

On the other hand, the neomonetarist policies implemented in Brazil and other newly industrialized countries during the 1990s included trade, financial and capital account liberalization. They were justified by the need to increase the efficiency of the financial and productive sectors and in order to eliminate high inflation. However, they require not only that domestic interest rates should rise, but also that they should exceed international rates by a substantial margin because of the political, currency and other risks associated with these countries.

It is impossible to determine the size of the interest rate differential that would be required to attract a given volume of foreign resources, because of the continuous changes in the domestic circumstances and in international liquidity. Excessively low margins or low international liquidity tend to be associated with insufficient capital inflows and, potentially, with capital flight and currency devaluation. In contrast, high margins or abundant liquidity are associated with large capital inflows, the accumulation of foreign reserves, deflationary pressures and currency overvaluation. The impact of the interest rate margins on aggregate demand is ambiguous and potentially shifting, because low (high) domestic interest rates can increase (reduce) consumption and investment through the usual Keynesian mechanisms, or reduce (increase) them because of the combined impact of the international capital movements and the ensuing changes in the exchange rate.

Only excessively high interest rate differentials can persist over long periods, but the consequences of chronic conditions may often be more serious than those of the acute variety. They may include deindustrialization (because of high financial costs and foreign competition), rapid growth of the domestic public debt (if the capital inflows are sterilized), and the creation of a 'casino' atmosphere in which financial strategies steadily shift from hedge towards speculative and, finally, Ponzi finance (Arestis and Glickman 2002). The next section shows that this brief outline of neomonetarism and its potential consequences provides a good summary of the Brazilian experience in the 1990s.

NEOMONETARISM IN BRAZIL

In the early 1990s, international liquidity increased substantially because of the sluggishness and financial fragility of the US economy. Relatively low interest rates in the main financial markets induced large capital outflows from the developed countries, in order to obtain higher returns in the so-called 'emerging' markets, or finance the expansion of production in these countries.[7] Several Latin American governments, including Brazil's, believed that these capital flows provided an opportunity to overcome the severe balance of payments constraint that had restricted growth and fuelled inflation since the 1982 debt crisis.

Attracting real and financial resources from the rest of the world was one of the most important objectives of the neomonetarist economic reforms in Brazil. In 1988, during the Sarney administration,[8] the domestic financial system was reformed and, from 1989, international capital flows were gradually liberalized (Studart 1999b). The exchange rate regime also became increasingly flexible, at least until the Real Plan (Banco Central do Brasil 1993). From 1990, during the Collor administration, Brazilian imports were liberalized incrementally, and the country implemented the resolutions of the GATT (General Agreement on Tariffs and Trade) Uruguay Round.[9] Between late 1991 and early 1994, the Collor and Franco administrations imposed strongly contractionary monetary policies in order to control demand and inflation, generate exportable surpluses and attract foreign capital. Finally, the Cardoso administration implemented a fully neomonetarist economic programme, especially through the Real Plan. These policies were partly successful. In 1992, in spite of the domestic political instability and high inflation, foreign capital inflows were restored for the first time since the foreign debt crisis, initially through the repatriation of Brazilian capital (Gonçalves 1999a, pp. 125–8). The economy began to grow strongly (see Table 6.1), and the availability of imported goods substantially expanded the possibilities of consumption.

Table 6.1 Brazil: GDP, 1990–1999

Year	US$ million	R$ million	Real growth rate (%)
1990	469 318	12	−5.53
1991	405 679	60	−0.57
1992	387 295	641	−2.06
1993	429 685	14 097	3.35
1994	543 087	349 205	4.33
1995	705 449	646 192	2.75
1996	775 475	778 887	1.24
1997	807 814	870 743	1.87
1998	787 499	914 188	−1.21
1999	536 600	963 969	−0.55

Sources: IBGE (Instituto Brasileiro de Geografia e Estatística (Brazilian Institute of Geography and Statistics)) and Bulletin of the Central Bank of Brazil.

In order to assess the impact of the neomonetarist policy shift, let us define *real* and *financial resource transfers* and the *monetary impact of the foreign sector*.

1. The *real resource transfers* (RT) are equal to the visible and invisible trade balance (net exports of goods and non-factor services). If RT > 0, the country transfers real resources (coffee, soya beans, minerals, autos and so on) to the rest of the world. These transfers generate a foreign currency inflow that can be accumulated as foreign reserves, or they can be used to transfer financial resources to the rest of the world, for example, to service the foreign debt. Alternatively, if the country is a net importer of goods and services its residents receive real resource

transfers (machines, oil, autos, freight services and so on) from abroad (RT < 0). In this case, the balance of payments can be in equilibrium only if there is, simultaneously, a transfer of financial resources from the rest of the world (for example, foreign investment or loans), providing the hard currency required to finance the trade deficit.

2. The *financial resource transfers* (FT) include the unilateral financial flows (UF) and the foreign debt flows (FDe). UF comprise the net flows of foreign direct and portfolio investment, profit and dividend remittances, payment of other factor services, unrequited transfers and the errors and omissions in the balance of payments.[10] FDe includes new loan disbursements and debt service payments (interest and amortization) by the central government and the private sector.[11]

3. If the private sector must surrender its hard currency holdings to the central bank, its external transactions directly affect the monetary base. For example, currency inflows due to exports or foreign investment expand the monetary base, while profit remittances and the foreign debt service contract the monetary base. The monetary impact of these transactions may be sterilized through open market operations. However, sterilization does not eliminate the monetary impact; it merely transfers it from the monetary base to the domestic public debt. Central government transactions are different. On the one hand, if central government borrows money abroad or issues sovereign bonds (in order to finance its foreign liabilities, increase the country's foreign reserves or to set market standards), the monetary base and the DPD are not affected. Similarly, central government foreign debt service payments do not reduce the monetary base or the DPD. In either case, only the foreign reserves change.

On the other hand, if the Ministry of Transport (for example) borrows abroad in order to finance a road-building programme, the monetary impact of this currency inflow is indirect. The loan expands the monetary base only when the ministry draws funds from the Treasury account at the central bank (its balance is not included in the money supply). Therefore, the monetization of the foreign loan appears through an increase in the fiscal deficit. When the Ministry of Transport repays the loan, its domestic expenditures fall and the fiscal deficit declines. In what follows, the *monetary impact of the foreign sector* is determined by the domestic currency value of the foreign transactions of the private sector, that is, the local currency value of the balance of payments surplus, minus the foreign currency transactions of the central government (presumably including only its foreign debt flows). The (indirect) monetary impact of the central government's foreign transactions, if it exists, is included either in the public expenditures or in the tax revenues (see below).

Let us return to the impact of neomonetarism. In 1990–91, Brazil made real resource transfers to the rest of the world (that is, Brazil had a trade surplus) of US$15.7 billion. The corresponding currency inflow was used to finance foreign debt repayments of US$14.4 billion and unilateral financial outflows of US$1.1 billion (the net foreign direct and portfolio investment inflow was only US$170.5 million).

The Brazilian balance of payments changed structurally in the following period (see Table 6.2). Between 1992 (when the liberalization of the capital account was concluded) and the first half of 1994 (that is, before the Real Plan), the transfer of real resources to the rest of the world reached US$27.7 billion. At the same time, the rescheduling of the foreign debt reduced net debt payments to only US$2.6 billion, while the unilateral financial inflows increased sharply, to US$11.4 billion (including net foreign investment of US$15.6 billion). As a result, Brazil's foreign reserves increased from US$9.4 billion to US$42.9 billion, and the monetary impact of the foreign sector was strongly expansionary, at US$41.4 billion.

Inflation increased slowly but relentlessly between 1992 and mid-1994, from under 20 per cent to over 40 per cent per month. Inflation control became essential for the political legitimacy and economic viability of the neomonetarist accumulation strategy.

High inflation was eliminated in Brazil through the Real Plan (see Figure 6.1).[12] The theoretical underpinnings of the Real Plan resembled those of other Latin American stabilization and economic reform programmes of that period. The plan presumed that the main cause of inflation was the public deficit, and that inflation persisted because of widespread indexation in the economy. This diagnosis synthesized monetarist views (where monetary expansion causes inflation) with a neostructuralist approach (which emphasizes the role of inflation inertia). In this case, contractionary policies are necessary but insufficient to reduce inflation; de-indexation coordinated by the state is also essential (Dornbusch and Simonsen 1983; Lopes 1986; Saad-Filho and Mollo 2002).

We have seen above that the liberalization of the capital account attracted large unilateral financial flows to Brazil, leading to the accumulation of substantial foreign currency reserves. In mid-1994, it had become clear that these inflows were sufficient to finance Brazil's foreign debt repayments, regardless of the real resource transfers to the rest of the world. At the same time, trade liberalization had become politically very important (see next section). Throughout this period, the economic authorities and their apologists in the press and in academia claimed that further trade liberalization was essential. It was hoped that it would curtail the power of the oligopolies and the labour unions (which would increase economic efficiency and help to reduce inflation), increase the supply of consumer and investment goods

Table 6.2 External sector of the Brazilian economy; selected variables, 1990.I–1991.IV and 1992.I–1994.II (US$ million)

Period	RT (a)	FDe (b)	UF (c)	FT (d = b+c)	BP (e = a+d)	IR (f)	Me (g)
1990.I	1 496.5	-3 854.2	-1 795.6	-5 649.8	-4 153.3	7 384.0	n.a.
1990.II	3 298.1	690.2	-396.6	293.6	3 591.7	10 173.0	n.a.
1990.III	2 369.0	-2 731.3	-24.9	-2 756.2	-387.2	10 171.0	n.a.
1990.IV	687.8	-1 195.2	276.8	-918.4	-230.6	9 973.0	n.a.
1991.I	2 805.4	-4 256.5	14.6	-4 241.9	-1 436.5	8 663.0	-3 110.4
1991.II	2 997.1	-1 539.5	826.6	-712.9	2 284.2	10 401.0	777.7
1991.III	1 037.2	-2 449.8	508.9	-1 940.9	-903.7	7 956.0	-2 951.5
1991.IV	981.6	947.8	-545.9	401.9	1 383.5	9 406.0	411.0
Total	15 672.7	-14 388.5	-1 136.1	-15 524.6	148.1	–	-4 873.2
1992.I	3 001.2	2 618.3	2 256.5	4 874.8	7 876.0	17 063.0	6 343.1
1992.II	3 284.9	1 555.3	477.9	2 033.2	5 318.1	21 703.0	4 973.4
1992.III	3 544.2	-2 527.2	-658.7	-3 185.9	358.3	21 964.0	-1 084.1
1992.IV	3 286.1	330.0	-34.8	295.2	3 581.3	23 754.0	3 090.0
1993.I	3 320.7	-4 879.3	-277.8	-5 157.1	-1 836.4	22 309.0	-1 379.1
1993.II	2 077.9	-531.4	400.4	-131.0	1 946.9	24 476.0	2 404.2
1993.III	1 730.4	228.7	76.6	305.3	2 035.7	26 948.0	2 493.0
1993.IV	2 346.9	-45.5	3 164.2	3 118.7	5 465.6	32 211.0	5 922.9
1994.I	2 083.4	255.0	3 637.3	3 892.3	5 975.7	38 282.0	6 833.2
1994.II	2 978.8	5 562.9	2 369.4	7 932.3	10 911.1	42 881.0	11 768.6
Total	27 654.5	2 566.8	11 411.0	13 977.8	41 632.3	–	41 365.3

Note: RT: real resource transfers to the rest of the world, FDe: foreign debt flows, UF: unilateral financial flows, FT: financial resource transfers from the rest of the world, BP: balance of payments surplus, IR: international reserves, Me: monetary impact of the foreign sector.

Source: Calculated from the Bulletin of the Central Bank of Brazil.

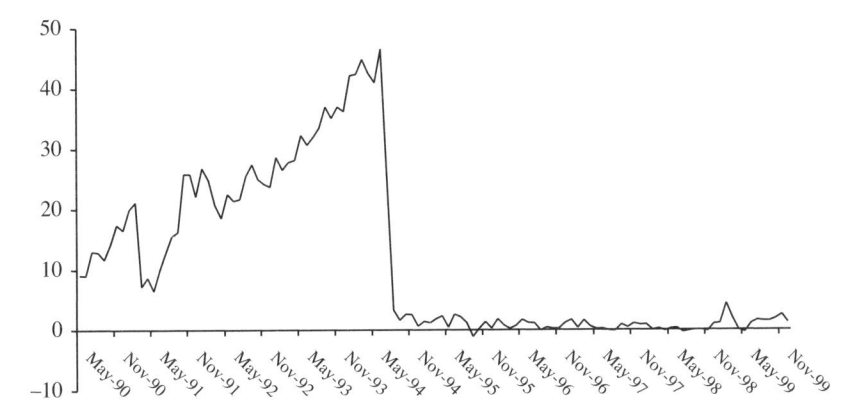

Figure 6.1   Brazil: monthly inflation rate, May 1990–December 1999 (%)

(reducing inflation even further), force industry to invest in new technologies (leading to growth and employment opportunities), and reduce the monetary impact of the foreign sector (curbing the growth of the DPD). In sum, as long as domestic policies were 'credible', cheap foreign savings would finance rapid capital accumulation in Brazil and bring back the 'historical' growth rates, above 5 per cent per annum.

GROWTH AND CRISIS

Economic stabilization and the neomonetarist policy shift were perceived to be highly successful in the immediate aftermath of the Real Plan. The steep decline of inflation and the simultaneous expansion of aggregate demand were the most evident achievements of neomonetarism. There were three main reasons for the demand increase: first, inflation stabilization and import liberalization stimulated investment and the growth of domestic trade and services; second, consumer credit expanded swiftly; credit demand for consumption and investment increased because the stabilization, while the banks increased credit supply in order to boost their revenues, badly dented by the Real Plan (see 'Fiscal and financial crisis' below); and third, dollar wages increased 15 per cent, reflecting the exchange rate appreciation and the elimination of inflation losses worth around US$16 billion annually.[13]

High international liquidity and high domestic interest rates (see Figure 6.2) contributed to a sharp increase in foreign capital inflows in early 1994 (in the first half of this year, the financial resource transfers to Brazil reached

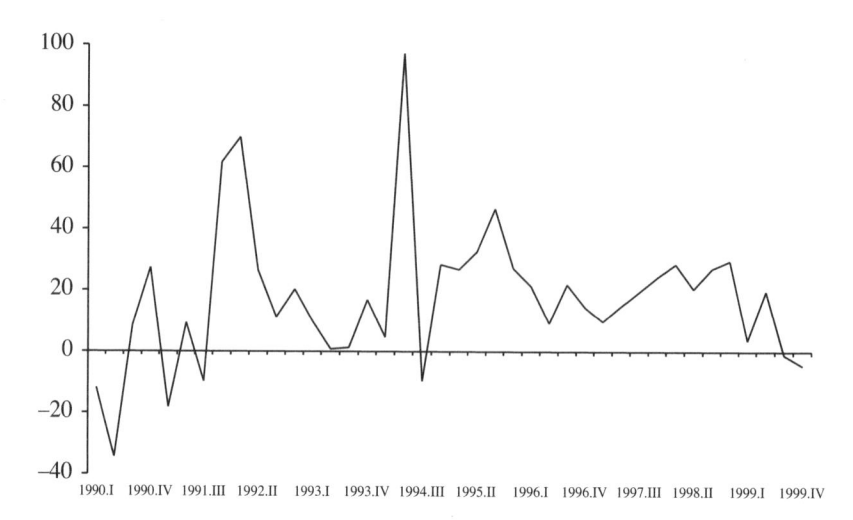

Note: * Annualized quarterly rates, deflated by the IGP-DI.

Source: Central Bank of Brazil.

*Figure 6.2 Brazil: real interest rate, 1990–1999 (%)**

US$11.8 billion). These currency inflows contributed to a substantial appreciation of the real, especially in the third quarter of 1994. On a trade-weighted basis, the Brazilian currency appreciated 16 per cent in the second half of the year and, between July and October, the dollar fell from R$1 to only R$0.82.[14] During the second half of 1994 the government abandoned its gradualist strategy, eliminated most export incentives and drastically liberalized imports, in order to abolish Brazil's trade surplus.[15]

Demand growth, trade liberalization and exchange rate overvaluation rapidly changed Brazil's trade flows. The real resource transfers to the rest of the world shifted from *plus* US$8.3 billion (that is, a trade surplus) in the first three quarters of 1994, to *minus* US$9.1 billion (that is, a trade deficit) in the next three quarters. This was a deliberate objective of the Brazilian authorities:

> [T]he logic of the exchange rate policy is to reduce exports, increase imports and the current account deficit and, therefore, make the country import capital again. These capital imports and the domestic savings accumulated by the private sector will finance economic growth. (Pedro Malan, Minister of Finance, *Gazeta Mercantil*, 24 October 1994)

The real resource transfers from the rest of the world and the accumulation of foreign reserves to support the real would be viable only if Brazil received substantial foreign capital inflows on a long-term basis and could borrow abroad extensively. However, international liquidity dried up in mid-1994. Between May and December, the US Federal Reserve raised the discount rate six times, from 3 to 4.75 per cent (the prime rate increased from 6 to 8.5 per cent, and the libor from 3.4 to 6.8 per cent). Higher international interest rates helped to shift international capital flows back to developed country markets, making it harder for the 'emerging' economies to finance their current account deficits. By the end of the year, the foreign reserves of several countries were already declining rapidly, leading to the Mexican crisis and to serious difficulties in Argentina. Capital flight from Brazil reduced the country's reserves by US$9.7 billion between the third quarter of 1994 and the first quarter of 1995 (see Table 6.3). Similar shifts also occurred after the Asian crisis, in 1997, and the Russian crisis, in 1998 (see 'Currency crisis' below).

These recurrent shifts in the international capital flows destabilized the neomonetarist accumulation strategy in Brazil. In early 1995, less than one year after its implementation, the Real Plan was no longer part of a viable growth strategy. Economic policy became synonymous with crisis management.

The international turbulence after the Mexican crisis made it difficult to control any attempted devaluation of the real. Under these circumstances, the government decided to support the overvalued currency through higher interest rates (which should reduce the capital outflows and curtail import demand) and expand the privatization programme, with incentives to bids by foreign companies in order to attract hard currency.[16] The exchange rate policy finally shifted in March 1995, when sliding bands were introduced, initially between R$0.86 and R$0.90 to the dollar. The government intended to devalue the real every month by half a percentage point in excess of the domestic rate of inflation, in order to increase export competitiveness and reduce the current account deficit incrementally. In addition, consumer goods imports were restricted, and export incentives were restored (Kume 1998).[17] Although the trade balance improved, these measures did not eliminate the real resource transfers to Brazil, and the government was unable to devise a viable strategy to finance the balance of payments.

High domestic interest rates and the restoration of international liquidity later in 1995 brought strong capital inflows to Brazil. The financial resource transfers reached US$25.0 billion in the last three quarters of the year, and Brazil's international reserves climbed by US$18.1 billion, to US$51.8 billion. High interest rates increased the opportunities for speculative gain in the open market, especially in the light of the industrial slowdown. Eventually, these high interest rates destabilized the central government budget and the balance sheet of the banking system and the local governments, leading to a severe fiscal and financial crisis (see 'Currency crisis' below).

Table 6.3 *External sector of the Brazilian economy, selected variables, 1994.III–1995.I and 1995.II–1995.IV (US$ million)*

Period	RT (a)	FDe (b)	UF (c)	FT (d = b+c)	BP (e = a+d)	IR (f)	Me (g)
1994.III	3 248.2	−2 608.3	−152.0	−2 760.3	487.9	43 455.0	1 345.4
1994.IV	−2 066.2	−3 421.9	1 098.4	−2 323.5	−4 389.7	38 806.0	−3 532.2
1995.I	−3 492.1	2 320.2	−3 888.1	−1 567.9	−5 060.0	33 742.0	−4 318.1
Total	−2 310.1	−3 710.0	−2 941.7	−6 651.7	−8 961.8	–	−6 504.9
1995.II	−3 529.9	486.9	2 834.0	3 320.9	−209.0	33 512.0	532.9
1995.III	−1 152.6	11 100.7	5 812.0	16 912.7	15 760.1	48 713.0	16 502.1
1995.IV	−1 369.1	2 699.4	2 111.7	4 811.1	3 442.0	51 840.0	4 184.0
Total	−6 051.6	14 287.0	10 757.7	25 044.7	18 993.1	–	21 219.0

Note: RT: real resource transfers to the rest of the world, FDe: foreign debt flows, UF: unilateral financial flows, FT: financial resource transfers from the rest of the world, BP: balance of payments surplus, IR: international reserves, Me: monetary impact of the foreign sector.

Source: Calculated from the Bulletin of the Central Bank of Brazil.

INDUSTRIAL RESTRUCTURING

Trade liberalization, high interest rates and exchange rate overvaluation expressed the policy bias towards foreign and financial capital at the expense of domestic productive capital. They introduced new forms of competition into the Brazilian economy, based on the microeconomic integration of Brazilian production and finance into transnational circuits. Their consequences for the industrial base, the level of employment, and the model of economic growth in Brazil were twofold.[18] First, the share of imported manufactured goods increased sharply (see Table 6.4).

Table 6.4 Brazilian manufacturing industry, import coefficient, 1993 and 1996 (%)

Sector	1993	1996
1. Standardized capital goods and electronic goods	29	65–75
2. Chemical inputs, fertilizers, resins	20–26	33–42
3. Auto parts, natural textiles, capital goods made to order, rubber	8–15	20–25
4. Pharmaceuticals, tractors, electric and electronic consumer goods, glass, chemical goods	7–11	13–16
5. Synthetic textiles, petrochemical inputs, cars, food, paper and cardboard	3–6	9–12
6. Beverages, shoes, plastics, dairy products, semi-processed foods	0.7–3	4–8
7. Non-tradable goods (cement, inputs and others)	0.5–2.5	1–4

Source: Coutinho et al. (1999, p. 70).

Second, foreign firms participated in 49.1 per cent of the 3276 mergers and acquisitions (M&As) registered in Brazil between 1990 and 1999. Both the number of M&As and the degree of foreign involvement increased continually after 1991. In that year, foreign companies participated in 47 out of 184 M&As (25.5 per cent). In 1999, they were involved in 341 out of 491 M&As (69.5 per cent).[19] The sectors most affected by this wave of transnational integration were those manufacturing electric and electronic goods, telecommunications equipment, car parts and processed foods. In these and in other sectors, large firms previously controlled by domestic capital were absorbed by transnational conglomerates, for example, Metal Leve, Lacta, Cofap, Freios Varga, Arno, Refripar, Renner, Agroceres and the banks Nacional, Garantia, Bamerindus and Real. Coutinho et al. (1999, pp. 66, 73) rightly argue that:

> [The] avoidance of industrial development policies by the state ... strongly contributed to the increasing exposure of domestic industry to imports, especially in high value added sectors and those with a high technological content ... [T]he explosion of imports 'hollowed out' the productive chains, and led to a large reduction in intra-industry demand ... which sharply reduced the economy's capacity to create jobs ... Frantic attempts to cut costs have led to successive rounds of innovation and rationalisation in the productive process, that generated strong tensions in the labour market ... [This is partly due to the] entry of new competitors and the redefinition of strategic alliances [that] have destabilised the oligopolic structures inherited from previous decades ... The 'modernisation' of [these] oligopolic structures has ruptured the existing supply chains, led to the entry of new [foreign] suppliers, reduced the degree of verticalisation and increased the import coefficients ... [The] higher coefficient of imported inputs and components (and, therefore, the substantially lower value creation in the country) means that the success of efforts to stimulate domestic demand for intermediate goods and employment will tend ... to be very modest.

The main cause of the declining trend of the GDP growth rates after 1994 was the combination of domestic demand restrictions with economic restructuring based on the microeconomic integration of domestic capital into transnational value chains.[20] They led to the hollowing out of Brazilian manufacturing industry and the dismantling of the existing supply chains, and to the rapid growth of unemployment because of both technological improvements and insufficient demand.

The Brazilian open unemployment rate increased from 3.9 per cent in December 1990 to 8.7 per cent in June 1998, according to the federal government's statistical service, IBGE.[21] In Greater São Paulo alone, 180 000 manufacturing jobs were lost in 1995 (Lacerda 1996, p. 19). In Brazil as a whole, there was a net loss of more than one million manufacturing industry jobs between 1989 and 1997, leading to a one-third decline of employment in the manufacturing sector (Bonelli 1999, p. 89). During the 1990s, the share of manufacturing industry in GDP declined from 33 to 22 per cent, and Brazil fell from eighth to eleventh place in the world ranking of manufactured output (Diniz 1999, p. 172; see also Coutinho et al. 1999, p. 75).

Certain sectors, such as the durable goods industry (especially automobiles) enjoyed substantial productivity gains due to increasing labour market 'flexibility',[22] technological modernization and changes in their product mix.[23] Manufacturing productivity increased, on average, by 7.6 per cent annually between 1990 and 1997 (Feijó and Carvalho 1998). In spite of this, the industrial base shrank and became more fragmented, with new industries starting up and old industries relocating towards poorer areas in the Northeast and the South (Bonelli 1999, pp. 95–7). These heavy blows to traditional manufacturing areas, especially the São Paulo metropolitan area, were softened by the expansion of trade within Mercosur and the transfer of several state-owned groups to Brazilian capital.[24] In sum,

Firms achieved substantial output growth after 1994, without any corresponding increase in their productive capacity. The productivity gains became possible not only through new management and organisational methods, specialisation in less complex products and increased efficiency, but also because of the reduction in the local content of the output. The current investment projects reproduce these features, and they have low capital and employment coefficients. (Laplane and Sarti 1999, p. 263).[25]

The restructuring of the productive sector achieved only partly the strategic objectives of the new accumulation strategy. For example, the stock of FDI in Brazil doubled from US$45 billion at the end of 1994 to US$90 billion four years later, while portfolio investment increased from US$25 billion to US$60 billion in the same period.[26] However, foreign investors did not target the export markets as had been expected:

[The] large majority of [domestic] investment projects was driven by the strong growth of the domestic market [in 1994–95], and they had a very small export component. With respect to foreign investment, it has been shown that the Brazilian market is also the main target of current foreign direct investment projects. (Coutinho et al. 1999, p. 72)

Moreover, it should not be expected that foreign investors will target export growth in the near future: 'There is no great interest in the verticalisation of production, showing that the [transnational] firms are not planning to review the specialisation and outsourcing efforts undertaken in this decade' (Laplane and Sarti 1999, p. 237).

FISCAL AND FINANCIAL CRISIS

The reduction of the rate of growth of the DPD in the first year of the Real Plan was one of the government's most important achievements (see Figure 6.3). This was mainly due to the increase in tax revenues because of the elimination of high inflation, and the reduction in the nominal interest rates, which cut substantially the cost of servicing the DPD. However, in mid-1995 the DPD started growing rapidly for three reasons: the sterilization of foreign capital inflows, central bank assistance to the financial system and to local governments (see below), and the impact of the high domestic interest rates on the cost of the DPD (see Carvalho 1999).[27]

The DPD increased by 134 per cent between the Mexican crisis and the end of 1996, when it reached US$171 billion (22 per cent of GDP). In the same period, the domestic debt of local governments increased from US$28.6 billion to US$48.1 billion, even though their primary deficit was only US$5.2 billion. Debt growth was mostly due to the high domestic interest rates,

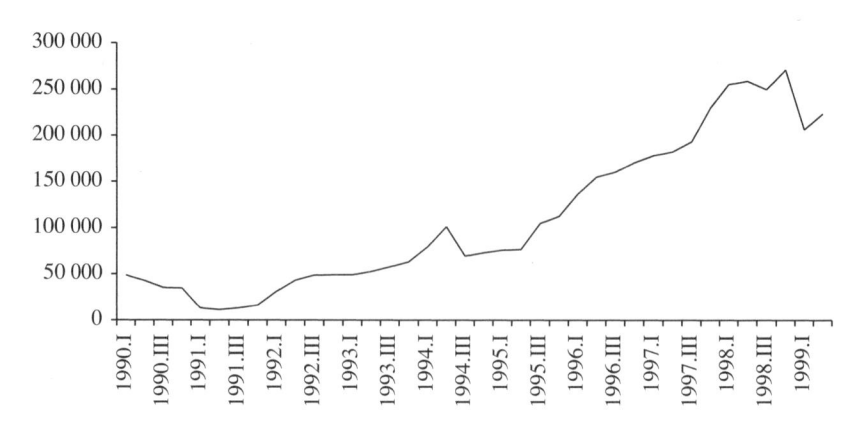

Source: Central Bank of Brazil.

Figure 6.3 Brazil: domestic public debt, 1990–1999 (US$ million)

revenue losses associated with the Real Plan and faltering tax revenues due to the economic stagnation. In 1997, several state governments had become unable to pay even debt interest. The impending devaluation of these securities persuaded the central government to swap new federal securities for virtually worthless local government bills. This debt swap reached US$84.0 billion by September 1999.

While the local government financial crisis developed, the domestic financial system entered into a period of severe instability (Cardim de Carvalho 1999). The sector had been seriously weakened by the elimination of its inflation gains (equivalent to 2.5 per cent of GDP, see Cysne 1994). Most banks reacted by expanding consumer credit (see 'Growth and crisis' above); however, this revenue source was limited by the credit restrictions imposed after the Mexican crisis. Moreover, several small- and medium-sized institutions faced liquidity problems as the foreign credit crunch took its toll. Finally, the increase in the domestic interest rates in 1995 reduced liquidity even further, increased the stock of bad debts and slowed down domestic economic activity (Studart 1999a, 1999b).

The collapse of two of the largest Brazilian banks, Econômico and Nacional, sparked a financial crisis that rapidly spread to smaller institutions. In order to contain the contagion, the central bank opened a credit line for troubled private banks in November 1995 (PROER, Programme of Incentives to Strengthen and Restructure the Financial System). In February 1997, a similar programme was launched for local government-owned banks (PROES, Programme of Incentives to Reduce Local Government Banking Activity), which aimed at their privatization or closure.

Through programmes such as these, in three years the central bank took control, closed or forced the sale of 72 of the 271 Brazilian banks that existed in July 1994 (Barros and Almeida Jr 1997; Cardim de Carvalho 1999; Studart 1999b).[28] Their assets were sold to other institutions, especially foreign banks. Consequently, the Brazilian financial system became substantially more concentrated and internationalized (Gonçalves 1999a, pp. 106, 134).

The opacity of the central bank's balance sheet makes it difficult to determine the cost of PROER. The loans were made using mainly compulsory bank deposits at the central bank that, in accounting terms, have zero cost. However, these loans expanded liquidity, which was generally sterilized through the sale of government securities at market interest rates. Their value should be included in the cost of the programme. These costs should also include the difference between the market value of the private assets and the value at which they were purchased by the central bank. This simple estimate indicates that the salvaging operation cost approximately R$6.4 billion in 1995 (0.9 per cent of GDP), R$6.0 billion (0.8 per cent of GDP) in 1996, and R$5.6 billion (0.7 per cent of GDP) in 1997.[29]

In 1996–97, the contractionary impact of the fiscal surplus and the smaller monetary impact of the foreign sector were more than compensated by the rediscount loans, local government debt swaps and the autonomous growth of the DPD due to the high domestic interest rates (Morais 1998; Rosar 1999).

Throughout the 1990s, the central government attempted to control the growth of the DPD mainly through expenditure cuts, and fiscal surpluses were achieved in every year except 1991 (see Table 6.5).[30] In spite of these surpluses, the DPD reached US$171.0 billion in 1996, US$230.0 billion in 1997 (an increase of US$59 billion, in spite of the fiscal surplus of US$16.8 billion), and US$270.9 billion one year later (a further increase of US$40.9 billion, despite the fiscal surplus of US$10.7 billion).

The neomonetarist policy of permanently high interest rates subsidized the accumulation of financial capital at the expense of industrial capital and employment creation. The most obvious way of capturing this subsidy was through interest rate arbitrage. Domestic and foreign investors borrowed heavily in the foreign markets, paying around 12 per cent per annum, and sold the hard currency to the central bank in order to purchase government securities paying around 30 per cent. In contrast, Brazilian reserves abroad received interest rates below 5 per cent. The difference between the interest paid to the holders of federal securities and the interest received on the new reserves (minus the depreciation of the exchange rate) was a government subsidy to the accumulation of financial capital (the next section shows that this exercise was riskless to the private sector).

The Brazilian foreign debt also increased because of the search for cheaper industrial finance, given the high cost of domestic loans. As a result, the

Table 6.5 Brazil: central government fiscal balance, 1991–1999*

Year	US$ million	% GDP
1991	–3 596	–0.93
1992	4 306	1.15
1993	3 363	0.78
1994	9 504	1.69
1995	4 899	0.68
1996	2 595	0.33
1997	16 850	2.10
1998	10 734	1.38
1999	22 672	2.36

Note: * Fiscal balance = cash balance of the Treasury and the social security system, excluding financial revenues and expenditures.

Source: Calculated from the Bulletin of the Central Bank of Brazil.

country's foreign debt doubled between 1991 and 1998, when it reached US$243.2 billion. A large part of this increase was due to purely financial accumulation, implying that it was probably not accompanied by a corresponding increase in the capacity of the borrowers to generate foreign exchange. This may generate pressures for the devaluation of the real in the medium and long terms, even though devaluation increases the domestic currency cost of the debt service.

The Mexican crisis showed that, if the international markets are unstable, it can be impossible to finance domestic consumption and investment through unilateral financial flows. The limitations imposed upon the neomonetarist accumulation strategy by the Mexican crisis had three important fiscal effects.

First, the rapid growth of the domestic public debt increased the central government's financial expenditures (see Figure 6.3 and Table 6.6). The drainage of productive and money capital and wages by the tax system in order to pay the domestic debt service demonstrates the financial priorities of neomonetarism.[31] These policies concentrate income (Kane and Morisett 1993; Bulmer-Thomas 1994; CEPAL 1999), and they reduce the country's long-term growth prospects (Saad-Filho et al. 1999).

Second, the conflict between monetary and fiscal policies became increasingly severe. Permanently contractionary monetary policies tended to relax the fiscal policy stance, because they increased the costs of the DPD and, at a further remove, the stock of the debt (since these costs were paid mostly through new security issues). In order to induce the financial markets to hold

Table 6.6 Brazil: central government financial expenditures, 1991–1998*

Year	US$ million
1991	19 791.2
1992	76 314.7
1993	130 244.9
1994	123 050.1
1995	36 165.1
1996	37 564.0
1997	44 264.9
1998	70 996.3

Note: * The financial expenditures include the cost of the domestic public debt and the costs of the contractual domestic and external debt of the central government.

Source: Calculated from the Bulletin of the Central Bank of Brazil and from unpublished data from the Office of the National Treasury (details available on request).

the growing stock of securities, the Treasury and the central bank increasingly issued dollar-indexed bills, and they sanctioned a substantial reduction in the maturity structure and an increase in the liquidity of these securities (see Table 6.7). The rapidly growing financial expenditures of the central government, and the increasing liquidity of the DPD, induced the government to engage in successive rounds of fiscal and monetary policy contraction, in a vicious circle that gradually increased its own financial fragility. The solution to this dilemma requires the continuous increase of the fiscal surplus (which is politically impossible), privatizations (which are limited by the availability of sellable assets) or, more realistically, lower interest rates (which may violate the balance of payments constraint; see next section and Calvo and King 1998).

Third, the discrepancy between domestic and international interest rates was one of the main reasons why the central government's primary liabilities (monetary base plus DPD) increased much more rapidly than the foreign reserves (Table 6.8). The stock of reserves increased by 120.1 per cent between 1994 and mid-1998, from US$32.2 billion to US$70.9 billion. In the same period, the primary liabilities increased by 317.2 per cent, from US$69.8 billion to US$291.2 billion. The decline in the foreign reserve cover, from 46.1 per cent to only 24.2 per cent, increased the vulnerability of the real to capital outflows, in spite of the growing size of the reserves (Garcia 1995; Nogueira Batista 1996). In short, interest rate rises can stem capital outflows temporarily, but they tend to increase the economy's long-term vulnerability to speculative attacks. The rapid growth of the DPD was one of the most

Table 6.7 Brazil: indexation and maturity of central government securities, 1991–1999

Period	Type of security (%)						Maturity (months)
	Index-linked securities				Fixed price securities	Total*	
	Daily rate[a]	Exchange rate	Prices[b]	Other[c]			
1991.IV	67.20	11.47	5.27	–	16.06	100.00	n.a.
1992.IV	9.00	3.00	23.60	9.60	54.80	100.00	n.a.
1993.IV	3.80	17.26	42.05	10.47	26.42	100.00	n.a.
1994.I	2.50	22.83	27.82	13.88	32.97	100.00	n.a.
1994.II	50.30	9.24	28.03	12.42	0.00	100.00	n.a.
1994.III	27.50	6.09	22.31	13.69	30.42	100.00	n.a.
1994.IV	16.00	8.30	12.53	22.96	40.20	100.00	n.a.
1995.I	24.44	9.23	11.99	17.58	36.75	100.00	n.a.
1995.II	24.38	9.24	11.55	27.79	27.03	100.00	n.a.
1995.III	40.61	5.93	8.80	12.17	32.48	100.00	n.a.
1995.IV	37.77	5.29	5.26	8.98	42.70	100.00	n.a.
1996.I	26.08	7.94	2.92	11.79	51.27	100.00	n.a.
1996.II	18.86	8.04	2.34	10.80	59.94	100.00	n.a.
1996.III	17.86	7.85	1.95	9.97	62.37	100.00	n.a.
1996.IV	18.61	9.38	1.75	9.26	61.00	100.00	n.a.
1997.I	19.13	12.47	1.54	8.88	57.98	100.00	n.a.
1997.II	19.39	9.28	2.33	8.95	60.05	100.00	n.a.
1997.III	18.82	9.72	0.97	12.11	58.38	100.00	5.82

1997.IV	34.78	15.36	0.34	8.61	40.91	100.00	6.48
1998.I	27.78	15.13	0.32	6.10	50.68	100.00	4.69
1998.II	42.73	16.49	0.41	5.23	35.13	100.00	4.49
1998.III	65.70	21.38	0.61	5.27	7.05	100.00	3.84
1998.IV	69.05	21.00	0.36	6.07	3.51	100.00	3.73
1999.I	68.19	25.48	0.23	4.88	1.22	100.00	4.53
1999.II	64.01	23.98	0.22	3.65	8.14	100.00	3.38
1999.III	59.50	26.28	0.28	3.16	10.78	100.00	3.31
1999.IV	59.60	25.60	0.20	3.10	11.50	100.00	3.84

Notes:
a. Overnight (Selic).
b. Price indices: IGP-DI and IGP-M.
c. TR, TBF, TJLP.
* Totals rounded.

Sources: Bulletin of the Central Bank of Brazil and central bank press releases.

Table 6.8 Brazil: foreign currency cover of the primary liabilities of the central government, 1991–1999

Period	International reserves (US$ million) (a)	Primary liabilities (US$ million) (b)	International reserve cover (c = a/b) (%)
1991.I	8 663.0	22 667.4	38.2
1991.II	10 401.0	20 247.7	51.4
1991.III	7 956.0	22 704.8	35.0
1991.IV	9 406.0	24 769.5	38.0
1992.I	17 063.0	36 931.7	46.2
1992.II	21 703.0	48 748.2	44.5
1992.III	21 964.0	54 213.0	40.5
1992.IV	23 754.0	56 716.1	41.9
1993.I	22 309.0	54 504.9	40.9
1993.II	24 476.0	57 291.4	42.7
1993.III	26 948.0	62 287.9	43.3
1993.IV	32 211.0	69 759.6	46.2
1994.I	38 282.0	84 186.4	45.5
1994.II	42 881.0	106 346.9	40.3
1994.III	43 455.0	83 936.5	51.8
1994.IV	38 806.0	94 032.7	41.3
1995.I	33 742.0	94 076.2	35.9
1995.II	33 512.0	92 196.6	36.3
1995.III	48 713.0	119 076.5	40.9
1995.IV	51 840.0	135 027.5	38.4
1996.I	55 753.0	152 805.8	36.5
1996.II	59 997.0	171 911.7	34.9
1996.III	58 775.0	180 861.7	32.5
1996.IV	60 110.0	190 205.7	31.6
1997.I	58 980.0	199 570.6	29.6
1997.II	57 615.1	205 744.9	28.0
1997.III	61 931.0	215 987.2	28.7
1997.IV	52 173.0	258 737.5	20.2
1998.I	68 594.0	281 993.6	24.3
1998.II	70 898.0	291 188.6	24.3
1998.III	45 811.0	277 422.4	16.5
1998.IV	44 556.0	303 733.2	14.7
1999.I	33 848.3	227 565.1	14.9
1999.II	41 345.5	242 902.4	17.0
1999.III	42 753.0	254 688.0	16.8
1999.IV	36 342.0	248 402.9	14.6

Notes:
a. International liquidity (IMF concept).
b. Monetary base plus domestic public debt.

Sources: Calculated from the Bulletin of the Central Bank of Brazil.

important consequences of the government's neomonetarist economic strategy. It was a symptom of the inefficacy of conventional fiscal and monetary policies, and it increased the financial fragility of the state and the external vulnerability of the economy.

CURRENCY CRISIS

During the 1990s, the Brazilian balance of payments constraint changed remarkably. In the past, this constraint emerged mainly through the scarcity of foreign exchange, leading to the accumulation of foreign debt and payments arrears. After the liberalization of the trade and capital accounts, the balance of payments constraint appeared through the level of the domestic interest rates and, later, through exchange rate volatility. The change in the balance of payments constraint reduced the significance of holding a large stock of reserves for the country's solvency.

In 1997, the feeling that the government's macroeconomic strategy was dangerously vulnerable led the monetary authorities to selling heavily dollar-linked securities and forward exchange rate contracts. The stock of dollar-linked securities increased from US$35.4 billion (15.4 per cent of the DPD) in December 1997, to US$56.9 billion (21.0 per cent) one year later (see Table 6.7). Moreover, the central bank, operating through Banco do Brasil, sold US$15–20 billion in futures contracts. In brief, the Brazilian government tried to stabilize the real through the nationalization of the exchange rate risk.

However, these measures were insufficient to stem the capital outflow after the Russian crisis, in the second half of 1998. The international reserves declined from US$70.9 billion, in June, to only US$33.8 billion nine months later. This was due mainly to short-term capital outflows and the difficulty of refinancing the foreign debt (the net foreign debt outflow reached US$43.5 billion). In these three quarters, the balance of payments deficit was US$46.5 billion (see Table 6.9). The monetary and fiscal policies were ineffective, and they transformed the government's domestic and external financing strategies into Ponzi schemes. Given the capital outflow, it became impossible to escape from this trap without a substantial currency devaluation.

Towards the end of 1998, the Brazilian government negotiated with the IMF and the G7 a financial support scheme including loans of US$41.3 billion over three years. The IMF agreement committed the Brazilian government to substantial primary budget surpluses, liberalizing the exchange rate and reducing the current account deficit. The central bank was also barred from operating in currency futures. This agreement had five main objectives: it should limit the impact of the Russian crisis, preserve the liberalization of

Table 6.9 External sector of the Brazilian economy; selected variables, 1996.I–1998.II, 1998.III–1999.I and 1999.II–1999.III (US$ million)

Period	RT (a)	FDe (b)	UF (c)	FT (d = b+c)	BP (e = a+d)	IR (f)	Me (g)
1996.I	−1 764.3	2 431.0	3 405.2	5 836.1	4 071.8	55 753.0	5 365.4
1996.II	−1 500.5	1 110.6	4 615.8	5 726.4	4 225.9	59 997.0	5 519.5
1996.III	−3 358.4	739.4	1 515.8	2 255.1	−1 103.3	58 775.0	190.3
1996.IV	−5 877.7	4 100.8	3 356.7	7 457.6	1 579.9	60 110.0	2 873.5
1997.I	−2 879.7	−1 388.5	3 380.8	1 992.3	−887.4	58 980.0	−337.0
1997.II	−3 259.3	−2 627.4	4 650.1	2 022.7	−1 236.6	57 615.1	−686.2
1997.III	−4 031.8	3 113.4	5 367.1	8 480.5	4 448.7	61 931.0	4 999.1
1997.IV	−4 981.4	−4 445.4	−771.0	−5 216.4	−10 197.8	52 173.0	−9 647.5
1998.I	−3 627.5	14 469.4	5 619.9	20 089.3	16 461.8	68 594.0	16 897.0
1998.II	−1 849.7	517.6	3 614.9	4 132.5	2 282.7	70 898.0	2 717.9
Total	−33 130.3	18 020.7	34 755.4	52 776.1	19 645.8	–	27 891.8
1998.III	−4 099.4	−16 946.2	−4 193.1	−21 139.2	−25 238.6	45 811.0	−24 803.5
1998.IV	−4 980.6	−10 654.1	4 829.8	−5 824.3	−10 804.9	44 556.0	−10 369.8
1999.I	−1 749.5	−15 916.8	7 210.0	n.d.	−10 456.3	33 848.3	−10 456.0
Total	−10 829.5	−43 517.0	7 846.7	−26 963.5	−46 499.9	–	−45 629.3
1999.II	−1 042.8	−4 272.6	4 416.6	n.a.	−898.9	41 345.5	−898.0
1999.III	−1 468.4	−6 924.0	9 619.1	n.a.	1 226.6	42 753.0	n.a.
Total	−2 511.3	−11 196.7	14 035.6	n.a.	327.7	–	−898.0

Notes: RT: real resource transfers to the rest of the world; FDe: foreign debt flows; UF: unilateral financial flows; FT: financial resource transfers from the rest of the world; BP: balance of payments surplus; IR: international reserves; Me: monetary impact of the foreign sector; n.d: no data; n.a.: not available.

Source: Calculated from the Bulletin of the Central Bank of Brazil.

Brazil's capital account, restore the country's foreign reserves, signal the 'credibility' of the domestic policies, and prevent the devaluation of the real (and the foreign capital invested in Brazil). These objectives, especially the commitment to international capital mobility, explain the IMF demand that Brazil should keep a minimum level of reserves of US$20 billion, *except* IMF resources (that is, IMF resources were unavailable for exchange rate management; they were held, ultimately, in order to preserve the possibility of capital flight). The IMF agreement completed the transformation of the central bank into the underwriter of the (foreign and domestic) financial capital invested in Brazil.

The impending currency crisis led to bitter policy debates in Brazil. Towards the end of 1998, newspaper headlines reported the previous day's decline in the country's reserves, government policies were criticized stridently, and lobbies for and against the devaluation clashed angrily in Congress, in public debates and in the press. Broadly speaking, the financial sector and the monetary authorities defended the exchange rate peg in order to facilitate industrial modernization, preserve the foreign currency value of the domestic assets owned by non-residents and to avoid upsetting the country's international integration. In contrast, the traditional manufacturing elites and the trade unions argued strongly for devaluation in order to increase external competitivity, stimulate the economic recovery and reduce unemployment.[32] (Both sides usually ignored the increasing risk of foreign takeovers because of the devaluation.)

In December, the central government's portfolio imbalance had become extremely serious. In spite of a fiscal surplus of US$10.7 billion, the domestic public debt increased by US$41 billion during the year, reaching US$270.9 billion (34.9 per cent of GDP). The average maturity of the federal securities had declined to only 3.3 months, and the country's reserves had declined by US$40 billion in six months. This decline, in spite of the interest rate increase to the politically feasible limit of 49.8 per cent, demonstrated the failure of neomonetarism both as an accumulation strategy and as a crisis management policy. In early January 1999, the central bank widened the exchange rate bands of the real, effectively devaluing the currency by 8 per cent, from R$1.21 to R$1.32 per dollar. The currency immediately collapsed, which forced the government to float the real. By the end of January the exchange rate reached R$1.98 per dollar (the real fell 40 per cent in 17 days; see Figure 6.4).

The devaluation of the real was very different from the other currency crises in the 1990s. These crises took most investors by surprise and led to substantial capital losses. In contrast, the collapse of the real was widely anticipated, and it brought substantial gains to the financial sector. The devaluation increased the net public sector debt by R$43.6 billion between December 1998 and June 1999 (mainly because of its impact on the

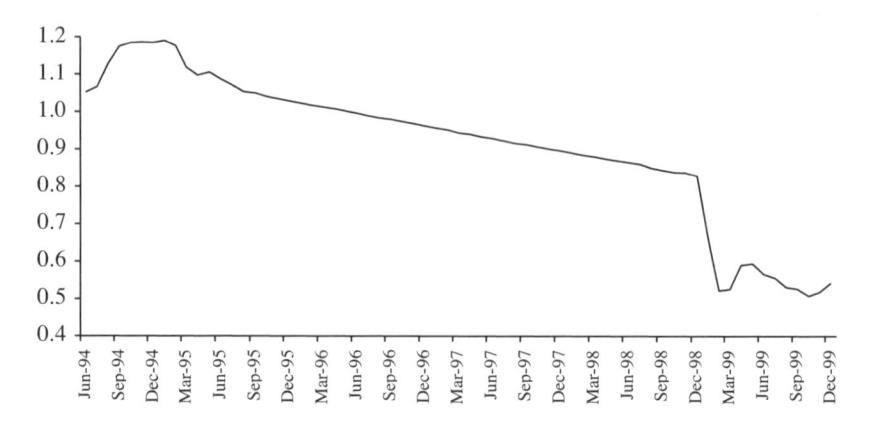

Note: * Monthly average rates.

Source: Central Bank of Brazil.

Figure 6.4 Brazil: nominal exchange rate, June 1994–December 1999 (US$/R$)*

dollar-linked federal securities).[33] In addition to this, the central bank lost around R$7.8 billion in the futures market, raising the direct cost of the devaluation for the central government to 5.6 per cent of GDP. In contrast, several financial institutions reported profits in *January* that were nearly twice as high as their previous *annual* profits.[34] The currency crisis showed that Brazil has a travesty of the welfare state, which protects financial capital efficiently, at the expense of the wage earners.[35]

In March 1999, the (new) board of the central bank introduced a policy of managed fluctuation of the real with inflation targets, in agreement with the IMF. The inflation targets were 8 per cent in 1999, 6 per cent in 2000 and 4 per cent in 2001, with bilateral margins of 2 per cent in each year. The actual rates were 8.9, 6.0 and 7.7 per cent – the inflation targets were hardly an unqualified success. The fluctuation of the real helped to consolidate the competitive advantage gained with the devaluation, expanded the scope for manufacturing output growth (and the expansion of export agriculture), and permitted a reduction in real interest rates.

The new exchange rate regime offered investors the opportunity to make a new speculative attack, this time against the dollar. At the end of February 1999 the real was clearly undervalued at R$2.06 per dollar. Interest rates were still around 40 per cent, in spite of the imminent disbursement of US$4 billion by the IMF. Moreover, the central bank extended the tax relief on capital gains by foreign investors, and reduced the minimum period for investment in Brazil. In March, the net capital inflows reached US$2.7 billion, mainly for investment in government securities and the stock market. This inflow appreciated the exchange rate to R$1.72 per dollar, bringing to the speculators gains of up to 20 per cent in one month.

The success of these speculative manoeuvres, first 'for' the real (in 1994–95), then 'against' it (in 1998), then 'for' once again (in 1999) demonstrate the rationale of the neomonetarist economic policies in Brazil. The monetary authority is committed to defending the short-term interests of the private financial institutions.[36] Substantial capital losses will be bailed out because of the need to avoid systemic risks, while long-term gains are guaranteed by the subsidies implicit in the monetary policy.

The devaluation of the real and the additional incentives provided to financial capital allowed the central bank to reduce the overnight interest rate from 43.2 per cent in March to 20.7 per cent in July. However, by mid-1999 the new exchange rate regime was already strained. In August, in order to reverse the creeping devaluation of the real and boost the foreign reserves (stagnant around US$40 billion, of which half was unavailable), the central bank started selling dollar-linked securities again. Only the sale of these securities allowed the exchange rate to settle below two per dollar without politically disastrous interest rate increases.[37]

CONCLUSION

The Brazilian economy grew slowly but changed substantially in the 1990s. This was largely due to the high cost of the neomonetarist economic strategy implemented in this period, especially through the Real Plan. The average rate of growth of GDP in the 1990s was only 1.7 per cent per annum, the lowest in the century. Investment declined from 22.1 per cent of GDP to 19.6 per cent, while domestic savings fell from 20.1 to 16.8 per cent of GDP. Manufacturing employment fell by one-third, and productive capacity declined in several important sectors, especially the capital goods industry. Industrial restructuring reduced the economy's employment generating capacity, and Brazil became more heavily dependent upon imports and foreign finance. Consequently, the balance of payments constraint became more severe.

This dismal performance was a direct result of the neomonetarist accumulation strategy implemented in the 1990s, especially under the Real Plan. The stabilization programme, although successful in reducing inflation, caused significant damage. Between 1990 and June 1994 Brazil transferred real resources to the rest of the world worth US$43.3 billion (see Table 6.10). Between July 1994 and December 1998 this transfer was reversed, and it reached US$50.6 billion: a shift of US$93.9 billion; both periods include 18

Table 6.10 Brazilian economy, selected variables, 1990.I–1994.II and 1994.III–1998.IV

Selected variables		1990.I–1994.II	1994.III–1998.IV
(a)	Trade balance (goods and services)	43 327.2	–50 572.1
(b)	Foreign debt flows (new loans minus interest and amortization)	–11 821.7	997.5
(c)	Unilateral financial flows	10 274.9	43 208.1
(d = b+c)	Financial resource inflows	–1 546.8	44 205.6
(e = a+d)	Balance of payments surplus	41 780.4	–6 366.5
(f)	International reserve increase[ae]	33 202.0	1 101.0
(g)	Foreign debt stock increase[bf]	24 856.0	94 870.0
(h)	Monetary base increase[ce]	–4 288.6	18 555.5
(i)	Domestic public debt increase[ce]	87 968.1	201 241.6
(j)	Monetary impact of the foreign sector[d]	36 492.1	7 432.5
(k)	Central government fiscal surplus[d]	6 249.8	42 404.7
(l)	Central government financial expenditures[d]	331 167.5	178 907.3
(m)	Foreign reserve cover (% change)[ce]	2.1	–37.1

Notes:
a. 1994.II minus 1989.IV.
b. 1994.IV minus 1990.IV.
c. 1994.II minus 1991.I.
d. Sum 1991.I–1994.II.
e. 1998.IV minus 1994.III.
f. 1998.IV minus 1994.IV.

Source: Central Bank of Brazil and Office of the National Treasury.

quarters. Partly for this reason, the current account shifted from balance to a deficit of US$108.7 billion. These deficits were financed through financial resource transfers from the rest of the world, which increased from nearly zero to US$44.2 billion. The most important element of these transfers was foreign direct and portfolio inflows, which quadrupled from US$15.8 billion to US$63.3 billion (however, profit and dividend remittances and the payment of factor services increased from US$11.0 billion to US$26.4 billion).

Largely for these reasons the balance of payments surplus (US$41.8 billion) turned into a deficit (US$6.4 billion), while the international reserves, which had increased by US$33.2 billion in the first period, were virtually stagnant during the Real Plan, in spite of the costly effort to attract foreign capital.

High interest rates were the main factor responsible for the rapid increase of the DPD. Between 1991 (after the Collor Plan) and mid-1994, the domestic public debt increased by US$88.0 billion, in spite of a fiscal surplus of US$6.2 billion. Under the Real Plan, the DPD increased by US$201.2 billion, in spite of the much larger fiscal surplus of US$42.4 billion. This increase in the domestic public debt was mostly due to the high cost of the DPD (US$178.9 billion), the local government debt swaps (US$78.7 billion), financial sector assistance (US$46.9 billion), and other central government debt costs (US$27.2 billion). The monetary impact of the foreign sector during the Real Plan was hardly significant (US$7.4 billion).

The financial priority of the new accumulation strategy worsened the balance of payments constraint, created economic instability and prevented sustained economic growth between 1995 and 1998. The devaluation of the real in early 1999 was a reflex of the partial collapse of this strategy. Certain social groups (especially the São Paulo manufacturing elite) tried to use the devaluation to reverse these disequilibria, and increase the weight of productive capital in the process of international integration of the Brazilian economy. They have failed, and neomonetarism remains the hegemonic economic policy in Brazil.

NOTES

*   We are grateful to Bruno Saraiva for his invaluable contribution to this chapter, and to Philip Arestis, Maria A. Baracho, Maria L. Mollo, Malcolm Sawyer, Marcio Valença and Howard Walker for their helpful suggestions. Responsibility for the remaining errors and omissions is our own. This project was partly funded by the Nuffield Foundation (SGS/LB/203) and by South Bank University Business School.

1. The system of accumulation is determined by the economic structures and institutional arrangements that typify the process of capital accumulation in a specific region, and in a certain period (Fine and Rustomjee 1996). This is a relatively concrete concept, with no direct relationship with more abstract concepts such as mode of regulation (Aglietta 1979; Boyer 1990). The accumulation strategy includes the economic policies associated with a given system of accumulation.

2. The study includes the years 1991–99, with emphasis on the 1994–98 period. The year 1990 has been excluded because of the transitory impact of the Collor stabilization plan.

3. In this chapter, the DPD includes the interest-bearing securities issued by the Treasury and the central bank, and held by the private sector or by state-owned funds and institutions, including BNDES (National Bank for Economic and Social Development) and FAT (Worker's Assistance Fund).

4. The emphasis, below, on the autonomous determinants of the central government's primary liabilities does not imply that Brazilian money supply is exogenous ('central government' is defined in note 12). The tensions between money demand (mediated by the financial system) and the autonomous determinants of money supply, analysed here through the changes in the stock of primary liabilities, are important causes of the high inflation and macroeconomic instability between the 1970s and the mid-1990s (see Saad-Filho and Mollo 2002). This chapter analyses only the primary liabilities of the central government, rather than the money supply. In particular, it does not investigate the behaviour of banks

(especially their liquidity preference or the impact of changes in compulsory reserves), or credit demand (see Studart 1999a, 1999b).
5. This section draws heavily upon Arestis and Sawyer (1998); see also Anderson (2000). The Brazilian case is analysed by Saad-Filho and Maldonado Filho (1998).
6. This argument is flawed because 'credibility' and 'investor confidence' are intangible and strongly influenced by their expected values. Policies designed to maximize 'credibility' almost invariably overestimate the levels of saving, investment and growth that can be achieved through the government's 'good behaviour' (Fine 1999a).
7. See Calvo et al. (1993), Fiori (1999) and Toporowski (2000). Between 1989 and 1993 the US federal funds rate declined from 9.2 to 3.0 per cent. The corresponding rates in Japan declined from 7.5 to 2.1 per cent, and in the UK from 14.8 to 5.8 per cent (see Coutinho et al. 1999, p. 65, n. 2).
8. José Sarney was president of Brazil between 1985 and 1990. His successor, Fernando Collor, was impeached in 1992, and vice-president Itamar Franco completed his term. One of his finance ministers, Fernando Henrique Cardoso, was elected president in 1994, and re-elected in 1998.
9. Brazilian industrial policies in the last two decades are surveyed by Cruz (1997) and Suzigan and Villela (1997).
10. These concepts aggregate categories in the Brazilian balance of payments which, at the time, did not conform to IMF or OECD standards.
11. The central government includes the federal government (Treasury), the social security system and the central bank of Brazil. Local (state and municipal) governments, state enterprises and federal trusts (except social security) are included in the private sector, because they enjoy financial autonomy and cannot monetize their own debts.
12. Governo do Brasil (1993); see also Nogueira Batista (1996), Bacha (1997), Dornbusch (1997), Saad-Filho and Maldonado Filho (1998), Almeida (1999), Saad-Filho et al. (1999) and Saad-Filho (2000).
13. The inflation losses of the wage earners are explained and measured by Kane and Morisett (1993), Bacha (1997) and Dornbusch (1997). They are mostly due to wage erosion because of inflation. The gains of the wage earners after the Real Plan largely explain the estimate that the real income of the poorest 50 per cent of the population increased by 30 per cent after the Real Plan. If this improvement did occur it was transitory, since this group's share of the national income declined from 12.2 to 11.6 per cent between 1993 and 1995. The improvement and the subsequent deterioration of the income distribution under the Real Plan are analysed by Neri and Considera (1996) and Gonçalves (1999b).
14. For estimates of the overvaluation of the real, see Kilsztajn (1996), Nogueira Batista (1996, p. 34), Bacha (1997, p. 201), Dornbusch (1997, p. 375) and Fishlow (1997).
15. Between January 1994 and January 1996, the price of tradables declined by one third *vis-à-vis* non-tradables (Bacha 1997, pp. 196–7). The price ratio continued to decline at least until mid-1998 (Castro 1999, p. 82).
16. The contractionary monetary policy raised the interest rates on personal loans to 237 per cent in May, while rates on short-term commercial loans reached 176 per cent (Nogueira Batista 1996, p. 48; see also Dornbusch 1997, p. 375).
17. 'At the beginning of the year [1995] the *policy of maintaining trade balance deficits was reevaluated*, in light of the uncertainty in foreign financial markets. Consequently, the government sought to define a strategy aimed at balancing trade flows. Initially, special attention was given to the export sector, so as to increase revenues through added foreign sales. Later on, steps were taken to regulate imports in sectors less detrimental to the process of price stabilization and industrial modernization. However, on several occasions, the priority accorded [to] the fight against inflation made it necessary to facilitate imports in order to offset supply deficiencies on the domestic market' (Banco Central do Brasil 1995, p. 103, original in English, emphasis added).
18. 'One of the most important aspects of the on-going transformation [of the Brazilian industry] is the deepening of foreign integration in the productive sector which is reflected, above all, in the large and increasing flow of foreign direct investment' (Laplane and Sarti 1999, p. 197).

19. PriceWaterhouse Coopers (*Folha de S.Paulo*, 21 January 2000, p. 2–1). For similar estimates, see Gonçalves (1999a, pp. 138–42).
20. Paraphrasing Joseph Schumpeter, Gustavo Franco, the central bank president, called this process 'creative destruction'. However, Tavares (1999) was closer to the mark when she criticized this government-sponsored 'non-creative destruction'.
21. IBGE data tend to underestimate the level of unemployment. According to the trade union-sponsored research institute, DIEESE, total (open and disguised) unemployment in São Paulo reached 20.3 per cent in April 1999. For an outstanding analysis of the dismantling of the formal labour markets in the wake of the new system of accumulation, see Pochmann (1999).
22. During the 1990s Brazilian labour markets became more 'flexible' in three ways. First, the right of labour unions to represent individual workers in court was curtailed. Second, a 1998 law allowed fixed-term contracts, which facilitated dismissal and reduced holidays and other benefits, and created 'overtime banks' allowing firms to impose overtime or reduce working hours at zero cost. Finally, throughout the decade small and medium-sized firms increasingly avoided the labour laws, for example, by refusing to register their employees. This process was facilitated by the declining bargaining power of the workers, and it was condoned by the government. The number of registered (legally protected) workers (*trabalhadores com carteira*) in Brazil declined by 15 per cent in the 1990s. In the manufacturing sector, the decline reached 25 per cent.
23. Machine imports increased from US$6.0 billion in 1990 to US$ 26.2 billion in 1997 (*Conjuntura Econômica*, November 1998). Their growth was partly due to the dislocation of domestic production (the capital goods sector was one of the worst hit by foreign competition, takeovers and 'rationalization').
24. See Cano (1999) and Laplane and Sarti (1999, pp. 222–4). '[The] flows of [Brazilian] exports to the Argentine market are concentrated on medium–high and medium–low technological intensity products, which include 70–75% of the sales of Brazilian industrial goods. The participation of these products in Brazilian exports to the rest of the world is less than 40%' (Machado and Markwald 1997, p. 197).
25. For a detailed analysis of the changes of productivity, structure of employment, increasing labour 'flexibility' and unemployment growth under the Real Plan, see CNI/CEPAL (1997) and Ramos and Almeida Reis (1998). For a long-term analysis, see Bonelli and Gonçalves (1998) and Urani (1998).
26. See Gonçalves (1999a, pp. 74–5). For a detailed analysis of the growing internationalization of Brazilian industry, see Laplane and Sarti (1999).
27. Real interest rates paid on federal securities between August and November 1994, before the Mexican crisis, were on average 1.7 per cent per month (23.3 per cent annually). In the first three months of 1995, they increased, on average, to 2.5 per cent (35.1 per cent annually).
28. Gonçalves (1999a, p. 163) estimates that the total number of banks in Brazil declined from 230 in 1994 to 179 in 1998. At least 25 medium and large Brazilian banks were sold off, of which at least 11 of them to foreign banks. Foreign participation among the 50 largest banks (which control 98 per cent of the assets and branches of the system) more than doubled from nine, in 1994, to 20, in 1998. Foreign control of the assets of the financial system reached 40 per cent in 1999.
29. See Bacha (1997, p. 190) and Nogueira Batista (1996, p. 56). Anecdotal evidence suggests that half of these costs will never be recouped.
30. In spite of this, conventional wisdom insists that fiscal profligacy was the main factor responsible for the explosive growth of the DPD. For a critique, see Munhoz (1994).
31. 'High average interest rates, and their instability ... are extremely damaging to the fiscal balance, economic growth, and economic competitivity ... *this is due to the financial priority of the economic policies, to the disadvantage of the real economy*' (IEDI 1998, p. 6, emphasis added).
32. In 1998 the manufacturing leader Eugênio Staub stated that '[the] dialogue of the private sector with the government is at its lowest level ever. The state bureaucracy has become self-sufficient and arrogant ... [T]hey do not listen to us and, when they listen, they do not

believe us'. His colleague Roberto Nicolau Jeha, was more incisive: 'We are on our knees. We are facing extinction. Brazilian manufacturers are finished and we have no dignity left. We are being taken to the slaughterhouse and keep praising modernisation' (Diniz 1999, pp. 172–3).

33. Bulletin of the Central Bank of Brazil, Table IV.13, December 1999.
34. Bank profit rates in Brazil are usually around 11 per cent. In January 1999, several banks' profit rates reached 200 to 400 per cent. Total bank profits in 1998 were R$1.8 billion; in the month of January 1999, these profits reached R$3.3 billion (Aloysio Biondi, *Folha de S.Paulo*, March 1999, p. 2–2).
35. George Soros declared that the devaluation of the real had only a small impact on the international financial system because it had been widely anticipated, and that Brazil offered protection mechanisms unavailable to investors elsewhere.
36. Armínio Fraga, the new president of the central bank, 'has shown that the government now thinks like the market, and this is good. Before, the president of the Central Bank was a bureaucrat' (Blairo Maggi, in *Dinheiro*, **121**, 22 December 1999, p. 30). This statement is incorrect; most previous central bank presidents were either academics or financial market executives.
37. For a critical analysis of the floating exhange rate regime, see Mollo and Silva (1999) and Saad-Filho and Morais (2002).

REFERENCES

Aglietta, Michel (1979), *A Theory of Capitalist Regulation: The US Experience*, London: Verso.

Almeida, Júlio G. (1999), 'Plano Real: do Sucesso ao Impasse', *Cadernos PUC Economia*, **8**, 11–47.

Anderson, Perry (2000), 'Renewals', *New Left Review*, **2** (1), 5–24.

Arestis, P. and M. Glickman (2002), 'Financial crisis in South East Asia: dispelling illusion the Minskyan way', *Cambridge Journal of Economics*, **26**, 237–60.

Arestis, P. and M. Sawyer (1998), 'New Labour, new monetarism', *Soundings: A Journal of Politics and Culture*, 9 (Summer), 24–41.

Bacha, Edmar (1997), 'Plano Real: Uma Segunda Avaliação', in IPEA/CEPAL (eds), *O Plano Real e Outras Experiências Internacionais de Estabilização*, Brasília: IPEA (Instituto de Pesquisa Econômica Aplicada (Institute of Applied Economic Research)).

Banco Central do Brasil (1995), *Relatório Anual*, Brasília: Banco Central.

Banco Central do Brasil (1993), *O Regime Cambial Brasileiro: Evolução Recente e Perspectivas*, Brasília: Banco Central.

Barros, J.R.M. and M. Almeida Jr (1997), 'Análise do Ajuste do Sistema Financeiro no Brasil', *Política Comparada*, **1** (2), May–August, 89–132.

Bonelli, Regis (1999), 'A Reestruturação Industrial Brasileira nos Anos 90: Reação Empresarial e Mercado de Trabalho', in OIT (International Labour Organisation) (ed.), *Abertura e Ajuste do Mercado de Trabalho no Brasil*, São Paulo: Editora 34.

Bonelli, R. and R.R. Gonçalves (1998), 'Para Onde Vai a Estrutura Industrial Brasileira?', in IPEA (ed.), *A Economia Brasileira em Perspectiva*, Brasília: IPEA (Instituto de Pesquisa Econômica Aplicada (Institute of Applied Economic Research)).

Boyer, Robert (1990), *A Teoria da Regulação: Uma Análise Crítica*, São Paulo: Nobel.

Bulmer-Thomas, Victor (ed.) (1994), *The New Economic Model in Latin America and Its Impact on Income Distribution and Poverty*, London: Macmillan.

Calvo, G. and M. King (1998), *The Debt Burden and Its Consequences for Monetary Policy*, London: Macmillan.
Calvo, G., L. Leiderman and C. Reinhart (1993), 'Capital inflows and exchange rate appreciation in Latin America: the role of external factors', *IMF Staff Papers*, **40** (1), 108–51.
Cano, Wilson (1999), 'América Latina: do Desenvolvimentismo ao Neoliberalismo', in J.L. Fiori (ed.), *Estados e Moedas no Desenvolvimento das Nações*, Petrópolis: Vozes.
Cardim de Carvalho, Fernando J. (1999), 'Sistema Bancário e Competitividade: Efeitos da Penetração do Capital Estrangeiro no Setor Bancário Brasileiro', in C.A.N. Costa and C.A. Arruda (eds), *Em Busca do Futuro: A Competitividade no Brasil*, Rio de Janeiro: Campus.
Carvalho, Carlos E. (1999), 'As Finanças Públicas no Plano Real', unpublished manuscript.
Castro, Antonio B. (1999), 'O Lado Real do Real: O Debate e Algumas Surpresas', in J.P.A. Magalhães, A.S. Mineiro and L.A. Elias (eds), *Vinte Anos de Política Econômica*, Rio de Janeiro: Contraponto.
CEPAL (UN Economic Commission for Latin America) (1999), *Panorama Social da América Latina, 1998*, New York: United Nations.
Chang, Ha-Joon (1994), *The Political Economy of Industrial Policy*, Cambridge: Cambridge University Press.
CNI/CEPAL (National Confederation of Industry/UN Economic Commission for Latin America) (1997), *Investimentos na Indústria Brasileira 1995–1999 – Características e Determinantes*, Rio de Janeiro: CNI.
Coutinho, L., P. Baltar and F. Camargo (1999), 'Desempenho Industrial e do Emprego sob a Política de Estabilização', in OIT (ed.), *Abertura e Ajuste do Mercado de Trabalho no Brasil*, São Paulo: Editora 34.
Cruz, Sebastião C.V. (1997), *Estado e Economia em Tempo de Crise: Política Industrial e Transição Política no Brasil nos Anos 80*, Campinas: Unicamp.
Cysne, Rubens P. (1994), 'Imposto Inflacionário e Transferências Inflacionárias no Brasil', *Revista de Economia Política*, **14** (3), July–September, 121–9.
Diniz, Ely (1999), 'Globalização, Elites Empresariais e Democracia no Brasil dos Anos 90', *Ensaios FEE*, **20** (1), 155–78.
Dornbusch, Rudiger (1997), 'Brazil's incomplete stabilization and reform', *Brookings Papers on Economic Activity*, **1**, 367–94.
Dornbusch, R. and M. Simonsen (eds) (1983), *Inflation, Debt and Indexation*, Cambridge, MA: MIT Press.
Feijó, C.A. and P.G.M. Carvalho (1998), 'Structural changes in the Brazilian economy: an analysis of the evolution of industrial productivity in the 1990s', unpublished manuscript.
Fine, Ben (1999a), 'Industrial policy and South Africa: a strategic view', unpublished manuscript.
Fine, Ben (1999b), 'Globalisation and finance', unpublished manuscript.
Fine, B. and Z. Rustomjee (1996), *The Political Economy of South Africa: From Minerals–Energy Complex to Industrialisation*, London: Hurst & Co.
Fiori, José Luís (1999), *Estados e Moedas no Desenvolvimento das Nações*, Petrópolis: Vozes.
Fishlow, Albert (1997), 'Is the Real Plan for real?', in S.K. Purcell and R. Roett (eds), *Brazil under Cardoso*, Boulder, CO: Lynne Rienner.
Garcia, Márcio G.P. (1995), 'Política Monetária e Cambial: Algumas Lições do

Período Recente para o Real', in IPEA/CEPAL (eds), *Transformação Produtiva com Equidade: O Debate no Brasil; Condicionantes Macroeconômicos*, Brasília: IPEA (Instituto de Pesquisa Econômica Aplicada (Institute of Applied Economic Research)).

Gonçalves, Reinaldo (1999a), *Globalização e Desnacionalização*, Rio de Janeiro: Paz e Terra.

Gonçalves, Reinaldo (1999b), 'Distribuição de Riqueza e Renda: Alternativa para a Crise Brasileira', in Ivo Lesbaupin (ed.), *O Desmonte da Nação: Balanço do Governo FHC*, Petrópolis: Vozes.

Governo do Brasil (1993), *Exposição de Motivos n° 393 do Ministro da Fazenda*, Brasília: Congresso Nacional.

IEDI (Institute for Industrial Development Studies) (1998), *Trajetória Recente da Indústria Brasileira*, Outubro: IEDI.

Kane, Cheikh and Jacques Morisett (1993), 'Who would vote for inflation in Brazil? An integrated framework approach to inflation and income distribution', World Bank Policy Research Working Paper 1183, September.

Kilsztajn, Samuel (1996), 'Ancoragem Cambial e Estabilização', in R.R. Sawaya (ed.), *O Plano Real e a Política Econômica*, São Paulo: Educ.

Kume, Honorio (1998), 'A Política de Importação no Plano Real e a Estrutura de Proteção Efetiva', in IPEA (ed.), *A Economia Brasileira em Perspectiva*, Brasília: IPEA (Instituto de Pesquisa Econômica Aplicada (Institute of Applied Economic Research)).

Lacerda, Antonio C. (1996), 'Os Paradoxos da Política Econômica do Real', in: R.R. Sawaya (ed.), *O Plano Real e a Política Econômica*, São Paulo: Educ.

Laplane, M.F. and F. Sarti (1999), 'O Investimento Direto Estrangeiro no Brasil nos Anos 90: Determinantes e Estratégias', in D. Chudnovsky (ed.), *Investimentos Externos no Mercosul*, Campinas: Papirus.

Lopes, Francisco L. (1986), *O Choque Heterodoxo: Combate à Inflação e Reforma Monetária*, Rio de Janeiro: Campus.

Machado, J.B.M. and R.A. Markwald (1997), 'Dinâmica Recente do Processo de Integração do Mercosul', in J.P. dos Reis Velloso (ed.), *Brasil: Desafios de Um País em Transformação*, Rio de Janeiro: José Olympio.

Mollo, Maria de Lourdes and Maria Luiza Silva (1999), 'A Liberalização do Câmbio no Brasil: Revisitando a Discussão dos Pressupostos Teóricos Embutidos nas Prescrições Cambiais Alternativas', *Estudos Econômicos*, **29** (2), 189–227.

Morais, Lecio (1998), 'A Crise Brasileira, a Dívida e o Déficit públicos: Para que Superávit Fiscal?', *Princípios*, **51**, 22–35.

Munhoz, Dércio G. (1994), 'Sobram Recursos ao Governo; Para Que o Ajuste Fiscal?', *Indicadores Econômicos*, **21** (4), January, 127–40.

Neri, Marcelo and Cláudio Considera (1996), 'Crescimento, Desigualdade e Pobreza: O Impacto da Estabilização', in IPEA (ed.), *A Economia Brasileira em Perspectiva*, Brasília: IPEA.

Nogueira Batista Jr., Paulo (1996), 'Plano Real: Estabilização Monetária e Desequilíbrio Externo', *Cadernos Temáticos*, 2, Sindicato dos Engenheiros do Rio de Janeiro.

Pochmann, Marcio (1999), *O Trabalho sob Fogo Cruzado: Exclusão, Desemprego e Precarização no Final do Século*, São Paulo: Contexto.

Ramos, L. and J.G. Almeida Reis (1998), 'Emprego no Brasil nos Anos 90', in IPEA (ed.), *A Economia Brasileira em Perspectiva*, Brasília: IPEA (Instituto de Pesquisa Econômica Aplicada (Institute of Applied Economic Research)).

Rosar, Orlando Oscar (1999), *Considerações Sobre a Evolução da Dívida Pública*

Brasileira nas Últimas Três Décadas, Anais do IV Encontro Nacional de Economia Política, Porto Alegre.
Saad-Filho, Alfredo (2000), 'Inflation theory: a review of the literature and a new research agenda', *Research in Political Economy*, **19**, 335–62.
Saad-Filho, A. and E. Maldonado Filho (1998), 'Inflation, growth and economic policy in Brazil', *Indicadores Econômicos*, **21**, September, 87–103.
Saad-Filho, A. and M. Mollo (2002), 'Inflation and stabilization in Brazil: a political economy analysis', *Review of Radical Political Economics*, **34** (2), 109–35.
Saad-Filho, A. and L. Morais (2002) 'Neomonetarist dreams and realities: a review of the Brazilian experience', in P. Davidson (ed.) *A Post Keynesian Perspective on Twenty-First Century Economic Problems*, Cheltenham, UK and Northampton, MA, USA: Edward Elgar.
Saad-Filho, A., L. Morais and W. Coelho (1999), 'Financial liberalisation, currency instability and crisis in Brazil: another plan bites the dust', *Capital and Class*, **68**, Summer, 9–14.
Silva, Sérgio S. (1976), *Expansão Cafeeira e Origem da Indústria no Brasil*, São Paulo: Alfa-Omega.
Studart, Rogério (1999a), *Estrutura e Operação dos Sistemas Financeiros no Mercosul: Perspectivas a Partir das Reformas Institucionais dos Anos 1990 e para a Integração Financeira das Economias do Bloco*, Rio de Janeiro: Relatório CEPAL/IPEA/IE-UFRJ.
Studart, Rogério (1999b), 'Financial opening and deregulation of Brazil's financial systems in the 1990s: possible effects on its pattern of development financing', unpublished manuscript.
Suzigan, Wilson (1986), *Indústria Brasileira: Origem e Desenvolvimento*, São Paulo: Brasiliense.
Suzigan, W. and A.V. Villela (1997), *Industrial Policy in Brazil*, Campinas: Unicamp.
Tavares, Maria da Conceição (1999), *Destruição Não Criadora*, Rio de Janeiro: Record.
Toporowski, Jan (2000), *The End of Finance*, Cheltenham, UK and Northampton, MA, USA: Edward Elgar.
Urani, André (1998), 'Ajuste Macroeconômico e Flexibilidade do Mercado de Trabalho no Brasil: 1981/95', in IPEA (ed.), *A Economia Brasileira em Perspectiva*, Brasília: IPEA (Instituto de Pesquisa Econômica Aplicada (Institute of Applied Economic Research)).

7. Macroeconomic policies of the Economic and Monetary Union: theoretical underpinnings and challenges

Philip Arestis and Malcolm Sawyer

INTRODUCTION

This chapter is focused on the macroeconomic policies of the European Monetary Union. It seeks to decipher the type of economic analysis and macroeconomic policies of the Economic and Monetary Union (EMU) theoretical and policy framework. It argues that the challenges to the EMU macroeconomic policies lie in their potential to achieve full employment and low inflation in the euro area. It is concluded that these policies as they currently operate have not performed satisfactorily since the inception of the EMU and are unlikely to operate any better in the future. The chapter presents some alternatives, which are based on a different theoretical framework and which propose different institutional arrangements and policies. The first main section is entitled 'Theoretical underpinnings of the EMU model', and deals with the nature of the economic model surrounding the EMU which is seen as essentially what has been termed the 'new consensus' in macroeconomics. The macroeconomic policies that emanate from this model are then deciphered in the section entitled 'EMU macroeconomic policies'. The key challenge is whether in the EMU these policies are adequate to deal with the problems of unemployment and inflation, and thus help to achieve and maintain a framework of full employment. The two sections that follow examine monetary policy and fiscal policy, respectively, within the EMU context. They are both found as unable to steer the euro area to a non-inflationary full-employment environment. In the section entitled 'Policies for full employment and low inflation', it is argued that the institutional and policy arrangements surrounding the EMU and the euro desperately need to be changed in that they are quite inadequate to deal with problems of unemployment and inflation. We propose alternative policies and institutional arrangements. A final section summarizes the argument and concludes.

THEORETICAL UNDERPINNINGS OF THE EMU MODEL

It is unlikely that economic policy pursued by any government or institution is fully consistent either internally or with some theoretical paradigm. However, in view of the approach adopted by the EMU, and the theoretical positions put forward by its officials (see, for example, European Commission 2000 and Issing 2003 for recent expositions), it can be thought of as embedded in the 'new consensus' macroeconomics paradigm. We argue that the approach can be viewed as 'new consensus' through its emphasis on the supply-side-determined equilibrium level of unemployment (the 'natural rate' or the non-accelerating inflation rate of unemployment, the NAIRU), its neglect of aggregate or effective demand (particularly in the long run), and of fiscal policy, and the elevation of monetary policy at the expense of fiscal policy.

We postulate that the economics of the EMU can be understood as based on the following elements listed below, which we would argue justify the description of a 'new consensus' variety. These elements are as follows:[1]

1. The market economy is viewed as essentially stable, and macroeconomic policy (particularly discretionary fiscal policy) may well destabilize the market economy. Markets, and particularly the financial markets, make well-informed judgements on the sustainability of economic policies, especially so in the current environment of open, globalized, capital and financial markets.

2. Monetary policy is taken as the main instrument of macroeconomic policy, with the view that it is a flexible instrument for achieving medium-term stabilization objectives: it can be adjusted quickly in response to macroeconomic developments. Indeed, monetary policy is the most direct determinant of inflation, so much so that in the long run the inflation rate is the only macroeconomic variable that monetary policy can affect (see, for example, ECB 2003c). Fiscal policy is no longer viewed as a powerful macroeconomic instrument (in any case it is subject to the slow and uncertain legislative process). It is recognized that the budget position will vary over the course of the business cycle in a counter-cyclical manner (that is deficit rising in downturn, surplus rising in upturn), which helps to dampen the scale of economic fluctuations (that is, act as an 'automatic stabilizer'). But these fluctuations in the budget position take place around a balanced budget on average over the

cycle. The budget (at least on current account) can and should be balanced over the course of the business cycle. Fiscal policies 'based on clear mandates and rules reflect a macroeconomic policy design that is generally preferable to the ad-hoc discretionary co-ordination of day-to-day policy action in the face of shocks' (ECB 2003c, p. 37). Monetary policy has, thus, been upgraded and fiscal policy has been downgraded.

3. Monetary policy can be used to meet the objective of low rates of inflation (which are desirable in this view, since low, and stable, rates of inflation are conducive to healthy growth rates).[2] However, monetary policy should not be operated by politicians but by experts (whether banks, economists or others) in the form of an 'independent' central bank (ECB 2003c, pp. 40–41). Indeed, those operating monetary policy should be more 'conservative', that is place greater weight on low inflation and less weight on the level of unemployment than the politicians (Rogoff 1985). Politicians would be tempted to use monetary policy for short-term gain (lower unemployment) at the expense of long-term loss (higher inflation). An 'independent' central bank would also have greater credibility in the financial markets and be seen to have a stronger commitment to low inflation than politicians do.[3]

4. Credibility is recognized as paramount in the conduct of monetary policy to avoid problems associated with time inconsistency. This is an argument that reinforces the requirement of central bank independence. It is argued that a policy which lacks credibility because of time inconsistency is neither optimal nor feasible (Kydland and Prescott 1977). The only credible policy is the one that leaves the authority no freedom as to how to react to developments in the future, and that even if aggregate demand policies matter in the short run in this model, a policy of non-intervention is preferable. It is precisely because of the time-inconsistency and credibility problems that monetary policy should be assigned to a 'credible' and independent central bank. Such a central bank should be given as its sole objective that of price stability.

5. Inflation targeting is preferred to money supply targeting. Inflation targeting is neither a rule nor discretion (in practice only degrees of discretion prevail): it is rather a framework for monetary policy whereby public announcement of official inflation targets, or target ranges, is undertaken along with explicit acknowledgement that low and stable inflation is monetary policy's primary long-term objective. This improves communication between the public and policy makers and provides discipline, accountability, transparency and flexibility in monetary policy. Inflation targeting has been described as 'constrained' or 'enlightened' discretion, in that inflation targets serve as a nominal anchor for monetary policy. As such, monetary policy imposes discipline on the central bank and the

government within a flexible policy framework. For example, even if monetary policy is used to address short-run stabilization objectives, the long-run inflation objective must not be compromised, thereby imposing consistency and rationality in policy choices (in doing so, monetary policy focuses public expectations and provides a reference point to judge short-run policies). Although the European Central Bank (ECB) allegedly does not pursue an inflation targeting policy (Duisenberg 2003a; Issing 2003; see, also, our discussion below), it does, none the less, pursue a monetary policy strategy with 'the clear commitment to the maintenance of price stability over the medium term' which 'implies a stable nominal anchor to the economy in all circumstances' (ECB 2001b, p. 49).

6. The level of economic activity fluctuates around the NAIRU, and unemployment below (above) the NAIRU would lead to higher (lower) rates of inflation. The NAIRU is a supply-side phenomenon closely related to the workings of the labour market.[4] The source of domestic inflation (relative to the expected rate of inflation) is seen to arise from unemployment falling below the NAIRU, and inflation is postulated to accelerate if unemployment is held below the NAIRU. However, in the long run there is no trade-off between inflation and unemployment, and the economy has to operate (on average) at the NAIRU if accelerating inflation is to be avoided. In the long run, inflation is viewed as a monetary phenomenon in that the pace of inflation is aligned with the rate of interest. Monetary policy is, thus, in the hands of central bankers. Control of the money supply is not an issue, essentially because of the instability of the demand for money that makes the impact of changes in the money supply a highly uncertain channel of influence.

7. The essence of Say's Law holds, namely that the level of effective demand does not play an independent role in the (long-run) determination of the level of economic activity, and adjusts to underpin the supply-side-determined level of economic activity (which itself corresponds to the NAIRU). Shocks to the level of demand can be met by variations in the rate of interest to ensure that inflation does not develop (if unemployment falls below the NAIRU).

Most of these general ideas can be seen as formalized (explicitly or implicitly) in what has become known as the 'new consensus' of macroeconomics (see, for example, Arestis and Sawyer 2002b). This 'new consensus' can be summarized in the following three equations:

$$Y_t^g = a_0 + a_1 Y_{t-1}^g + a_2 E(Y_{t+1}^g) - a_3[R_t - E_t(p_{t+1})] + s_1 \qquad (7.1)$$

$$p_t = b_1 Y_t^g + b_2 p_{t-1} + b_3 E_t(p_{t+1}) + s_2 \quad \text{(with } b_2 + b_3 = 1\text{)} \tag{7.2}$$

$$R_t = RR^* + E_t(p_{t+1}) + c_1 Y_{t-1}^g + c_2(p_{t-1} - p^T) \tag{7.3}$$

where Y^g is the output gap, R is nominal rate of interest, p is inflation, and p^T is inflation target, RR^* is the 'equilibrium' real rate of interest (that is the rate of interest consistent with zero output gap which implies from equation (7.2) a constant rate of inflation), and s_i (with $i = 1, 2$) represents stochastic shocks.

Equation (7.1) is the aggregate demand equation; equation (7.2) is a Phillips curve; and (7.3) is a monetary policy operating rule which replaces the old LM (liquidity–money supply) curve. There are three equations and three unknowns: output, interest rate and inflation. This model has a number of additional, and relevant, characteristics. Equation (7.1) resembles the traditional IS (investment–savings), but expenditure decisions are seen to be based on intertemporal optimization of a utility function. There are both lagged adjustment and forward-looking elements; the model allows for sticky prices (the lagged price level in the Phillips curve relationship) and full price flexibility in the long run. The term $E_t(p_{t+1})$ in equation (7.2) reflects central bank credibility. A central bank that credibly signals its intention to achieve and maintain low inflation will be 'rewarded' by lower expectations on the rate of inflation. The inclusion of term $E_t(p_{t+1})$ in equation (7.2) indicates that it may be possible to reduce current inflation at a significantly lower cost in terms of output than otherwise. This is an important element in ECB monetary policy (see, for example, Duisenberg 1999; Issing 2003). The operating rule implies that 'policy' becomes a systematic adjustment to economic developments rather than an exogenous process. Also, it contains no stochastic shock implying that monetary policy operates without random shocks. It contains the neutrality of money property, with inflation determined by monetary policy (that is, the rate of interest), and equilibrium values of real variables are independent of the money supply. The final characteristic we wish to highlight is that money has no role in the model; it is merely a 'residual', and this is more extensively discussed in Arestis and Sawyer (2003a, 2003b).

The three relationships that summarize the 'new consensus' contain all the essential elements of the theoretical framework of the EMU (see, also, ECB 2003a). There are, however, two important differences worth highlighting here though pursued further in the section on monetary policy. The first is that arguably the ECB does not pursue inflation targeting. Duisenberg (2003a) is adamant that the ECB approach does not entail an inflation target: 'I protest against the word "target". We do not have a target … we won't have a target'. The second is that in the ECB view the demand for money in the euro area is a stable relationship in the long run – most central banks would suggest the opposite in the case of their economies.[5]

EMU MACROPOLICIES

The launch of the euro as a 'real' currency (since January 2002), rather than as a 'virtual' currency (since January 1999), took place against an economic environment of slowing growth and rising unemployment across the world and the euro area, adding to the already high levels of unemployment. Table 7.1 illustrates this point. Since the second quarter of 2000, there has been a continuous slowdown in real GDP growth rate in the euro area. The forecasts for the years 2003 and 2004 and the ECB projections for the same years is that this slowdown will continue in 2003, with some recovery expected in 2004. A similar pattern is evident in the cases of the US economy and Britain (where the situation does not appear to be as bad). However, it is the US growth rate expected at 3.4 and 3.6 per cent in 2003 and 2004, respectively, against the euro area's 1.0 and 2.3 per cent, respectively, which might lead the world economy out of the present slowdown, though the recent rise in the value of the euro may knock down the rate of growth further. In terms of unemployment and inflation the situation is no better. The euro area unemployment is already high at around 9 per cent, through 2003 and 2004, and though the rate is much lower in the United States and Britain, it is now increasing in all three countries (and quite rapidly in the US case).[6] Inflation may not be a problem in the United States and Britain but in the euro area it has been above the 2 per cent limit set by the ECB though dipping below 2 per cent in May 2003. The forecasts for inflation and the ECB projections relating to inflation tell a similar story: the situation may improve by the year 2004, although it is likely to be above the 2 per cent ECB inflation target.

The challenges to the EMU macropolicies surrounding the euro arise from the extent to which they can tackle the problems just summarized. These are embedded in the monetary policy operated by the ECB, and in the Stability and Growth Pact (SGP).[7] Can they deliver full employment without inflationary pressures? We now attempt to answer this question and begin by briefly locating the key economic policy ingredients of the EMU system.

Monetary policy has been removed from national authorities and from political authorities and placed with the ECB, and fiscal policy will be permanently constrained by the SGP. The ECB and the national central banks are linked into the European System of Central Banks (ESCB) with a division of responsibility between them. The ECB has the responsibility for setting interest rates in pursuit of the inflation objective and the national central banks' responsibility for regulatory matters. Central banks are viewed as having no discernible effects on the level or growth rate of output in the long run, but do determine the rate of inflation in the long run. Thus, inflation is still seen as a

Table 7.1 Real GDP growth rates, inflation rates and unemployment rates

Real GDP growth rates[1]

Year	1999				2000				2001				2002				GDP forecasts	
Quarter	1Q	2Q	3Q	4Q	1Q	2Q	3Q	4Q	1Q	2Q	3Q	4Q	1Q	2Q	3Q	4Q	2003	2004
Euro area	1.7	1.8	2.6	3.3	3.5	3.7	3.2	2.8	2.5	1.6	1.3	0.5	0.3	0.7	0.8	0.7	1.0	2.3
US	4.0	3.9	4.2	4.3	4.2	4.9	3.7	2.3	1.5	−0.1	−0.4	0.1	1.4	2.2	3.3	2.9	3.4	3.6
Britain	2.2	1.9	2.4	3.2	3.4	3.6	3.0	2.3	2.6	2.0	1.9	1.9	1.2	1.6	2.2	2.2	2.2	2.6

Inflation rates[2]

Year	1999				2000				2001				2002				Inflation forecasts	
Quarter	1Q	2Q	3Q	4Q	1Q	2Q	3Q	4Q	1Q	2Q	3Q	4Q	1Q	2Q	3Q	4Q	2003	2004
Euro area	0.8	1.0	1.1	1.5	2.1	2.1	2.5	2.7	2.6	3.2	2.7	2.2	2.6	2.1	2.0	2.3	2.1	1.7
US	1.7	2.1	2.4	2.6	3.2	3.3	3.5	3.4	3.4	3.4	2.7	1.9	1.3	1.3	1.6	2.2	2.0	2.1
Britain	1.0	1.5	1.3	1.2	0.8	0.6	0.9	1.0	0.9	1.5	1.5	1.0	1.6	1.0	1.0	1.5	1.9	1.8

Unemployment rates

Year	1999				2000				2001				2002				Unemployment forecasts	
Quarter	1Q	2Q	3Q	4Q	1Q	2Q	3Q	4Q	1Q	2Q	3Q	4Q	1Q	2Q	3Q	4Q	2003	2004
Euro area	10.3	10.1	10.0	9.7	9.5	9.2	9.0	8.5	8.5	8.4	8.4	8.0	8.1	8.2	8.3	8.5	8.8	8.8
US	4.3	4.3	4.2	4.0	4.0	4.0	4.0	4.0	4.2	4.5	4.8	5.6	5.6	5.8	5.8	5.9	5.7	5.5
Britain	6.3	6.1	6.0	5.9	5.9	5.6	5.5	5.3	5.2	5.1	5.2	5.3	5.2	5.2	5.4	5.2	5.1	5.1

Notes:
1. Growth rates = $100 \, (X_t/X_{t-1} - 1)$, where X_t = is value in quarter t, and X_{t-1} = is value in quarter of a year ago.
2. Inflation is defined as the overall harmonized index of consumer prices (HICP) for the euro area and the UK; consumer price index (CPI) for the USA.

Sources: Euro area: ECB *Monthly Bulletin*, various issues; USA: Bureau of Labor Statistics (CPI and Unemployment, April 2003), Bureau of Economic Analysis (GDP, March 2003); UK: National Statistics (March 2003). Forecasts: European Commission Spring Forecasts (2003) for the euro area and the UK; *Economic Report of the President* (February 2003) for the USA.

monetary phenomenon and ultimately it is central banks that determine the inflation rate.

The ECB is set up to be independent of the European Union (EU) Council and Parliament and of its member governments. There is, thus, a complete separation between the monetary authorities, in the form of the ECB, and the fiscal authorities, in the shape of the national governments comprising the EMU. It follows that there can be little coordination of monetary and fiscal policy. Indeed, any attempt at coordination would be extremely difficult to implement, for apart from the separation of the monetary and fiscal authorities, there is also the constitutional requirement that national governments (and hence the fiscal authorities) should not exert any influence on the ECB (and hence the monetary authorities). Any strict interpretation of that edict would rule out any attempt at coordination of monetary and fiscal policies.

The ECB is the only effective federal economic institution, and it has the one policy instrument of the 'repo' rate to pursue the main objective of low inflation. The ECB is clear on this issue. For example, ECB (2003a) states:

> In the field of monetary-fiscal policy co-ordination, the emphasis has shifted away from the joint design of short-term policy responses to shocks towards the establishment of a non-discretionary, rule-based regime capable of providing monetary and fiscal policy-makers with a time-consistent guide for action and thus a reliable anchor for private expectations. ... Therefore there will generally be no need for further co-ordination of day-to-day policy moves. (p. 38)

National fiscal policy is subject to the requirements of the SGP (with no fiscal policy at the level of the EU with a balanced budget requirement and EU expenditure set at 1.24 per cent of EU GDP). The official rationale for the SGP is twofold. The first is that a medium-term balanced budget rule secures the scope for automatic stabilizers without breaching the limits set by the SGP (see below for more details). Second, since a balanced budget explicitly sets the debt ratio on a declining trend, it reduces the interest burden and improves the overall position of the government budget. Underlying the approach to SGP, though, is the notion of sound public finances. The European Commission (2000) is emphatic on this issue:

> Achieving and sustaining sound positions in public finances is essential to raise output and employment in Europe. Low public debt and deficits help maintain low interest rates, facilitate the task of monetary authorities in keeping inflation under control and create a stable environment which fosters investment and growth ... The Maastricht Treaty clearly recognises the need for enhanced fiscal discipline in EMU to avoid overburdening the single monetary authority and prevent fiscal crises, which would have negative consequences for other countries. Moreover, the loss of exchange rate instrument implies the need to create room for fiscal policy to tackle adverse economic shocks and smooth the business cycle. The

stability and growth pact is the concrete manifestation of the shared need for fiscal discipline. (p. 1)

It is further argued that these views spring from experience in that both emphases on fiscal prudence and stability in the founding Treaty of the EMU spring from the firm conviction that:

> [T]he deterioration of public finances was an important cause behind the poor economic performance of many EU countries since the early 1970s. The subsequent decades taught Europe a salutary lesson of how economic prosperity cannot be sustained in an unstable economic policy environment. Inappropriate fiscal policies frequently overburdened monetary policy leading to high interest rates. On the supply-side, generous welfare systems contributed to structural rigidities in EU economies and fuelled inappropriate wage behaviour. The net effect was a negative impact on business expectations and on investment, thus contributing to a slower rise in actual and potential output. As a result, employment stagnated. (European Commission 2000, p. 9)

The level of NAIRU is viewed as being favourably affected by a 'flexible' labour market, but is unaffected by the level of aggregate demand or by productive capacity. The thrust of the European Employment Pact agreed in Cologne by the European Council in June 1999 is very much based on the theoretical construct we expounded in the first section of this chapter. Interestingly enough, recent theoretical and empirical contributions suggest that capital stock is an important determinant of NAIRU (see, for example, Arestis and Biefang-Frisancho Mariscal 2000), thereby establishing the importance of aggregate demand in curing unemployment. Baker et al. (2002) provide evidence that supports the view that those 'inflexible' euro-area labour markets cannot be held responsible for the high unemployment rates there (see Table 7.1). Union strength, the severity of employment protection legislation, unemployment benefits replacement ratios and labour market deregulations of the 1990s, cannot be held responsible for the euro-area unemployment rates. They conclude that 'the empirical case has not been made that could justify the sweeping and unconditional prescriptions for labour market deregulation which pervade much of the policy discussion' (p. 56).

We may turn our attention next to the EMU policy framework, and discuss first monetary policy as implemented by the ECB, followed by the fiscal policy aspects.

MONETARY POLICY

Institutional and Policy Arrangements

ECB monetary policy has been assigned a quantitative definition of price stability in the form of a 0–2 per cent target for the annual increase in the Harmonized Index of Consumer Prices (HICP) for the euro area (preferably hovering in the lower range of 0–2 per cent). The ECB, however, announced at a press conference on 8 May 2003, its intention to maintain inflation 'close to but below 2 per cent' over the medium term. Issing (2003) insists on the 'clarification' aspect as being 'totally different from what is normally seen as inflation targeting'.

Furthermore, the 'close to but below 2 per cent' inflation 'is not a change, it is a clarification of what we have done so far, what we have achieved – namely inflation expectations remaining in a narrow range of between roughly 1.7% and 1.9% – and what we intend to do in our forward-looking monetary policy'.[8] This 'clarification' may have become necessary in view of 'deflation' fears in the euro area, in that the ECB would worry about deflation if it were to arise. The president of the ECB at the press conference on 8 May 2003, expressed 'the ECB's commitment to provide a sufficient safety margin to guard against the risks of deflation', although he insisted: 'We do not share this fear for the euro area as a whole' (Duisenberg 2003a). Issing (2003) concurs when he suggests that 'it is clear enough that we are not blind in the eye which identifies deflationary problems. We have both eyes ... watching deflationary as well as inflationary developments'. And yet Duisenberg in a subsequent press conference, 5 June 2003, argued strongly: 'We are convinced that we don't have to prepare ourselves for deflation because we don't see deflation coming. And that's what I have said, I think, loud and clear' (Duisenberg 2003b).[9]

The official doctrine of the ECB is based on a 'two-pillar' monetary strategy, which has been adopted. The 'first pillar' is a commitment to analyse monetary developments for the information they contain about future price developments. This is the quantitative reference value for monetary growth, where a target of 4.5 per cent of M3 has been imposed. Being a reference level, there is no mechanistic commitment to correct deviations in the short term, although it is stated that deviations from the reference value would, under normal circumstances, 'signal risks to price stability'. The 'second pillar' is a broadly based assessment of the outlook of price developments and the risks to price stability. This broad range of indicators includes: the euro exchange rate; labour market indicators, such as wages and unit labour costs; fiscal policy indicators; and financial market indicators, such as asset prices.

The rationale of the 'two-pillar' approach is based on the theoretical premise that there are different time perspectives in the conduct of monetary policy that require a different focus in each case. There is the short- to medium-term focus on price movements that requires economic analysis. In this analysis, a '[b]road range of economic/financial developments are analysed, to assess economic shocks, dynamics and perspectives and the resulting risks to price stability over the short to medium term' (Issing 2003). There is also the focus on long-term price trends that requires monetary analysis.[10] There is, thus, a strong belief in the long-term link between money (M3 in this case) and inflation. Issing leaves no ambiguity of the ECB belief in this relationship, when he argues that there is '[n]o evidence that long-run link between money and prices has broken down in euro area; many studies show good leading indicator properties'; and that '[e]xcess money/credit may provide additional information for identifying financial imbalances and/or asset price bubbles, which ultimately may impact on price developments'. The ECB also conducts 'cross-checking' between the two analyses so that consistency is ensured (Issing 2003).[11]

Policy Defects with the ECB Monetary Policy Arrangements

These policy arrangements we have just discussed suffer from a number of defects. First, if inflation is induced by a demand shock (that is, a higher level of demand pushes up inflation) then a policy to influence aggregate demand, and thereby, it is hoped, inflation may have some validity. But such a policy is powerless to deal with cost inflation or supply shock inflation. A supply shock would lower (raise) output while raising (lowering) inflation. Further, the extent to which the domestic interest rate can be changed is circumscribed by exchange rate considerations and it is likely to take some time before it has any impact on aggregate demand (and then the impact may be rather small). Indeed the British monetary authorities (and others) talk in terms of a two-year lag between the change in interest rates and the resulting impact of changes in aggregate demand on the rate of inflation. Interest rates are likely to influence investment expenditure, consumer expenditure, market interest rates and asset prices, expectations and the exchange rate. These changes in turn influence domestic and external demand, and then inflationary pressures. In addition, interest rate changes can also have distributional effects, whether between individuals or between economic regions (see, for example, Arestis and Sawyer 2002a).

Second, changes in interest rates have only a limited impact on aggregate demand. But further, in so far as interest rates do have an impact it comes through effects on investment and on the exchange rate. High interest rates have long-term detrimental effects through reducing future productive capacity and through the impact of foreign trade. We have surveyed elsewhere (Arestis and Sawyer 2002b) the results of simulations of the effects of monetary policy using macroeconometric models. The survey is based on work undertaken for the ECB, the US Federal Reserve System and the Bank of England. The conclusion of that survey is that the effects of interest rate changes on inflation tend to be rather small – typically a 1 percentage point change in interest rates may dampen inflation by 0.2 to 0.3 per cent after two years.

Third, monetary policy is a 'one policy fits all' approach. Within the euro area there has to be a single central bank discount rate. It is well known that the setting of that single interest rate poses difficulties – the rate which is appropriate for a country experiencing high demand and perhaps inflationary pressures is not the same as that appropriate for one facing low demand. Indeed, monetary policy may address the average inflation picture but cannot address differences in inflationary experience across the euro area countries. In late 2003, there is evidence of significant disparities in inflationary experience despite the convergence of inflation that was required by the Maastricht criteria (and indeed a number of countries would not now satisfy the inflation convergence conditions of the Maastricht Treaty).[12] Further, the impact of interest rate changes is likely to differ markedly across countries.

Fourth, the ECB assessment of the level of economic activity is completely impervious to the behaviour of interest rates. Bibow (2003) puts it aptly: 'Ex ante interest rate policies never seem to conflict with economic growth in ECB policy communications and assessments. Ex post economic developments do not appear to have been related to interest rate developments either' (p. 5). The ECB rationale is that monetary tightening would not pose any risk to economic activity. Such policy keeps inflationary expectations under control, thereby sustaining confidence in price stability, which stimulates economic activity. This is rather surprising in view of the work undertaken on the transmission mechanism in the euro area (ECB 2002d, October), which shows that monetary policy has strong real effects, especially so in 'that investment is a main driving force, with a contribution of more than 80 percent to the total response of GDP after three years' (p. 47).[13]

Problems with the ECB Monetary Policy

The management, operation, communication and potential efficacy of monetary policy within these institutional arrangements by the ECB have entailed many problems. In terms of the management aspect, the response of monetary policy decisions to evolving events has been slow. It is of some interest to note in this context the reluctance of the ECB to reduce the 'repo' rate of interest when a downturn in economic activity in 2001, not just in the euro area, became rather obvious. In particular, the ECB can be faulted for underestimating the impact of the US recession on the euro area, and for not reacting on time in terms of reducing interest rates. After signalling in April 2001 an imminent cut in interest rates, it never implemented it; however, when in May it signalled no change, the ECB subsequently cut interest rates! It is of considerable importance to note that the ECB (2001b) in March 2001 was claiming:

> The general outlook for this year and next remains positive. Economic activity in the euro area is mainly determined by domestic factors. The conditions on the domestic side ... have remained favourable ... This notwithstanding, an element of uncertainty with regard to the outlook for euro area continues to be the world economy and its potential impact on euro area developments. However, at this juncture there are no signs that the slowdown in the US economy is having significant and lasting spillover effects on the euro area. (p. 5)

In the May issue of the *Monthly Bulletin*, the ECB (2001d) was declaring that 'economic growth supported by domestic demand, will be broadly in line with estimates of potential growth in 2001' (p. 5). As mentioned above, the ECB cut its key interest rate on 10 May 2001, thereby throwing the financial markets into widespread confusion (see, also, Bibow 2002).[14]

ECB monetary policy since then has been no less confusing. In the January issue of the *Monthly Bulletin*, the ECB (2002a) was stating that 'no fundamental economic imbalances have built up in recent years in the euro area which would require a long correction process' (p. 5), thereby attempting to let the financial markets believe that there was no intention for further interest rate cuts. If anything, increases in interest rates were implied. In April 2002 the 'thread' of interest rate increase was evident enough: 'the persistence of excess liquidity in the economy could become a concern once the economic recovery in the euro area gathers pace' (ECB 2002b, p. 5). Similarly, in May 2002 the ECB (2002c) was more explicit about 'the prospects for price stability', which 'appear to be somewhat less favourable than they were towards the end of last year' (p. 5). In the meantime, on the other side of the Atlantic the Federal (Reserve) Open Market Committee (FOMC) kept lowering interest rates aggressively. It took the ECB until December 2002 to lower interest rates on the premise that 'the evidence has increased that inflationary pressures are easing, owing in particular to the sluggish economic expansion. Furthermore, the downside risks to economic expansion have not vanished' (ECB 2002e, p. 5).

The Federal Reserve System had already reduced interest rates on a number of occasions (no less than 13 times between 3 January 2001 and 25 June

2003). Still in March 2003 a 25 basis point reduction in the 'repo' rate prompted the ECB to argue:

> Overall, ECB interest rates have reached very low levels. On the basis of currently available information, this policy stance, while contributing to the preservation of price stability over the medium term, provides some counterbalance to the factors which are currently having an adverse effect on economic activity. (ECB 2003b, p. 6)

However, the sharp euro appreciation since April 2002 would suggest the opposite: relative interest rates have not reached very low levels; so much so that '[t]he euro area's immediate problem is overly tight monetary and fiscal policy' (*The Economist*, 3 May 2003, p. 71). And yet, the ECB president at a press conference on 8 May 2003, declared that 'the euro at the moment – is about at the level which ... better reflects the fundamentals and it is roughly at average historical levels. So, there is not yet anything excessive about the level' (Duisenberg 2003a). As a result, the euro jumped to its highest level against the dollar and the pound sterling for four years.[15]

The ECB's methods of operation and communication have been confusing to the financial markets. In the 'two-pillar' strategy, there is uncertainty as to the value attached to the M3 reference value. The target has rarely been met, and yet this does not seem to impact on official strategy. As Fitousi and Creel (2002) have put it, 'In its communication with the public, the ECB consistently highlights its "reference value" for inflation and – often in a confusing way – its monetary policy target. This may well have undermined the ECB's credibility, rather than added to it' (p. 67). The 'clarification' offered on 8 May 2003, appears to downplay the importance of the money stock, and yet it reaffirmed its long-run importance.

There is, indeed, the further question of whether the aim of inflation being 'close to 2 per cent' is not too restrictive, and it suffers from not being symmetrical. Let alone the confusion it has created by the statement 'close to but below 2 per cent'; is there no change as the ECB suggested, or is it a move to a 2 per cent mid-point target (flatly denied by the ECB as noted above)? The ECB has been reluctant to manipulate the rate of interest sufficiently and for other purposes, when it is abundantly clear that such a move is paramount. In practice most central banks do not concentrate on inflation to the exclusion of any other policy objective (they usually take unemployment into account). In any case, it actually becomes more and more obvious that the 'close to 2 per cent' formulation is by far too low. Especially so currently when it is apparent that this policy stance 'provides an inadequate cushion against the risk of deflation in the event of a serious slump in demand' (*The Economist*, 28 September 2002, p. 11). Clearly, the ECB believes that it is an adequate cushion as evidenced by the 8 May 2003, 'clarification' of monetary policy by its officers (Duisenberg 2003a; Issing 2003; see, also, above for relevant discussion).

The problem with the ECB's methods of operation is partly the bank's secretiveness for it does not publish minutes of its meetings. This is compensated to some extent by the ECB president's news conference once a month after the monetary policy meetings, by the president's testimony to the European Parliament on a regular basis, by the monthly publication of the ECB's *Monthly Bulletin*, and by the ECB's GDP growth and inflation projections twice a year. The trouble is that the ECB has not learned to communicate its methods of operation, essentially because it does not publish minutes of the monetary policy meetings.

A further problem is that of the voting behaviour of the ECB Governing Council, and the real possibility of the ECB policy decisions being affected by national loyalties.[16] Meade and Sheets (2001) argue that they are so affected. They formulate a hypothesis that each council member would vote on the basis of the differential between national and euro-area inflation rates in the month prior to the monetary policy meeting. They also hypothesize that if the national inflation rate of a country is higher than the euro-area average in the given month by more than a threshold value, then the council member from that country will vote for monetary tightening or against monetary easing; and conversely if national inflation is below the euro-area average. They investigated all the ECB policy changes since January 1999, and calculated the aggregate number of Governing Council members who would have dissented from the actual policy change, given the authors' voting rule and different threshold values. They concluded that voting behaviour reflects their hypothesis. There is, thus, national bias in the ECB policy making, and reform of the ECB's structure appears inevitable.[17]

Reservations Regarding the Efficacy of ECB Monetary Policy

A number of reservations may be raised in terms of the efficacy of this monetary policy. First, there is the problem of the 'one size fits all' monetary policy. For example, the governor of the Bank of England argued, in an interview on German television on 20 December 2001, that such policy is risky and that '[t]he same monetary policy is not necessarily the best for every country at the same time' in such a diverse economic area. The governor also suggested in an interview on BBC radio on 21 December 2001, that unlike monetary policy in a single country where 'mitigating factors' exist, such as labour migration and fiscal redistribution, these factors 'are not present to any significant degree at the euro area level'. There is, thus, no way a country can offset undesirable effects of a too high or a too low rate of interest imposed by the ECB.

The second impinges crucially on the problem of the transmission mechanism of monetary policy in the euro area since, as Duisenberg (1999) concedes, 'Relatively little is known as yet' about it. Consequently, 'One important challenge for the Eurosystem is to obtain better knowledge of the structure and functioning of the euro area economy and the transmission mechanism of monetary policy within it, so that policy actions can be implemented accordingly' (p. 189).

Third, considerable doubt may be cast on the effectiveness of monetary policy in terms of responding to recession and as a means of controlling inflation (for an extensive discussion on this general point, see Arestis and Sawyer 2002b). There has been a reluctance to cut interest rates in the face of recession (with the United States a notable exception in this regard). The ECB has failed to meet its inflation target of below 2 per cent for three years (and has presided over widely differing inflation rates within the euro area).

Fourth, the inflation target of below 2 per cent can be argued to be too low. The consequence is that deflationary policy is continuously pursued. This has a number of implications, of which two stand out here. The first is that it is very difficult to see how full employment with no inflation can be achieved. The deflationary thrust to the policies not only ensures that unemployment rises in the present but it also serves to depress investment and capital formation, thereby harming future prospects for employment. The second is a serious concern about the distributional effects of contractionary policies. Moderate rates of inflation improve the relative position of low-income groups, and deflationary policies cause it to deteriorate (Nordhaus 1973). Blinder (1987) concurs with the contention that contractionary monetary policies distort income distribution against low-income groups (see, also, Forder 2003).

Fifth, in terms of the impact of interest rates on expenditure, there are questions relating to the magnitude of the impact, timing and variability of the time lags involved.

Sixth, since interest rate policy has a range of effects, such as on aggregate demand and on the exchange rate, and also has distributional effects, the objectives of monetary policy should reflect that, and should, thus, be recast to include growth and high levels of employment alongside inflation.

Seventh, exchange rate changes are expected to have small effects on the EMU economy. Its relatively closed nature in terms of international trade (with imports and exports amounting to less than 10 per cent of GDP) means that variations in the exchange rate of the euro will have much less impact on prices than in more open economies.

Further Critique

Despite all these problems and criticisms, the ECB president went to new lengths in early October 2002, when testifying before the European Parliament, to defend the prevailing high level of interest rates in the euro area despite its economic problems (see Table 7.1, above). He defended his decision arguing:

> I, perhaps unkindly, compare the euro area economy with the other major economies in the world, which have followed, what I would call more-aggressive interest rate policies. If one looks at the results of these policies, then I am positively convinced that our policy stance, which implies historically low real interest rates and nominal interest rates, but also presents an image of stability, forward-looking and creating no hindrance whatsoever to the resumption of growth in both investment and consumption; with a liquidity situation which can be described as ample and a monetary policy stance which can be characterized as accommodative, is one which deserves to be greatly valued. (Duisenberg 2002, p. 4)

The policy the ECB president was referring to was the reduction of the key euro-area interest rate by 1.5 percentage points, to 3.25 per cent in November 2002 from the height of 4.75 per cent in October 2001 (though the interest rate had been raised from 3.50 per cent in March 2001). By contrast, the US Federal Reserve System cut its equivalent rate by 4.75 percentage points, to 1.75 per cent, between January 2001 and October 2001, and then by a further 1.25 per cent in the period to November 2002. The results of the ECB policy as compared to the Federal Reserve System's are not complementary to the president's argument, to say the least – compare the GDP annualized growth rates in the first three quarters of 2002, 0.3, 0.7 and 0.8 per cent in the case of the euro area, respectively, and 1.4, 2.2 and 3.3 per cent in the United States; also the annualized unemployment rate of 8.1. 8.2 and 8.3 per cent, respectively, in the euro area, as compared to 4.0, 4.0 and 5.8 per cent, respectively, in the United States.[18] Furthermore, the dollar did not suffer over the period the kind of decline suggested by the ECB president's comparisons. On the contrary, following the statement of the ECB president referred to above, the dollar moved higher than the euro at that time.[19] Clearly the claims of the ECB president could not be sustained.

But the ECB continue to insist that the current level of interest rate in the euro area is the 'right' one. The euro has appreciated substantially since October 2002 and three of its major countries, Germany, Italy and the Netherlands appear to be on the brink of recession (and Portugal has already experienced two quarters of negative growth). Recent data, European Commission (2003), reveal that Germany contracted by 0.03 per cent in the last quarter of 2002 (at an annualized rate), and by 0.2 per cent in the first quarter of 2003, thus experiencing two consecutive quarters of negative growth. Italy reported 0.1 per cent contraction in 2003 quarter 1 (although it had expanded by 0.4 per cent in 2002 quarter 4), the Netherlands shrank by 0.3 per cent in the same quarter having contracted by 0.2 per cent in the fourth quarter of 2002. France experienced a 0.1 per cent contraction in the fourth quarter of 2002, but a 0.3 per cent expansion in the first quarter of 2003, while the whole euro-area growth was zero in the first quarter of 2003, following growth of 0.1 per cent in the fourth quarter of 2002. The dangers of 'deflation' in the euro area are very clear indeed, and yet the ECB (2003d) argues that 'the monetary policy stance remains consistent with the preservation of price stability in the medium term' (p. 5). Duisenberg (2003b) goes even further when responding to a press conference question relating to the 50 basis points interest rate reduction on 5 June 2003, 'There is nothing linked to deflation. It is only linked to, what in itself is, a very favourable outlook for price developments. It's so favourable that we can afford to lower interest rates without endangering our projection and goal of price stability, which is close to but below 2%'.

FISCAL POLICY

Institutional and Policy Arrangements

The core elements of SGP are three: (a) to pursue the medium-term objectives of budgetary positions close to balance or in surplus; (b) the submission of annual stability and convergence programmes by the member states; and (c) the monitoring of the implementation of the stability and convergence programmes. The main feature of the core elements is the requirement that the national budget deficit does not exceed 3 per cent of GDP, and failure to meet that requirement could lead to a series of fines depending on the degree to which the deficit exceeds 3 per cent. It is also necessary for national budgetary policies to 'support stability oriented monetary policies. Adherence to the objective of sound budgetary positions close to balance or in surplus will allow all Member States to deal with normal cyclical fluctuations while keeping the government deficit within the reference value of 3% of GDP'. Furthermore,

> Member States commit themselves to respect the medium-term budgetary objective of positions close to balance or in surplus set out in their stability of convergence programmes and to take the corrective budgetary action they deem necessary to meet the objectives of their stability or convergence programmes, whenever they have information indicating actual or expected significant divergence from those objectives. (Resolution of the European Council on the Stability and Growth Pact, Amsterdam, 17 June 1997)

A country's budgetary data become available for the Commission to scrutinize on 1 March each year when the stability programmes are submitted. Each programme contains information about the paths of the ratios of budget deficit to GDP and national debt to GDP. The Council (ECOFIN) examines the stability reports and deliver an opinion within two months of their submission. If the stability programme reveals that a country is significantly diverging from its medium-term budgetary objective, then the Council will make relevant recommendations to strengthen the stability programme. If the situation persists then the member state is judged to have breached the reference values. The SGP details 'escape' clauses, which allows a member state that has an excessive deficit to avoid sanction. If there is an economic downturn and output has fallen by more than 2 per cent, then the member state will escape sanction automatically but the deficit should be corrected once the recession has finished. If output falls between 0.75 and 2 per cent then the Council can exercise discretion when making a decision on an 'excessive' deficit; other factors will be taken into account such as the abruptness of the downturn, the accumulated loss of output relative to past trends and whether the government deficit exceeds government investment expenditure. The scale of the downturn which would be involved if the 'escape clauses' were to be invoked occurs rarely and would involve a very severe economic downturn. If a country is found to have breached the reference values, then it has four months to introduce the corrective measures suggested by the Council. If the country follows the Council's recommendations, then the 'excessive' deficit can continue, but the budget deficit must be corrected within a year following its identification. A country which chooses not to introduce corrective measures will be subject to a range of sanctions, at least one or more must be imposed, of which one must be in the form of a non-interest-bearing deposit lodged by the national government. In this instance, it will fall upon EMU members, excluding the member country under consideration, to reach a decision on sanctions. The non-interest-bearing deposit consists of a fixed component (0.2 per cent of GDP), and a variable component (one-tenth of the difference between the deficit ratio and the 3 per cent reference value). If the budget deficit is not corrected within two years, the deposit is forfeited and becomes a fine, whereas if the deficit is corrected within two years the deposit is returned and the penalty becomes the forgone interest.

Flaws of the SGP

These SGP institutional arrangements point to a general deflationary bias in the operation of the SGP. It is illustrated by the response of the ECB president at a press conference on 6 December 2001, after the ECB's policy-making council, to an Italian request to delay target dates for budget balance in view of the projected downturn in economic activity. He argued that 'it is of the greatest importance to enhance confidence with both consumers and investors if governments stick to their medium-term strategy, whatever happens' (Duisenberg 2001). The ECB president was more forthcoming at a similar press conference on 8 May 2003, when he argued:

> Looking ahead, it is crucial to underpin the fiscal policy framework with decisive action, strong peer pressure and consistent implementation of the rules of the Treaty and of the Stability and Growth Pact. Countries should maintain budgetary positions close to balance or in surplus over the cycle, and, where this is not the case, take the required structural consolidation measures. (Duisenberg 2003a)

There are serious flaws in the management of the SGP. One illustration of this is the predictions made in January 2002 by the European Commission for the year 2002 relating to budget deficits under the terms of the SGP. Those predictions prompted the possibility of the 'early warning' mechanism in the case of Germany and Portugal in particular. ECOFIN ignored the European Commission's recommendation for Germany and Portugal to be censured in view of the size of their deficits, which were creeping close to the SGP 3 per cent ceiling (it stood at 2.7 per cent of GDP in the case of Germany and 2.2 per cent in the case of Portugal, though it later transpired that the figure for 2001 was 4.2 per cent). ECOFIN chose, instead, to strike a deal whereby no formal warning was issued, but the two countries made pledges to keep within the rules of the SGP.[20] This accord raises questions about the governance of the euro area, and provides fertile ground for financial markets to question the credibility of the EMU institutions. Furthermore, it could substantially weaken the credibility of the fiscal constraints that are imposed on the prospective new EU entrants in the period leading to their accession. It also supports the charge that the EMU does not keep to its own rules and pledges. The comparison with the episode of the application of the Maastricht criteria in the period leading to the introduction of the virtual euro, when the criteria were fudged to ensure that a large number of countries could join the euro, is telling (Arestis et al. 2001).

More Flexible SGP Fiscal Rules?

In September 2002, the European Commission admitted for the first time that the SGP fiscal rules relating to the single currency need to be changed. They would be more flexible in the future in view of the euro-area economic weaknesses. The European Commission actually relaxed the deadline of 2004 by which Germany, Portugal and France should balance their budgets. These countries were given until 2006 to balance their budgets. In return the Commission demanded that the members reduce their deficit by 0.5 per cent a year starting in 2003. It was at the 2002 summer summit in Seville of the 15 EU members when they all signed a commitment 'to achieve budgetary positions close to balance or in surplus as soon as possible in all Member States and at the latest by 2004' (Council of the European Union 2002, p. 8). The European Commissioner for Economic and Monetary Affairs admitted at the time that it was of great concern to them that the original political commitment of national governments to uphold the SGP was substantially weakening.

The Commission also said that they would pay more attention to structural deficits so that a country's fiscal deficit would be judged in relation to cyclical conditions. These changes have taken place alongside Germany, Portugal and France showing evidence of having breached the conditions of the SGP. Portugal became the first country to breach the 3 per cent rule, and admitted to a budget deficit in excess of the 3 per cent of GDP upper limit in 2002. Italy's 2002 budget deficit was also criticized by the European Commission for reaching 'dangerous proportions', and the charge was made that the Italian government were massaging the figures. France, too, was criticized by the European Commissioner for Economic and Monetary Affairs, for its 2003 tax and spending plans; the commissioner expressed concern that France may not be able to meet the new deadline of 2006. In fact France initially refused to adhere even to the 2006 deadline, arguing that its expenditure plans were affordable. These incidents have raised the validity of the use of a 'one size fits all' approach to fiscal policy, without accounting for the different circumstances of the countries involved and the differential impact which recession can have. They further illustrate that the SGP serves to operate in a deflationary manner.

The ECB president in his early October 2002 testimony to the European Parliament actually blamed France, Germany and Italy for being responsible for the uncertainty surrounding the economic recovery in the euro area; he argued: 'Three of the larger countries have not used the time when there were good economic conditions … to consolidate their budgets. Now they bear the burden of it' (Duisenberg 2002). In fact, the SGP has been the focus of growing controversy within the euro-area member countries. There is still the argument, mainly from the ECB, that reforming the SGP, especially relaxing its rules, would damage the euro's credibility. It can be argued, though, that the opposite may be nearer to reality. In any case, the relaxation that has been implemented is too small by far to create any serious problems of credibility. It is our view that a great deal more is needed if fiscal policy is to help the euro area to speedily lead towards a real recovery. Under these circumstances, credibility might be enhanced rather than reduced.

More recently (April 2003), when it became apparent that France had a public deficit of 3.1 per cent in 2002, with European Commission provisional forecasts putting it at 3.7 per cent for 2003 and 3.6 per cent for 2004, and Germany (where the budget deficit is thought to rise to 3.6 per cent in 2003) and Portugal (with an expected 3.2 per cent deficit in 2003), all three could very well be fined. In fact the Commission is of the opinion that 'an excessive government deficit' already exists in France. It has recommended that France should eliminate the deficit by the end of 2004, with the necessary measures being in place by October 2003. In 2004, France should also bring back to a declining path its government to GDP ratio.

It has become apparent that the slowdown in economic growth has brought about, largely through the operation of the 'automatic stabilizers' rather than discretionary fiscal policy, the scale of budget deficits which could readily be predicted from the size of the slowdown. Buti et al. (1997) had found that a 1 per cent change in GDP produced on average a 0.5 per cent change in the average budget deficit in the EU countries.

The economic slowdown in the eurozone has clearly shown that the fiscal rules of the SGP are counterproductive during a slowdown and the budget rules cannot cope with the effects of recession. Moves to enforce the fiscal rules will inevitably add further deflationary pressures.

Flaws Relating to the Balanced Budget Requirement

Further reservations relate to the requirement of a balanced budget over the cycle. Even if it is accepted that the budget should be balanced over the cycle, there is little reason to think that the extent of the swings in the budget position will be similar across countries. What reason is there to think that a swing in the deficit to a maximum of 3 per cent of GDP is relevant for all countries? Countries will differ in the extent to which their GDP varies in the course of a business cycle and in the extent to which the budget position is sensitive to the business cycle. Buti et al. (1997) found that the budget balance is negatively linked to GDP growth, but in a way which varies between countries with estimates of changes in the deficit to GDP ratio of up to 0.8 and 0.9 per cent for the Netherlands and Spain, respectively, for a 1 per cent slowdown in growth. The notable feature is the differences among countries.

The next question is whether there is any reason to think that a (on average) balanced budget is compatible with high levels of employment – indeed whether it is compatible with any level of employment (including the NAIRU). A well-known identity (though generally forgotten by advocates of the SGP) drawn from the national income accounts tells us that: (Private Savings minus Investment) plus (Imports minus Exports) plus (Tax Revenue minus Government Expenditure) equals zero, which is in symbols:

$$(S-I)+(Q-X)+(T-G)=0. \tag{7.4}$$

Individuals and firms make decisions on savings, investment, imports and exports. For any particular level of employment (and income), there is no reason to think that those decisions will lead to:

$$(S-I)+(Q-X)=0. \tag{7.5}$$

But if they are not equal to zero, then (G – T), the budget deficit, will not be equal to zero, since:

$$(G-T)=(S-I)+(Q-X). \tag{7.6}$$

The SGP in effect assumes that any level of output and employment is consistent with a balanced budget ($G - T = 0$), and hence compatible with a combination of net private savings and the trade position summing to zero. But no satisfactory justification has been given for this view. Two possible arguments could be advanced. First, it could be argued that budget deficits cannot be run for ever as the government debt to income ratio would continuously rise and that would be unsustainable. Hence governments eventually have to run balanced (on average) budgets. However, that depends on whether the post-tax rate of interest (on government bonds) is greater or less than the growth rate, the debt to income ratio being unsustainable in the former case but not in the latter. Further, it relates to the size of the primary deficit, which is the deficit that excludes interest payments. It is the overall budget deficit which is targeted by the SGP, and it can be readily shown that an *average* 3 per cent budget deficit and a 60 per cent debt ratio are compatible and sustainable, if the rate of growth of money GDP is 5 per cent (which is not an unreasonable assumption and could arise from, for example, 2.5 per cent inflation and 2.5 per cent real growth).[21] In general a 3 per cent budget deficit would be compatible with a sustainable debt ratio of $3/g$ where g is nominal growth rate.

Second, some form of Say's Law could be invoked to the effect that intended savings and investment are equal at full employment (or modified for foreign trade, domestic savings plus trade deficit equals investment). Even if Say's Law held (which we would dispute), what is required here would be that the level of private demand could sustain the supply-side equilibrium – that is the non-accelerating inflation rate of unemployment, and the NAIRU does not correspond to full employment. In particular, there is no reason to think that a balanced budget position is compatible with employment at the level given by the NAIRU.

This equality can be viewed in another way. Suppose that the condition of balanced budget is imposed; it then follows that:

$$(S-I)+(Q-X)=0. \tag{7.7}$$

If (as is likely) $S > I$, then $Q < X$. Hence a country would be required to run a trade surplus (and hence run a capital account deficit with the export of capital to other countries). A budget in balance would imply that net private savings $(S - I)$ is equal to the trade surplus $(X - Q)$, which in turn is equal to the capital account deficit. It can first be noted only some countries can run a trade surplus, and that must be balanced by others which run a deficit. This would then imply that some countries would have positive net private savings and others negative private savings. Countries that are able to run a trade surplus (at high levels of employment) can, in effect, export their 'excess' savings, but that cannot be the case for all countries.

The imposition of an upper limit of 3 per cent of GDP on the size of the budget deficit and the declaration of the aim of a balanced budget over the cycle represented a significant tightening of the fiscal position as compared with the 3 per cent of GDP target for the budget deficit in the Maastricht Treaty convergence conditions. In those conditions, the 3 per cent was to be achieved at a particular point in time: under the SGP the 3 per cent limit is to be exceeded only under extreme conditions. Although no justification was ever given by the European Union for the choice of 3 per cent in the convergence conditions, two were advanced by others. Buiter et al. (1993), for example, suggested that the choice of the 3 per cent figure for the deficit to GDP ratio arose from a combination of advocacy of the so-called 'golden rule' (that current expenditure should be covered by current revenue) and that 'EC public investment averaged almost exactly 3% of EC GDP during 1974–91' (p. 63).

Others have suggested that the 3 per cent figure corresponded to the range of deficits run by a number of countries, notably Germany, and was achievable.[22] These possible justifications remind us of two points. The first is that typically governments have run budget deficits. The imposition of a balanced budget requirement represents a major departure from what governments have done in the past. The second is that governments invest, and it is generally accepted that governments can and should borrow to fund their investment programmes. The SGP imposes the requirement that governments generally fund their investment programmes from current tax revenue.

A balanced budget (on average) means, of course, that current government expenditure will be much less than tax revenue since that tax revenue would also need to cover interest payments on debt and to pay for capital expenditure. In the UK, this has been cast in terms of the so-called 'golden rule' of public finance, which is taken to be that 'over the economic cycle the Government will borrow only to invest and not to fund current expenditure' (Treasury 1997, p. 1), though capital consumption (depreciation) is regarded as current spending so that it is net capital formation which can be financed by borrowing. The 'public debt as a proportion of national income will be held over the economic cycle at a stable and prudent level' (p. 1). Furthermore, 'The fiscal rules focus on the whole of the public sector, because the debts of any part of the public sector could ultimately fall on the taxpayer. Looking at the whole public sector also removes incentives to reclassify activities simply to evade prudent constraints on borrowing' (p. 16). Thus, the use of fiscal policy to regulate aggregate demand in the economy is much reduced, if not entirely removed, especially in the direction of stimulating the economy. It is, thus, argued that '[d]iscretionary fiscal changes should only be made if they are demonstrably consistent with achievement of the Government's fiscal rules over the economic cycle' (p. 16).

The general stance of the SGP with its requirement of an overall balanced budget and maximum deficit of 3 per cent of GDP is a deeply flawed one. There is no reason to think that a balanced budget position is consistent with high levels of employment (or indeed with any particular level of employment). Further, there is little reason to think that the 3 per cent limit can permit the automatic stabilizers to work, and striving to reach the 3 per cent limit in time of recession is likely to push economies further into recession. The balanced budget requirement does not allow governments even to borrow to fund capital investment projects.

Further reservations include the separation of the monetary authorities from the fiscal authorities. The decentralization of the fiscal authorities inevitably makes any effective coordination of fiscal and monetary policy difficult. Since the ECB is instructed to focus on inflation while the fiscal authorities will have a broader range of concerns, there will be considerable grounds for conflict. A serious implication of this is that the SGP is in danger of becoming the 'instability' pact. This suggests a need for the evolution of a body, which would be charged with the coordination of EMU monetary and fiscal policies. In the absence of such a body, tensions will emerge in the real sector when monetary policy and fiscal policy pull in different directions. The SGP in effect resolves these issues by establishing the dominance of the monetary authorities (ECB) over the fiscal authorities (national governments).

The SGP seeks to impose a 'one size (of straitjacket) fits all' fiscal policy – namely that over the course of the cycle national government budgets should be in balance or slight surplus with a maximum deficit of 3 per cent of GDP. It has *never* been shown (or even argued) that fiscal policy should be uniform across countries. The SGP imposes a fiscal policy, which in the end fits nobody. For there is no reason to think that what is in effect a single fiscal policy (balanced budget over the cycle) is appropriate for all. The April 2003 *Monthly Bulletin* of the ECB is, none the less, very explicit. It clearly, and forcibly, suggests:

> [T]he Stability and Growth Pact provides a robust and flexible framework within which any strains on public finances can be addressed and budgetary discipline is secured ... It remains essential that both the commitments made in the stability programmes and the requests to further improve fiscal positions, as subsequently agreed in the ECOFIN Council, be implemented in full. This will help to build confidence in the fiscal framework and anchor expectations about the future macroeconomic environment. (ECB 2003c, p. 6)[23]

POLICIES FOR FULL EMPLOYMENT AND LOW INFLATION

If current EMU policy arrangements cannot produce full employment and low inflation within the euro area, then the obvious question is the extent to which necessary changes to the existing framework are required to achieve this objective. This section attempts to answer this question.

Institutional Changes

The slowdown in economic activity in the euro area has exposed the serious faultlines in the SGP. The present policy stance would seem to be untenable in the longer term. As detailed above, for fiscal policy, the 3 per cent budget deficit limit and on average balanced budget remain in place, but as countries approach the 3 per cent limit in practice the limit has been relaxed, though not in all cases. Some countries now have four years to meet the balanced budget requirements with a resulting lack of clarity over the operation of the SGP. One response has been to call for some slackening of the restraints of the SGP; for example, modify the limits to permit borrowing for capital investment. Another response has been to decry the 'flexibility' that has been in the interpretation of the SGP, and to seek ways of making the balanced budget requirement really bite. This would simply be a disaster, and would turn the SGP into the 'Instability and No Growth Pact'.

The response of the ECB is worrying when they argue:

> It is natural for an economic slowdown to have adverse effects on member countries' budget position. However, for countries with a budget position still not close to balance or in surplus, it is important to adhere to their medium-term consolidation plans. A short-lived slowdown should not significantly change the scope for reaching the targets set in the countries' stability programmes.

Further, 'as adjustment needs are likely to become more visible in periods of less vigorous economic growth, policy makers must now step up the reforms' rather than allowing efforts to abate' (ECB 2001f, p. 6).

The draft of the European Convention (2003a, 2003b) does not indicate any proposals for change in the fiscal and monetary policies of the eurozone. Working Group IV in their preliminary publication begins by suggesting 'the Union's economic and social objectives should be included in a new constitutional treaty' (European Convention 2002, p. 2). Indeed, 'Some members of the group have emphasized the importance of including a reference to sustainable growth and productivity. Others attach more importance to highlighting full employment, social and regional cohesion, and a better balance between competition and public services in a social market economy' (p. 2). The final draft proposals stipulate: 'The Union shall work for a Europe of sustainable development based on balanced economic growth, with a social market economy aiming at full employment and social progress' (European Convention 2003a, p. 3). Furthermore, some of the members felt that the objectives of growth and development should be included in the mandate of the ECB, although 'A large number of the group considers that the tasks, mandate and statute of the European Central Bank should remain unchanged, and should not be affected by any new treaty provisions' (p. 3). Transparency and accountability of the ECB, enhancing the reporting of the ECB to the European Parliament and the publication of the ECB minutes are further recommendations. In the event, the proposals in the final EU draft constitution confirms the current objective of the ECB without further recommendations. It merely restates the previous Treaty agreements when it says: 'The primary objective of the Bank shall be to maintain price stability. Without prejudice to the objective of price stability, it shall support general economic policies in the Union with a view to contributing to the achievement of the Union's objectives' (European Convention 2003a, p. 20).

In terms of the SGP, Working Group IV of the European Convention (2002) did not offer much of a change:

> [A]s far as the Treaty provisions on excessive deficit procedures (Article 104) are concerned, a majority of the Group wish to see these amended in order to allow the Commission to issue first warnings of excessive deficits directly to the Member State concerned. In the subsequent phases, the Council should take decisions by QMV (Qualified Majority Voting) on the basis of a Commission proposal, always excluding from voting the Member State concerned. (p. 4)

The Working Group went on to suggest that 'some propose that the deficit criteria should take into account structural elements, as well as the "golden rule" on public investments' (p. 4). But in the draft constitution (as revised in June 2004), the existing arrangements are reiterated without any serious attempt to tackle the thorny and disturbing issue of SGP. Not surprisingly, the president of the European Commission has been quoted in the *Financial Times* (29 May 2003) as being unhappy with the whole exercise of a

European Constitution: 'It is in some respects a step backwards. Despite all the hard work we have put into this, the text that is now before us simply lacks vision and ambition' (p. 9).

Another assessment of the situation, and a set of proposals, comes from the Centre for European Reform. A recent publication (Fitousi and Creel 2002) suggests:

> Meanwhile, the Growth and Stability Pact is in crisis. While the European economy is grinding to a halt, euro area governments are less and less willing to comply with the strict fiscal limits of the Pact. Their attempts to evade its rules have undermined the Pact's credibility. There can now be no doubt that a thorough overhaul is necessary ... For the European policy mix, this 'liberation' of fiscal policy would be a breath of fresh air. It would ease the constant pressure on the ECB to adopt a more active style of macro-economic management, and remove many of the constraints that are currently inhibiting economic policy co-ordination in the EU. (p. 68)

The UK Treasury has recently published a set of proposals to reform EMU fiscal policy. The Treasury (2003) proposes to endow fiscal policy with a stabilization objective along with a trigger point for discretionary action. This would be a rule whereby discretionary fiscal policy is undertaken when the output gap exceeded a certain percentage of GDP, or when expected inflation deviates from the target. Credibility and transparency would be ensured through the publication of a 'stabilization report' along the lines of the current 'inflation report' of the Bank of England. However pertinent this proposal may be, it does not tackle the serious constraint of the SGP and the 3 per cent ceiling on fiscal deficit.

Svensson (2003) calls for the ECB to modify its monetary policy strategy in the manner of some other central banks. It is, thus, argued that the ECB should abandon completely the two-pillar strategy and 'just adopt the much superior international-best-practice strategy of flexible inflation strategy, as it is demonstrated by the Reserve Bank of New Zealand, the Bank of England, the Riksbank and the Bank of Norway' (p. 5). The 'clarification' arguments rehearsed above may very well constitute an attempt towards this objective, although by no means does it address entirely the Svensson recommendation. The problem with this particular proposal is whether the premise of its argument is acceptable. It is rather debatable whether the 'international-best-practice strategy' is represented by flexible inflation targeting (European Convention 2002). Ball and Sheridan (2003) provide evidence that suggests that this need not be the case. They conclude that there is 'no evidence that inflation targeting improves a country's economic performance' (p. 29).

Some of these proposals, especially the one by Fitousi and Creel (2002), do open the way to improve the institutional set-up of the euro area, but they are incomplete in a serious sense. Although they begin to address the issue of institutional revisions, they do not go far enough to cure the fundamental problem of inherent deflationary bias in the current institutional system. The problems identified above with the operation and management of the ECB remain, save for attempts at accountability and transparency. The objectives of the ECB, and, thus, the deflationary bias in its operation remain intact. Similarly, in the case of the SGP, the stance taken is to essentially accept the current arrangements, other than making the point that 'budgetary and financial coordination of the Member States with the objective of monetary stability as a basis for sound economic growth is of utmost common concern' (Fitousi and Creel, 2002, p. 4). It is essentially the failure of the European Convention to address the issue of the deflationary bias of the euro-area institutional arrangements where we find its recommendations incomplete.

Our own response is to call for the abolition of the Stability and Growth Pact in anything like its present form. In other words, we call for the removal of the artificial limits on budget deficits and stop seeking to impose a 'one size fits all' policy on all countries. A substantial EU budget (of the order of 5 per cent or more of GDP), which could be used to provide fiscal stimulus (as recommended in the MacDougall Report, European Commission 1977) with coordinated national fiscal policies, would be a good way of addressing problems of low demand in the euro area. But in the absence of a significant EU budget capable of providing automatic stabilizers and stimulating the EU economies, active fiscal policy must remain in the hands of national governments.[24]

It is often argued that the budget position of each country has to be restrained for there are in effect externalities or spillover effects. This sometimes takes the form that a national government's spending puts upward pressure on interest rates (more specifically on bond rates), which is perceived to raise the cost of borrowing for other governments. It can take the form that government expenditure pushes up demand, which pushes up inflation at least in the country concerned. This may then spill over into other countries and/or lead the ECB to raise interest rates to damp down inflation. Without accepting that government expenditure would have these effects, we would observe that the expansion of private sector expenditure could be expected to have similar effects to those of public expenditure. The fluctuations in the overall level of expenditure come in practice predominantly from fluctuations in private expenditure and particularly investment. The logic of imposing limits on public sector expenditure (budget deficit) would also apply to imposing limits on private sector expenditure. Perhaps there should be limits on the size of the private sector deficit or on the trade account!

The objectives and mode of operation of the ECB must also be changed. The objectives of the ECB should conspicuously include growth and employment variables, and not merely inflation. The reformulated ECB should be required to act as lender of last resort and not merely possess the potential to act as such. Moreover, the ECB should adopt a more proactive stance regarding bank surveillance and supervision. The proposal for the reformulation of objectives readily follows from what has been said previously: the ECB should be charged with setting interest rates in a manner that encourages growth and full employment, rather than merely inflation. Further, EMU institutional arrangements are required for the operation of an EMU fiscal policy, and to ensure that monetary authorities do not dominate economic policy making; serious coordination of monetary and fiscal policies is paramount, just as the European Convention suggests, but it would have to go hand in hand with the other changes to which we have just alluded. These are important institutional changes. In terms of economic policy further changes are required.

Economic Policy Changes

The achievement of full employment does require an appropriate high level of aggregate demand. This translates into some combination of increased demand for consumption, for investment, for public expenditure, and for exports. Whether such a level of aggregate demand would require a substantial budget deficit inevitably depends on what happens to the other sources of demand in the equation. But a high level of aggregate demand is only one condition for the achievement of full employment. In the context of the euro area, there are further significant obstacles to the achievement of full employment. The first is the lack of productive capacity in many regions to provide high levels of employment. Estimates by the OECD of the 'output gap' for 2002 are –0.8 per cent, that is, actual output is slightly below potential output; yet this is combined with over 8.2 per cent unemployment. In a similar vein, the OECD's estimates of the non-accelerating wage rate of unemployment (NAWRU) average of 8.1 per cent for the European Union, is again close to the actual experience of 8.25 per cent.[25] Interpreting the NAWRU as an indicator of a capacity constraint, suggests capacity problems.[26] In this context, higher levels of aggregate demand would place pressure on capacity and could well have some inflationary consequences. The second obstacle is the disparity of unemployment, in that a general increase in demand would push some regions to or even above full employment. The third problem is that there has been incomplete convergence of business cycles across euro-area countries, suggesting the need for differentiated policies across countries (and specifically differentiated fiscal policies). But even if there were convergence of business cycles, the cyclical movements would be around with quite different levels of unemployment.

These considerations suggest that the restoration of full employment in the euro area will take much more than a level of aggregate demand. It will require the creation of sufficient capacity to support full employment, and the substantial reduction of regional disparities. But the creation of high levels of aggregate demand remains a necessary, though not sufficient, condition for the creation of full employment. At the present time, the euro area lacks any significant policies that address the unemployment issue: it lacks the power to create high levels of aggregate demand to promote investment or to reduce regional disparities.

The achievement of high levels of economic activity without inflationary pressures, then, requires three elements, in addition to high levels of aggregate demand. First, institutional arrangements for collective wage determination and price setting which are conducive to low inflation. Wage determination within the EU is currently undertaken on a decentralized and fragmented basis, even where it is (or has been) centralized within a particular national economy. The institutional arrangements for collective wage determination at the EU level do not currently exist, and this effectively rules out any possibilities for the operation of incomes policy or similar for the next few years. There are a number of examples in Europe (within and outside the EU) of centralized institutional arrangements that have been conducive to relatively low inflation: for example, Austria, Germany, Norway and Sweden.[27]

Second, in addition to the construction of the relevant institutional arrangements discussed so far, it is necessary to construct a well-functioning real economy, which is also conducive to combining low inflation with high levels of economic activity. We take the view that a major element of that would be the construction of a level and location of productive capacity that is capable of providing work to all that seek paid employment. This would require not only that the general level of productive capacity be raised, but also that much of that increase be directed towards the less prosperous regions of the EMU. This would require the enhancement of the functions of the European Investment Bank (EIB), or a similar institution, to ensure high rates of capital formation, appropriately located across the EMU.

Third, the present disparities in regional unemployment levels (and also in labour market participation rates) within the EU would suggest that even if full employment were achieved in some regions, there would still be very substantial levels of unemployment in many others. In the presence of such disparities in unemployment, the achievement of a low level of unemployment overall (not to mention full employment) would be difficult. This problem is compounded by the fact that within the EMU not only is there high unemployment on average, but there is at the same time a severe shortage of highly qualified labour in many member countries. On top of all these problems, there is still very low or even negligible mobility within the EMU

(Fertig and Schmidt 2002). Inflationary pressures would build up in the fully employed regions even when the less prosperous regions were still suffering from significant levels of unemployment. Interest rates would then rise to dampen down the inflationary pressures in the prosperous regions without consideration for the continuing unemployment in other regions.

Therefore, a further recommendation would be to have a revamped EIB to supplement the activities of the ECB, with the specific objective of enhancing investment activity in those regions where unemployment is acute. Enhanced investment activity will, thus, aim to reduce the dispersion of unemployment within the framework of reducing unemployment in general. This could be achieved through encouraging long-term investment whenever this is necessary by providing appropriate finance for it.

SUMMARY AND CONCLUSIONS

In this chapter, we have sketched the theoretical foundations of the EMU model. We have examined the policy implications of the EMU, along with its theoretical and institutional dimensions surrounding monetary and fiscal policies. The real challenges to EMU macropolicies lie in their ability to move the euro area to a full-employment situation with low inflation. They are actually unsatisfactory to withstand the challenge. They are overtly deflationary. We have proposed a number of changes that would include the following elements. First, any political constraints on national budget positions should be removed, and national governments set fiscal policy, as they deem appropriate. Second, institutional arrangements for the coordination of national fiscal policies be strengthened. Third, EU institutional arrangements are required for the operation of an EU fiscal policy, and to ensure that monetary authorities do not dominate economic policy making. Fourth, serious coordination of monetary and fiscal policies is paramount. Above all, though, the current mix of fiscal and monetary tightening along with currency appreciation, cannot deliver a healthy macroeconomic landscape. Especially so, in an environment that is geared to stagnation,[28] not to say deflation in some of its major economies (Germany and France).[29]

NOTES

1. More details on the euro-area theoretical framework may be found in Duisenberg (1999), Arestis et al. (2001), Tsakalotos (2001), Bibow (2003) and Issing (2003), to mention only but a few relevant examples. Our approach extends that in Arestis et al. (2001).
2. Issing (2003) puts it in the following way: 'Widespread consensus: even low inflation entails significant costs'. This statement should be judged against evidence provided by

Ghosh and Phillips (1998), where a large panel set that covers IMF countries over the 1960–96 period is utilized, to conclude that 'there are two important nonlinearities in the inflation–growth relationship. At very low inflation rates (around 2–3 per cent a year, or lower), inflation and growth are positively correlated. Otherwise, inflation and growth are negatively correlated, but the relationship is convex, so that the decline in growth associated with an increase from 10 per cent to 20 per cent inflation is much larger than that associated with moving from 40 per cent to 50 per cent inflation' (p. 674). However, the point at which the nonlinearity changes from positive to negative is thought to deserve a great deal more research. Issing's (2003) statement should also be judged in terms of statements like 'there is an optimal rate of inflation, greater than zero. So ruthless pursuit of price stability harms economic growth and well-being. Research even questions whether targeting price stability reduces the trade-off between inflation and unemployment' (Stiglitz 2003b).

3. See Forder (2000) for an extensive discussion and critique of the notion of credibility.
4. The March 2003 issue of the ECB's *Monthly Bulletin* puts it as follows: 'the outlook for the euro area economy could be significantly improved if governments strengthen their efforts to implement structural reforms in labour and product markets. Such reforms are important to ultimately raise the euro area's production potential, improve the flexibility of the economy and make the euro area more resilient to external shocks' (ECB 2003b, p. 6). A point repeated in the April 2003 issue of the *Monthly Bulletin* (ECB 2003c, p. 6).
5. Our own empirical work (Arestis et al. 2003) suggests that the demand for money differs between the component countries of the EMU and that such demand is unstable in a number of those countries.
6. Forecasts from European Commission Spring Forecasts (European Commission 2003).
7. For more details on the EMU institutional macroeconomic framework, see, for example, ECB (1999, 2001b, 2003a, pp. 37–49).
8. It can, though, be noted that the inflation rate in the eurozone has generally been above the 2 per cent level.
9. The ECB vice-president made similar noises at a conference in Vienna on 13 June 2003. He put it this way: 'We have repeatedly stressed that there is no risk of deflation in the euro region as a whole – or in other words, if there is risk, it is judged to be weak' (reported in *New York Times*, 13 June 2003, p. W7).
10. It is for this reason that the ECB 'decided to discontinue the practice of conducting the review of the reference value for M3 on an annual basis' (ECB 2003d, p. 5).
11. The ECB has recently stressed this argument when it states that what the cross-checking implies is that its Editorial 'will first present the economic analysis, which identifies short to medium-term risks to price stability, and then turns to the monetary analysis, which assess medium to long-term trends in inflation. It will conclude by cross-checking the analyses conducted under these two pillars' (ECB 2003d, p. 5).
12. In the year to May 2003, the highest annual rates were recorded in Ireland (3.9 per cent), Portugal (3.7 per cent) and Greece (3.5 per cent); the lowest rates were observed in Germany (0.6 per cent), Belgium and Austria (both 0.9 per cent). Thus there was a near 3 per cent differential between the three countries with the highest inflation and the three with the lowest inflation.
13. See also, Arestis and Sawyer (2002b) and Kuttner and Mosser (2002).
14. In the June *Monthly Bulletin* (ECB 2001e), the picture changed to one that suggested: 'Real GDP growth in the euro area in 2001 is expected to come down from the high level reached in 2000 ... primarily as a result of the less favourable external environment' (p. 5). However, 'the contribution to real GDP growth from domestic demand is expected to remain robust. This is consistent with the favourable economic fundamentals of the euro area' (p. 5). The November 2001 *Monthly Bulletin* (ECB 2001g), reverts to: 'The conditions exist for a recovery to take place in the course of 2002 and economic growth to return to a more satisfactory path. The economic fundamentals of the euro area are sound and there are no major imbalances which would require prolonged adjustment. The uncertainty currently overshadowing the world economy should diminish over time' (p. 6). This ought to be contrasted to the Bank for International Settlements *Annual Report* (BIS

2002) which stated: 'On balance, it seems that the synchronised downturn in 2001 mainly represented the effects of common shocks, reinforced by the high trade intensity of the demand components most severely affected' (p. 16).

15. The euro exchange rate jumped to $1.1506 against the dollar. It had been at $1.1360 against the dollar ahead of the ECB's decision.

16. The Governing Council comprises 18 members as follows: there are six policy makers based in Frankfurt (they are from Finland, France, Germany, Italy, the Netherlands and Spain); and 12 heads of national central banks (members of the EMU) in the euro area. All 18 members have equal say. There are, thus, six countries with two representatives on the Governing Council.

17. In the same paper, Meade and Sheets (2001) provide evidence that enables them to conclude that in the case of the US Federal Reserve System, policy makers' regional unemployment plays a significant role in monetary policy decisions. Thus, regional factors play an important role in monetary policy decisions.

18. The US also had fiscal stimulus first from the Bush tax cuts of mid-2001 and then the increased expenditure on security measures in the aftermath of September 11th.

19. The *Financial Times* (Wednesday, 9 October 2002) explained that dollar rise as 'traders expressing disappointment at the outlook for euro area growth'; this was essentially due to: 'Comments by ... the president of the European Central Bank' which 'dampened tentative hopes that the ECB had been braced to support growth with a cut in interest rates'.

20. On 30 January 2002, the European Commission issued for the first time a recommendation with a view to giving an early warning to Germany and Portugal in an attempt to avoid excessive budgetary deficits. On 12 February 2002, ECOFIN decided to abrogate the early warning in view of the commitment by Germany and Portugal to take action to avoid the occurrence of an excessive deficit.

21. The general formulation is $d = b/g$ where b is the budget ratio, d the debt ratio and g the rate of nominal growth.

22. In the decade up to 1992 the German general government financial balance averaged 1.8 per cent deficit, and the euro area as a whole averaged 4.45 per cent deficit (calculated from OECD *Economic Outlook*, various issues).

23. A further disturbing, and highly objectionable implication of the monolithic focus on price stability and on the 3 per cent SGP rule, is the manner in which it is thought appropriate 'to address the fiscal challenges of population age' (ECB 2003c, p. 46). The ECB (2003c) paper actually warns that free health care, as for example in many euro-area countries, will have to be restricted to emergency services only. This is so in view of the high and rising 'ratio between the number of pensioners and the number of contributors'; for 'otherwise the cost would overwhelm economies and lead to rising inflation' (p. 39). Although the report recognizes that raising the retirement age should produce large gains, funded-pension arrangements are thought to carry potentially larger benefits for economic growth. These relate to the beneficial effects on the labour market (social security contributions would thereby be perceived as savings for retirement rather than as taxes) and capital market (higher capital accumulation of capital). This absurd suggestion is not unrelated, of course, to the SGP ideas, to which we have objected vehemently in this study.

24. An interesting case was made by Joseph Stiglitz in *The Guardian* (8 May 2003a) under the title 'Don't trust the bankers' homilies: the EU stability pact destabilises by cutting spending in a downturn', that 'The lesson for Europe is clear: the EU should redefine the stability pact in terms of the structural or full employment deficit – what the fiscal deficit would be if the economy were performing at full employment. To do otherwise is irresponsible'.

25. The figures in this and the preceding sentence derived from OECD, *Economic Outlook* databank (accessed June 2003).

26. In this context it is worth quoting the ECB chief economist, who suggested at a press conference in Berlin on 16 April 2002 that the return in 2002 of the euro area to its average growth after the 2001 economic slowdown 'is an indication that the euro area and

Europe in general still have low potential growth' (reported in the *Financial Times*, 18 April 2002).
27. The idea of a state-funded 'buffer fund' to stabilize employment in cases of difficulties is a relevant suggestion. The trade union movement in Sweden has proposed this idea, recently. Finland has already been operating such a 'buffer fund', but it is not state funded and it is only a tenth of the one suggested in the case of Sweden.
28. Interestingly enough, the OECD (2003) cut its forecasts sharply for the euro-area growth for 2003 (from 1.8 per cent in its December 2002 forecasts to 1.0 per cent in its April 2003 forecasts), and for 2004 (from 2.7 per cent in its December 2002 forecasts to 2.4 per cent in its April 2003 forecasts), while trimming its forecasts for the United States in 2003 only to 2.5 per cent in its April 2003 forecasts (from 2.6 per cent in its December 2002 forecasts) and raising expected GDP growth for 2004 to 4 per cent in its April 2003 forecasts (from 3.6 per cent in its December 2002 forecasts).
29. A relevant table published in *The Economist* (3 May 2003, p. 70) clearly indicates that forecasts for core inflation (inflation that excludes energy, food and tobacco) for the period March 2003 to June 2004, portray Germany moving into deflation with France being on the margin.

REFERENCES

Arestis, P. and I. Biefang-Frisancho Mariscal (2000), 'Capital stock, unemployment and wages in the UK and Germany', *Scottish Journal of Political Economy*, **47** (5), 487–503.

Arestis, P., I. Biefang-Frisancho Mariscal, A. Brown and M. Sawyer (2003), 'Asymmetries of demand for money functions amongst EMU countries', *Investigación Económica*, **62** (245), July–September, 15–32.

Arestis, P., A. Brown and M. Sawyer (2001), *The Euro: Evolution and Prospects*, Cheltenham, UK and Northampton, MA, USA: Edward Elgar.

Arestis, P. and M. Sawyer (2002a), 'The Bank of England macroeconomic model: its nature and implications', *Journal of Post Keynesian Economics*, **24** (4), 529–45.

Arestis, P. and M. Sawyer (2002b), 'Can monetary policy affect the real economy?', Working Paper No. 355, Levy Economics Institute of Bard College, September.

Arestis, P. and M. Sawyer (2003a), 'The nature and role of monetary policy when money is endogenous', Working Paper No. 374, Levy Economics Institute of Bard College, March.

Arestis, P. and M. Sawyer (2003b), 'Does the stock of money have any significance?', *Banca Nazionale Del Lavoro Quarterly Review*, **56** (225), 113–36.

Baker, D., A. Glyn, D. Howell and J. Schmitt (2002), 'Labour market institutions and unemployment: a critical assessment of the cross-country evidence', Working Paper 2002-17, Center for Economic Policy Analysis, New School University, New York: USA.

Ball, L. and N. Sheridan (2003), 'Does inflation targeting matter?', NBER Working Paper, No. 9577, National Bureau of Economic Research: Cambridge, MA.

Bank for International Settlements (BIS) (2002), *Annual Report*, Basle: Switzerland.

Bibow, J. (2002), 'The monetary policies of the European Central Bank and the euro's (mal-) performance: a stability oriented assessment', *International Review of Applied Economics*, **16** (1), 31–50.

Bibow, J. (2003), 'Is Europe doomed to stagnation? An analysis of the current crisis and recommendations for reforming macroeconomic policymaking in Euroland', Working Paper No. 379, Levy Economics Institute of Bard College, May.

Blinder, A. (1987), *Hard Heads, Soft Hearts*, Reading, MA: Addison-Wesley.
Buiter, W. G. Corsetti and N. Roubini (1993), 'Excessive deficits: sense and nonsense in the Treaty of Maastricht', *Economic Policy*, **16**, 58–90.
Buti, M., D. Franco and H. Ongena (1997), *Budgetary Policies During Recessions: Retrospective Application of the 'Stability and Growth Pact' to the Post-War Period*, Brussels: European Commission.
Council of the European Union (2002), *Council Recommendation of 21 June 2002 on the Broad Guidelines of the Economic Policies of the Member States and the Community*, Brussels: Council of the European Union.
Duisenberg, W.F. (1999), 'Economic and monetary union in Europe: the challenges ahead', in *New Challenges for Monetary Policy*, proceedings of a symposium sponsored by the Federal Reserve Bank of Kansas City, Jackson Hole, WY, 26–28 August, pp. 185–94.
Duisenberg, W.F. (2001), 'Introductory statement, and questions and answers', ECB Press Conference, 6 December, Frankfurt.
Duisenberg, W.F. (2002), *Testimony to the European Parliament*, 8 October, Brussels, www.ecb.int.
Duisenberg, W.F. (2003a), 'Introductory statement, and questions and answers', ECB Press Conference, 8 May, Frankfurt.
Duisenberg, W.F. (2003b), 'Introductory statement, and questions and answers', ECB Press Conference, 5 June, Frankfurt.
European Central Bank (ECB) (1999), 'The institutional framework of the European System of Central Banks', *Monthly Bulletin*, July, 55–63, Frankfurt.
European Central Bank (ECB) (2001a), *Monthly Bulletin*, January, Frankfurt.
European Central Bank (ECB) (2001b), *Monthly Bulletin*, March, Frankfurt.
European Central Bank (ECB) (2001c), *Monthly Bulletin*, April, Frankfurt.
European Central Bank (ECB) (2001d), *Monthly Bulletin*, May, Frankfurt.
European Central Bank (ECB) (2001e), *Monthly Bulletin*, June, Frankfurt.
European Central Bank (ECB) (2001f), *Monthly Bulletin*, October, Frankfurt.
European Central Bank (ECB) (2001g), *Monthly Bulletin*, November, Frankfurt.
European Central Bank (ECB) (2001h), *Monthly Bulletin*, December, Frankfurt.
European Central Bank (ECB) (2002a), *Monthly Bulletin*, January, Frankfurt.
European Central Bank (ECB) (2002b), *Monthly Bulletin*, April, Frankfurt.
European Central Bank (ECB) (2002c), *Monthly Bulletin*, May, Frankfurt.
European Central Bank (ECB) (2002d), *Monthly Bulletin*, October, Frankfurt.
European Central Bank (ECB) (2002e), *Monthly Bulletin*, December, Frankfurt.
European Central Bank (ECB) (2003a), 'The relationship between monetary policy and fiscal policies in the euro area', *Monthly Bulletin*, February, 37–49, Frankfurt.
European Central Bank (ECB) (2003b), *Monthly Bulletin*, March, Frankfurt.
European Central Bank (ECB) (2003c), 'The need for comprehensive reforms to cope with population ageing', *Monthly Bulletin*, April, 5–6, Frankfurt.
European Central Bank (ECB) (2003d), *Monthly Bulletin*, May, Frankfurt.
European Commission (MacDougall Report) (1977), *Report of the Study Group on the Role of Public Finance in European Integration*, Brussels: European Commission.
European Commission (2000), 'Public finances in EMU – 2000', *European Economy – Reports and Studies*, No. 3, Brussels.
European Commission (2003), 'Flash estimates for the first quarter of 2003', http://europa.eu.int, accessed May 2003.

European Convention (2002), 'Economic governance', Working Group IV, Working Document 19, 7 October, Brussels.
European Convention (2003a), *Draft Constitution*, Vol. 1, 26 May, Brussels.
European Convention (2003b), *Draft Constitution*, Vol. 2, 26 May, Brussels.
Fertig, M. and C.M. Schmidt (2002), 'Mobility within Europe – what do we (still not) know?', IZA (Institute for Study of Labour) Discussion Paper, No. 447, March.
Fitousi, J-P. and J. Creel (2002), *How to Reform the European Central Bank*, London: Centre for European Reform.
Forder, J. (2000), 'The theory of credibility: confusions, limitations, and dangers', *International Papers in Political Economy*, **7** (2).
Forder, J. (2004), 'Central bank independence: economic theory, evidence, and political legitimacy', in P. Arestis and M. Sawyer (eds), *The Rise of the Market*, Cheltenham, UK and Northampton, MA, USA: Edward Elgar.
Ghosh, A. and S. Phillips (1998), 'Warning: inflation may be harmful to your growth', *IMF Staff Papers*, **45** (4).
Issing, O. (2003), 'Evaluation of the ECB's monetary policy strategy', ECB Press Conference and Press Seminar, 8 May, Frankfurt.
Kuttner, K. and P. Mosser (2002), 'The monetary transmission mechanism: some answers and further questions', *Economic Policy Review*, Federal Reserve Bank of New York, New York.
Kydland, F. and E.C. Prescott (1977), 'Rules rather than discretion: the inconsistency of optimal plans', *Journal of Political Economy*, **85** (3), 473–92.
Meade, E.E. and N.D. Sheets (2001), 'Regional influences on US monetary policy: some implications for Europe', Discussion Paper No. 523, Centre for Economic Performance, London School of Economics.
Nordhaus, W. (1973), 'The effects of inflation on the distribution of economic welfare', *Journal of Money, Credit, and Banking*, **5**, 465–504.
Organisation for Economic Co-operation and Development (OECD) (1999), *Economic Outlook*, May, Paris: OECD.
Organisation for Economic Co-operation and Development (OECD) (2003), *Economic Outlook*, May, Paris: OECD.
Rogoff, K. (1985), 'The optimal degree of commitment to an intermediate monetary target', *Journal of International Economics*, **35**, 151–67.
Stiglitz, J. (2003a), 'Don't trust the bankers' homilies', *The Guardian*, 8 May.
Stiglitz, J. (2003b), 'Too important for bankers: central banks' ruthless pursuit of price stability holds back economic growth and boosts unemployment', *The Guardian*, 10 June.
Svensson, L.E.O. (2003), 'How should the eurosystem reform its monetary strategy?', Briefing paper for the Committee on Economic and Monetary Affairs of the European Parliament, available at www.princeton.edu/~svensson.
Treasury (1997), *Pre Budget Report*, Cmnd. 3804, London: HMSO.
Treasury (2003), *Fiscal Stabilization and EMU*, available at www.hm-treasury.gov.uk.
Tsakalotos, E. (2001), 'European employment policies: a new social democratic model for Europe?', in Arestis and Sawyer (2001a), pp. 26–45.

Index

Ackum Agell, S. 107
Agell, J. 91, 92
aggregate demand, and unemployment 203
Akerlof, G.A. 86, 91, 92
Almeida, M. Jr 175
Amsden, A.H. 55, 56, 57, 60
Andersson, L. 101
Arai, M. 95, 100
Arestis, P. 47, 49, 161, 162, 197, 198, 203, 205, 206, 210, 214
Argondoña, A. 123
Aukrust model 86
Aukrust, O. 87

Backus, D. 11, 18
Baker, D. 203
Ball, L. 222
Banco de España 130, 142
Bank of England 209
bank finance 39
banks 51–2
  crashes 49
  and the development process 40
  lending 44, 45, 48–9
bargaining models 90, 91, 96
Barro, R. 9–10, 17
Barros, J.R.M. 175
Benston, G.J. 49
Beveridge curve 101
Bewley, T. 91
Bibow, J. 207
Biefang-Frisancho Mariscal, I. 203
Blanchard, O. 139
Blanchflower, D.G. 76, 90, 94, 107
Blinder, A. 210
Bonelli, R. 172
borrowing 44–5
Bosworth, B.P. 93
Brazil 3, 158–93
  accumulation strategy 158

aggregate demand 167
balance of payments 165
balance of payments constraint 181, 185
banks' collapse 174
capital account, liberalization 159, 165
capital flight from 169
capital flows 162, 169
capital outflow 181
competition 171
consumer credit 174
currency crisis 181–5
domestic financial system 174–5
  reform 162
domestic public debt (DPD) 173–4, 175, 176, 177, 181, 187
economic growth 163
exchange rate policy 169
financial crisis 174–5
financial resource transfers (FT) 164, 167–8, 169, 186
fiscal policy, conflict with monetary policy 176–7
foreign debt 175–6
foreign direct investment (FDI) 159, 173
GDP growth rate 158, 172, 185
IMF agreement 181, 183
import-substituting industrialization (ISI) 158
imports 171, 172
  liberalization 162
industrial restructuring 171–3
inflation 158, 165, 167
interest rate arbitrage 175
interest rates 160, 167, 169, 174, 175, 177, 185, 187
local government financial crisis 174
manufacturing industry 172

233

mergers and acquisitions 171
monetary impact of the foreign sector 164–5
monetary policy 163
  conflict with fiscal policy 176–7
neomonetarist policies 159, 162–7
productivity gains 160
PROER (Programme of Incentives to Strengthen and Restructure the Financial System) 174, 175
PROES (Programme of Incentives to Reduce Local Government Banking Activity) 174
real 168, 169, 181
  devaluation 183–4, 187
  managed fluctuation policy 184–5
Real Plan 158, 159, 162, 163, 165, 167, 187
real resource transfers (RT) 163–4, 165, 168
reserves 177, 181
speculation 184–5
trade deficit 159
trade flows 168
trade liberalization 165, 167
unemployment 159, 172
and the Uruguay Round 162
welfare state 184
Bricmont, J. 27
Buiter, W. 218
Bulmer-Thomas, V. 176
Buti, M. 216

Calmfors, L. 91, 92, 93, 128
Calonge, S. 151
Calvo, G. 177
Caprio, G. 49
Cardim de Carvalho, F.J. 174, 175
Carvalho, C.E. 173
Carvalho, P.G.M. 172
'cautious expansionism' 28
central bank independence 1–2, 3, 4, 5, 14, 15, 18, 19, 20, 30, 31
central banks
  'conservative central banker' 13
  and inflation 199, 202
central wage agreements, and wage drift 92–3
central wage bargaining, in Rehn–Meidner model 77

Centre for European Reform 222
CEPAL (UN Economic Commission for Latin America) 176
Chakravarty, S. 59
Chang, H.-J. 161
Cho, Y. Je 41, 55, 56, 58
Choong-Hwan, R. 59
Christofides, L.N. 90, 94
Cole, D. 55, 56, 57
competition 40
competitive atmosphere 44
competitive equilibrium level 91
'conservative central banker' 13
'consistent plan' 25
Council of the European Union 215
Coutinho, L. 171, 172, 173
credibility 2, 31, 161
  and elections 16–20
  and European Monetary Union 196
  and financial markets 29
  theory of 4–37
credibility problem 9–15
'credible', use of word 10
credit, and investment growth 42–3
credit risk 43–4, 48
credit standard 43, 44, 45, 52
Creel, J. 208, 222, 223
Cuadrado, J.R. 132
currency, revaluations of 74
Cysne, R.P. 174

Datta-Chaudhuri, M. 52
Davis, J.S. 104
De Gregorio, J. 47
deflation 212
deindustrialization 162
Del Rio, C. 132
Demetriades, P.O. 41
democracy 29–30
deregulation 1
developing countries
  capital accumulation 50
  intervention 49–50
development process
  and banks 40
  and financial fragility 38–70
  and savings 51
Diaz-Alejandro, C.F. 47
Diniz, E. 172
discount functions 24, 26

discount rate 23, 169
discretion 5, 6, 13, 21
discretionary policy 7, 13
disinflation 10, 12
domestic public debt 162
Dornbusch, R. 165
Driffill, J. 11, 18
Duisenberg, W.F. 197, 198, 204, 208, 209, 210, 211, 212, 214, 215

ECB (European Central Bank) 14, 31, 32, 196, 197, 198, 202, 219, 220
   defects in monetary policy arrangements 205–6
   deflationary bias 223
   Governing Council 209
   and inflation 205
   inflation targeting 208–9, 210
   and interest rates 205–6, 207–8, 211
   monetary policy 199, 204–12
      calls to modify 222
      efficacy 209–10
      problems with 206–9
      and recession 210
      transmission mechanism 210
   proposed changes to 223–4
   transparency and accountability 221
   'two pillar' monetary strategy 204–5, 208
ECOFIN 213, 214, 220
economic fluctuations 195
economic growth, and low profit levels 104
economic policy, 'third way' 71
economies of scale 51
The Economist 208
Edgren, G. 87
Edin, P.-A. 100, 101, 102, 103
Edquist, C. 102
Edquist, H. 102, 106
efficiency wage theory 90–91
EFO model 86
EIB (European Investment Bank) 225, 226
elections 30–31
   and credibility 16–20
Elster, J. 24
employment
   EU 108
   euro area 224–5

EMU (European Monetary Union) 3, 108, 194–231
   and credibility 196
   economic policy changes 224–6
   exchange rate changes 210
   inflation targeting 196–7, 204
   institutional changes 220–24
   macropolicies 199–203
   and the market economy 195
   monetary policy 195–6, 204–12
   'new consensus' 195
   policies for full employment and low inflation 220–26
   see also ECB; Stability and Growth pact
EMU model
   Phillips curve in 198
   theoretical underpinnings 195–8
endogenous growth model 39
equity 77, 79
Erixon, L. 72, 78, 83, 84, 85, 93, 99, 101, 102, 103, 104, 105, 106
ESCB (European System of Central Banks) 199
Espina, A. 131
EU (European Union), employment 108
Euh, Y.-D. 57, 60
euro 199
   appreciation 208, 211
euro area
   employment in 224–5
   impact of US recession 207
European Commission 202, 203, 211, 214
   MacDougall Report 223
European Convention 221, 222
European Employment Pact 203
European Monetary System 125
European Monetary Union *see* EMU
European single currency 3

Faxén, K.O. 100
Federal (Reserve) Open Market Committee (FOMC) 207
Feijó, C.A. 172
Fellner, W. 10
Ferreiro, J. 123
Fertig, M. 226
financial fragility, and the development process 38–70

financial liberalization 38
  South Korea 2
financial markets, and credibility 29
financial resource transfers (FT) 164
  Brazil 167–8, 169, 186
Financial Times 221
Fine, B. 159
firm performance, and wages 94
firms, intertemporal dependence
  between 50
fiscal policy 195
  and Stability and Growth pact 202–3,
  212–20
Fitousi, J.-P. 208, 222, 223
Flanagan, R.J. 93, 95
flexible labour market 203
Flórez, I. 134
Forder, J. 14, 15, 210
'foreign savings' 159, 161
foreign sector, monetary impact of
  164–5
Forslund, A. 91, 94, 107
France, public deficit 215–16
frictional unemployment 103
Friedman, M. 5, 6, 9, 21–22
Fries, H. 101
Fry, M.J. 41
future policy 25

García Durán, J.A. 123
García, M.A. 151, 152
Garcia, M.G.P. 177
GATT, Uruguay Round 162
GDP (gross domestic product) 22
  growth rate 47
General Theory 73, 86, 91
Giovannini, A. 41
Glickman, M. 47, 49, 162
globalization 161
GNP (gross national product) 39
Goldsmith, R.W. 39
Gómez, M.C. 123
Gonçalves, R. 163, 175
Goodhart, C.A.E. 49
Gordon, D. 9–10, 17
growth 38, 39–40
  impediments to 51
  and technical progress 51
Guidotti, P.E. 47
Gupta, K.L. 41

Gurley, J.G. 55

Hansen, B. 83
Hansson, P. 102
Harmonized Index of Consumer Prices
  (HICP) 204
Henrekson, M. 104, 106
Hernández, G. 124
Hibbs, D.A. Jr 95, 96, 100, 102, 103
Hohohan, P. 49
Holmlund, B. 93, 94, 95–6, 103

IMF agreement, Brazil 181, 183
incomes policy 74
  failure 88–90
'inconsistent time preferences' 24
INE (Instituto Nacional de Estadíctica)
  136
inflation 1, 2, 6, 9, 16, 22, 199, 225
  and central banks 199, 202
  controls 74
  and ECB 205
  and monetary policy 4
  and real wage flexibility 72
  in the Rehn–Meidner (R–M) model
  85–8
  Rehn–Meidner theory 82–96
  Scandinavian model of 128
informal credit market 52
  South Korea 57
insider–outsider theory 137
interest rates 40–41, 169
  and ECB 205–6, 207–8, 211
  and investment 46–8
  and liberalization 43, 45
  as a neomonetarist policy tool 161–2
  and savings 41–2
international financial institutions 161
international labour mobility 107
international liquidity 162, 167, 169
internationalization 106–7, 159
intertemporal dependence, among firms
  50
intervention 38, 49–54
inventories 41
investment, and interest rates 46–8
investment decisions 50–51
investment growth, and credit 42
irrational behaviour 24
Issing, O. 197, 198, 204, 205, 209

Jackman, R. 101
Jaramillo, F. 45
Jimeno, J.F. 13
Johnson, G.E. 93
Jonsson, L. 100

Kane, C. 176
Kaufman, G.G. 49
Keynes, J.M. 42, 73
Keynesian growth theory 99
Keynesian policy, definitions 73
Keynesianism, shortcomings 73–6
Khatkhate, D. 41
King, M. 177
King, R.G. 40
Krueger, A.B. 107
Kume, H. 169
Kuznets, S. 50
Kydland, F. 5–9, 16, 21, 196
Kydland and Prescott equilibrium 12

labour, regional mobility 101
labour market 1, 72, 98
  flexible 203
labour market mobility
  international 107
  Sweden 100–101
labour market policy 78–9
Lacerda, A.C. 172
Laplane, M.F. 173
Latin America 47
Lawrence, R.Z. 93
Layard, R. 84, 90, 93
Lee, S.J. 60
Leibenstein, H. 99
Levine, R. 40
liberalization 1
  and interest rates 43, 45
  limitations 39–49
Lindbeck, A. 72, 137
LO Congress 74
Locking, H. 95, 96, 100, 102, 103
Lommerud, K.E. 92
Lopes, F.L. 165
Lucas, R. 5, 6
Luintel, K.B. 41
Lundberg, E. 83
Lundberg, L. 102
Luxembourg process 108

Maastricht Treaty 4, 31, 147, 202, 206
MacDonald, I.A. 90
MacDougall Report, European Commission 223
McKinnon, R.I. 39
macroeconomics, 'new consensus' of 197–8
Maddison, A. 104
Malan, P. 168
Manresa, A. 151
marginal employment subsidies 74, 80
Marín, J. 124
market economy, and European Monetary Union 195
Marshall, A. 42
Marshallian model of structural change 98
Martín, C. 151, 152
Meidner, R. 71, 74, 75, 77, 79, 84, 89, 100
Mercosur 172
Metcalf, D. 139
Mexican crisis 176
Michl, T.R. 104
Milner, S. 139
Mishkin, F.S. 47
modern wage theory 90–93
Modigliani, F. 41
Moene, K.O. 92
Moghadam, R. 100
Mollo, M. 165
monetary impact of the foreign sector 164–5
monetary policy 1, 17
  ECB 199, 204–12
  and European Monetary Union 195–6
  and inflation 4
  problems and effects 15
monetary rule 9
monetary transmission lags 27
money supply 7
Monthly Bulletin (ECB) 207, 209, 219
Morais, L. 175
Morisett, J. 176

neomonetarism
  Brazil 159, 160–7
  implementation of policies 161
  interest rates as a policy tool 161–2
  macroeconomic level 160

microeconomic level 160–61
'new consensus' of macroeconomics 197–8
Nickell, S. 84, 90
Nilsson, C. 100, 101
Noguira Batista, P. Jr 177
non-accelerating inflation rate of unemployment (NAIRU) 119, 195, 197, 203, 217
non-accelerating wage rate of unemployment (NAWRU) 224
Non-Banking Financial Intermediaries (NBFI) 39, 40
Nordhaus, W. 15, 17, 210
Nurkse, R. 50
Nurkse–Rosensstein-Rodan–Scitovsky model 52

Odysseus problem 24, 26
OECD 224
OECD countries
  comparative wage development studies 93
  growth rates 53
Öhman, B. 93
Oswald, A.J. 90, 94

Park, Y.C. 55, 56, 57
pay equalization 100
Peñalosa, J. 124
Phillips curve 7, 8, 9, 11, 13, 18, 28
  in EMU model 198
  'short-run Phillips curve' 20
Pissarides, C. 100
policy, 'cautious expansionism' 28
policy failure 9
policymakers, types of 11, 12, 14, 18, 19
Ponzi finance 162
Poret, P. 93
Posen, A. 27
'precommitment' 25
preferences, change of 24
Prescott, E. 5–9, 16, 21, 196
price stability 4, 12, 16, 32, 79
private return 51
private sector 6, 8, 9–10, 11, 23, 28
production 51
productivity 97
productivity growth 99
profit margins 77

profits
  and nominal wages 84
  and wage drift 82–5
'prudence' 28
pseudo-credibility theory 4, 5, 26–32
public saving, Rehn–Meidner (R–M) model 79

rational expectations 18, 19
real resource transfers (RT), Brazil 163–4, 165, 168
Recio, A. 121, 123, 145
Rehn, G. 71, 73, 74, 75, 76, 77, 79, 80, 81, 82, 83, 84, 89, 98, 100, 103
Rehn–Meidner (R–M) model 2–3, 71–2
  central wage bargaining in 77
  content 73–82
  inflation in 85–8
  labour market policy 78–9, 81
  marginal employment subsidies 80
  means and objectives 75
  and the modern wage theory 90–93
  public saving 79
  relative wage-preferences 72
  restrictive fiscal policy 75–6, 81
  solidaristic wage policy 76–8, 82, 100, 101
  uniqueness 80–82
  validity 106–9
  wage formation 72
Rehn–Meidner theory of growth 96–106
  relevance of 100–106
  solidaristic wage policy and structural change 96–9
Rehn–Meidner theory of inflation 82–96
  evidence of 93–6
relative wage preferences 91
reputation 10, 11–12, 17–18, 18–19, 25, 28
  and unemployment 29
restrictive fiscal policy 75–6
revaluations, of currency 74
Revenga, A. 139
Roca, J. 121, 123, 145
Rogoff, K. 12–14, 196
Romer, D. 91
Romer, P. 39
Rosar, O.O. 175
Rosenstein-Rodan, P.N. 50
Russia, financial crisis 181

Rydén, B. 105

Saad-Filho, A. 165, 176
Salter, W.E.G. 97
Sarti, F. 173
savings
  and the development process 51
  and interest rate 41–2
  mobilization 41
Sawyer, M. 161, 197, 198, 205, 206, 210
Say's Law 197, 217
Scandinavian model of inflation 128
Schager, N.H. 93, 95
Schmidt, C.M. 226
Scitovsky, T. 50
self-finance 106
self-financing capacity 84
Serrano, F. 142
share prices 48
Shaw, E. 39
Sheridan, N. 222
short-termism 4, 20–26
Silva, S.S. 158
Simonsen, M. 165
Siven, C.-H. 100
Skedinger, P. 93, 95–6
Snower, D.J. 137
social objective function 16
'social responsibility' 89–90
social return 51, 52
Sokal, A. 27
Solchaga, C. 121, 125, 126
solidaristic wage policy 76–8, 100, 101, 108–9
  and structural change 96–9, 102–3
Solow, R.M. 51, 91, 97
South Korea
  Bank of Korea 55, 60
  corporate bonds 60
  debt/equity ratio 57
  devaluation 57
  development programme 55–6
  economic performance 38
  entrepreneurial capital 58
  export-led growth policy 52–3
  exports 53, 57
  financial liberalization 2
  financial reform (1965) 55, 56
  foreign debt 56, 59
  foreign loans 58
  GNP 59, 60
  heavy and chemical industries 59
  import substitution 52
  informal credit market 57–8
  interest rate 56
  nationalization of banks 54
  overinvestment 58, 60
  Presidential Emergency Decree (1972) 58
  private banks 53
  privatization of commercial banks 60
Spain 3
  budget deficit 145, 146
  collective bargaining 128, 138, 139, 141, 145
  debt service 147
  economic crisis 118, 119, 120–21
  economic policy during the 1980s and 1990s 117–57
  employment contracts 133–4, 135–6, 139, 142
  entry into EEC 120, 131
  expenditure on health and education 149
  financial sector, liberalization 132
  fiscal revenues, evolution 147
  GDP 125, 131, 134, 147
  In-House Labour Rules 139
  income distribution 149–51
  income tax 152
  incomes policy 118, 119
    (1977–1986) 122–3
  Industry White Paper 131
  inflation 117, 119, 120, 121, 122, 123, 125, 128, 133, 152
  labour costs 129
  labour market reforms 118–19, 132–45, 152–3
    first labour market reform 133–8
    second labour market reform 138–44, 144–5
    third labour market reform 144–5
  labour market segmentation 141, 142
  labour turnover 142
  manufacturing production 119
  manufacturing sector 121, 127, 128, 132
  modernization 117
  monetary policy 119, 123–32, 152
  National Employment Institute 142

non-accelerating inflation rate of unemployment (NAIRU) 119
Partido Popular 117, 131, 133, 144, 151, 152, 153
permanent employment 144
private consumption and saving 143–4
Public Pension Scheme 148
real interest rates 125
Reconversion Act 121
service sector 127, 128, 129, 131, 132
social pacts 122
Socialist Party 117, 118, 145
  general strategy of economic policy 120–32
Tax Studies Institute 149
taxation system 151
temporary employment 135, 136, 137, 142
trade unions 119, 137, 139, 142
unemployment 117, 118, 119, 122, 123, 125–6, 132
unemployment compensation 148–9
wage growth 120, 126, 129, 138
wage-setting process 139
wages 137
welfare state 117, 145–52
  financing 151
  plans for reform 148
Workers' statute 133
speculation 162
Stability and Growth Pact (SGP) 108, 147, 199
  balanced budget requirement 216–20
  changes to 220–21, 223
  core elements 212
  deflationary bias 213–14
  and fiscal policy 202–3, 212–20
  fiscal rules 214–16
  flaws in management 214
  and structural deficits 215
Stiglitz, J. 28
Strotz, R.H. 24
structural change 98
Studart, R. 162, 174, 175
Suen, A. 90
Summers, L.H. 91, 103
sunk costs 46, 47, 48
supply shocks 13
Suzigan, W. 158

Svensson, L.E.O. 222
Sweden 2–3, 71–116
  Beveridge curve 101
  devaluation policies 105
  exports 104
  firm performance and wages 94
  inflation 73
  labour market mobility 100–101
  labour market policy programmes 107
  pay equalization 100
  production 104
  productivity growth 106
  research and development (R&D) 102
  Social Democrats 107–8
  solidaristic wage policy 103–4
  structural change 101–2
  transformation pressure 105
  unemployment 107
  wage differences 94–5
  wage drift 83, 93
  wage drift and increase studies 93
  wages 72
  see also Rehn–Meidner (R–M) model
Swedish Productivity Commission 105
switching cost 46–7

technical progress, and growth 51
temptation 10, 20
theory of credibility 4–37
theory of transformation pressure 99
'third way', in economic policy 71
time-consistency problem 4, 5–9, 31
Tobin, J. 88
Topel, R. 100, 101, 102, 103
trade union models 91
trade unions 72, 73, 74, 89, 203
  in Rehn–Meidner model 76, 77
  Spain 119
Trade Unions and Full Employment 74
transformation pressure 73, 99, 104–5
Treasury 218, 222

uncertainty 42
unemployment
  and aggregate demand 203
  Brazil 159, 172
  causes 1, 199
  frictional 103
  'natural' rate 5, 6, 22
  regional levels 225–6

and reputation 29
Spain 117, 118, 119, 122, 123, 125–6, 132
Sweden 107
theory of frictional unemployment 103
United States
  Federal Reserve System, interest rates 211
  growth rate 199
  recession, impact on euro area 207
  wages 102

Villela, A.V. 158

wage drift 73–4, 80, 95–6
  and central wage agreements 92–3
  and central wage increases 95
  and profits 82–5
wage gaps 92, 94
wage restraint 08, 74
wage-earner funds 74
wages
  and firm performance 94
  and market forces 86
  solidaristic wage policy 76–8
wage–employment mechanisms 92
wage–wage–price spirals 86, 88
Wohlin, L. 105
world trade 53

X-inefficiency 72, 84–5, 90, 91, 94, 99

Yellen, J.L. 86, 91, 92

Zetterberg, J. 94, 101, 103